GRAMMAR EXPLORER 2

TEACHER'S GUIDE

Catherine Mazur-Jefferies & Kristin Sherman

NATIONAL GEOGRAPHIC LEARNING | **CENGAGE Learning**

Australia • Brazil • Japan • Korea • Mexico • Singapore • Spain • United Kingdom • United States

Grammar Explorer Teacher's Guide 2
Catherine Mazur-Jefferies and Kristin Sherman

Publisher: Sherrise Roehr

Executive Editor: Laura Le Dréan

Managing Editor: Eve Einselen Yu

Development Editor: Mark Brunswick

Associate Development Editor: Alayna Cohen

Assistant Editor: Vanessa Richards

Senior Technology Product Manager: Scott Rule

Director of Global Marketing: Ian Martin

Executive Marketing Manager: Ben Rivera

Sr. Director, ELT & World Languages:
Michael Burggren

Production Manager: Daisy Sosa

Content Project Manager: Andrea Bobotas

Senior Print Buyer: Mary Beth Hennebury

Cover Designer: 3CD, Chicago

Cover Image: Brian J. Skerry/National
Geographic Creative

Compositor: Cenveo® Publisher Services

> For product information and technology assistance, contact us at
> **Cengage Learning Customer & Sales Support,**
> **1-800-354-9706**
>
> For permission to use material from this text or product,
> submit all requests online at **www.cengage.com/permissions.**
> Further permissions questions can be e-mailed to
> **permissionrequest@cengage.com.**

Teacher's Guide 2: 978-1-111-35112-0

National Geographic Learning
20 Channel Center Street
Boston, MA 02210
USA

Cengage Learning is a leading provider of customized learning solutions with office locations around the globe, including Singapore, the United Kingdom, Australia, Mexico, Brazil and Japan.

Cengage Learning products are represented in Canada by Nelson Education, Ltd.

Visit National Geographic Learning online at **ngl.cengage.com**

Visit our corporate website at **www.cengage.com**

Printed in the United States of America
Print Number: 01   Print Year: 2014

CONTENTS

Message from the Series Editors

As the series editors, we are pleased to introduce the exciting new *Grammar Explorer* series. Throughout the process of developing these materials, our goal has been to provide students and teachers with a solid and thorough grammar experience that is easy for teachers and engaging for learners.

We do not take the word *explorer* lightly. We want to provide students and teachers with fascinating global content that acknowledges the incredibly diverse world we live in. This content allows students to explore the world and discuss their roles in it through meaningful communication. Students also explore language. They encounter the grammar in rich listening, speaking, reading, and writing activities that focus on a wide variety of topics—from science and innovation to ancient history. Students develop communicative skills that will serve them beyond the classroom.

Rob Jenkins and Staci Johnson

Introduction to *Grammar Explorer*

Grammar Explorer is a three-level grammar series starting at high-beginning and moving through low-advanced. Each unit of *Grammar Explorer* has two to four well-structured lessons that introduce and practice the target grammar gradually, with control and *without* overwhelming students.

Each *Grammar Explorer* lesson will captivate students with its content and engage them with a series of thought-provoking activities. The lesson starts with a short high-interest text where students *discover* the grammar. It continues with controlled practice of the target grammar point, and gradually moves toward open-ended speaking and/or writing activities.

Students learn, construct meaning, and practice using **all four skills**, with the goal of communicating fluently while using the target grammar accurately and appropriately. Each activity serves a purpose and provides a step in the path to student success. Furthermore, the series assists teachers by providing well-thought-out lessons that make teaching and learning both more effective *and* more fun.

Why does *Grammar Explorer* work?

Real-World Content

Relevant up-to-date topics and photos capture students' attention and bring learning to life. Students immediately have a reason to communicate on themes that reflect the world they live in. Grammar discovered through interesting content, as it is throughout *Grammar Explorer*, provides a common starting place for all learners and eventually leads seamlessly to application.

Integrated Skills in Controlled Lessons

Every unit of *Grammar Explorer* provides numerous opportunities to read, write, listen, and speak. Charts are simple and do not provide more information than a student can grasp at one time. After warming up with the *Explore* section, students do the controlled practice in *Learn* to ensure that they have a sufficient understanding of the structure before moving on to more open-ended and communicative activities in *Practice*.

Application of Knowledge

Each lesson and unit in *Grammar Explorer* ends with an application exercise. Teachers everywhere know that students not only need to master rules but also try out those rules by speaking and writing on their own. Carefully designed application exercises aim to help students gain the confidence they need to successfully transfer what they have learned to real life. Application exercises ask students to **critically think** about a variety of topics, **synthesize** information they have learned in a lesson or unit, and **use English** to discuss and communicate their ideas.

Flexible Learning

1. **Flipped Classrooms:** The readings, controlled practice activities, and listening activities can be assigned as out-of-class work, allowing teachers to focus on interactive and productive activities in class, while students work at their own pace at home.

2. **Blended or Online:** The Online Workbook and interactive eBook provide options for teaching a blended or fully online course.

SERIES COMPONENTS

Grammar Explorer components support a variety of classrooms, including traditional, flipped, blended, and online.

For the Student

Student Book
Also available in:
- split editions
- eBooks

Audio CD
Students can listen to:
- all *Explore* readings
- all listening activities
- all pronunciation activities

eBook
eBooks give learners fully integrated online, downloadable, and mobile access to their programs. With eBooks you can:
- complete and save activities
- listen to embedded audio
- search for keywords or phrases
- skip to any section with a functional table of contents
- highlight text and make notes
- view on devices running Mac®, Windows®, iOS™, and Android™

Online Workbook
The Online Workbook has both teacher-led and self-study options and includes:
- extensive additional practice of grammar in each lesson
- review exercises, including a "Unit Challenge" game
- interactive, automatically-graded activities
- independent practice for self-study, or results reported to instructor in MyELT
- additional listening practice
- additional pronunciation practice

For the Teacher

Teacher's Guide
In addition to presenting a general guide for teaching a unit, the Teacher's Guide provides:
- detailed teaching notes and background information for each unit
- suggestions for online activities to engage students with lesson themes
- extension activities and alternative writing exercises
- tips for flipped classrooms: activities can be assigned as homework, allowing teachers to focus on interactive activities in class
- answer keys and audio scripts

Teacher's eResource
The Teacher's eResource can be used as a reference and a Classroom Presentation Tool. With the Teacher's eResource, instructors can:
- project the Student Book pages and reveal answers
- challenge students to provide new example sentences in customizable grammar charts
- play embedded audio in the classroom
- reference the complete Teacher's Guide in an electronic version

Assessment CD-ROM with ExamView®
Assessment CD-ROM with ExamView® is an easy-to-use test generating program that:
- provides pre-made test questions for every unit
- allows teachers to customize their tests or create quizzes in as little as three minutes

Unit Opener

Each unit begins with an engaging National Geographic photo, the unit theme, and a list of the lessons and target grammar structures.

Using the Photo

- Direct students' attention to the photo and the photo caption. Ask them level-appropriate questions such as: *Who are the people? What do you see? Where is this? What is the theme of the unit? What does the photo say about the theme?*
- Ask students to write three questions about the photo. Then, if they have Internet access or are previewing at home, see if they can find answers to their questions online or in another reference.
- Read the Unit-Specific Teaching Tips to find background notes on the photo and theme-specific questions to ask.

Using the Table of Contents

- Draw students' attention to the table of contents in the box on the lower right. You may want to check their previous knowledge of the grammar by asking them: *Which grammar do you already know? What is an example?* Write any examples on the board and ask other students if they are correct. Don't provide any explanation at this point. This is a good way to get a sense of where your students are.
- If the grammar is new or if you want to be sure they understand the grammar-related language, you can preview the grammar terms that students will see in the unit. For your convenience, the Unit-Specific Teaching Tips provide a list of grammar terms and definitions for each unit. Also be sure to tell students to refer to the Glossary of Grammar Terms in the back of their Student Book any time they are unsure of a grammatical term.

Orienting Students to the Unit Theme

- Tell students to flip through the unit for one minute, looking at the pictures and reading any titles and captions. Then, ask students what they think the unit will be about and have them write their three guesses on a piece of paper. After they discuss their ideas with a group for two minutes, ask each group for their "best" answer.

- For three- or four-lesson units, tell students to flip through and look at the *Explore* readings at the beginning of each lesson in the unit. Ask them to rank the readings in order of interest. If possible, they can explain why.

Lessons

Each unit has two to four lessons.

- See the Unit-Specific Teaching Tips for student learning outcomes (SLOs) for each lesson. The **SLOs** help you and your students see more concretely what they will learn, or have learned. Write or project the SLOs on the board before you begin a new lesson and after you finish a lesson or a unit.

EXPLORE

1 READ.

This section provides a model reading in one of many genres, including magazine articles, websites, conversations, blog posts, radio shows, and others.

- Have students skim the text quickly and call out any words they don't understand. Write them on the board and, as a group, define each one using an example sentence or a drawing. **Option:** On the board, write only those words you feel are necessary for students to know. See if a student can provide a definition or an example sentence for each. Write your students' correct definitions or example sentences on the board. Write your own if they do not have any.
- See the Unit-Specific Teaching Tips for "Be the Expert," which provides background information on the content and often includes ideas on how to use the information in class.
- Play the audio as students follow along silently. Try stopping at the end of each paragraph and asking students comprehension questions.
- Play the audio again or have students read in pairs. Reading more than once will help students become more familiar with the content, vocabulary, and grammar.

Photo Tips: In addition to the unit opener, the Student Book features many photos. Some illustrate the text, while others provide context for listening activities.

- Direct students' attention to a photo and use it to illustrate any vocabulary.
- Use photos to recycle target grammar from previous lessons or units.
- Be sure to draw students' attention to captions as these will provide additional important information and provide context for the exercise.

General Reading Tips

The reading activities provide students with grammar in context, help them expand their vocabulary, and engage them with interesting content. While the Unit-Specific Teaching Tips offer information for individual passages, for further expansion and exploitation, you can also:

- have students create additional comprehension items about the passage;
- have students do paired readings of the passage to practice oral fluency;
- photocopy and cut up the passage into pieces for students to put in order, jigsaw-style:
  1. Cut reading passage into three or four parts. If it's a conversation, consider cutting after each line or group of lines.
  2. Put students into groups of three or four (See *Tips for Grouping* on page 6) and give each student one part of the text.
  3. Students read their part and learn the general ideas. Then, they tell their groupmates what is in their part.
  4. As a group, they decide which part is first, second, and so on. This can be a good opportunity to point out discourse markers such as topic sentences, introductions, and conclusions.

General Vocabulary Tips

Both the reading passages and the audio inputs expose students to vocabulary that may be unfamiliar to them. Incorporating the following techniques into the classroom will help students acquire language better and develop study habits that will help them outside and beyond the classroom.

- Suggest that students keep a vocabulary notebook and add unfamiliar words as well as definitions and sentences. Tell them to write down sentences

they hear or find online. This will help them see the common collocations and grammar patterns that often occur with certain words.

- Facilitate dictionary skills by having students look up new words.
- Help students acquire these words by suggesting that they practice them in speaking and writing activities.
- At lower levels, encourage students to make flashcards and practice them in pairs. Be sure to tell them to focus on commonly used words as opposed to highly specialized words. For beginners, for example, the word *mangrove* is not as important as *forest*.

Front

explore (verb)
/ɛksplôr/

Back

Translation: (students first language)

Collocation: explore a place/a topic/ideas

Other forms:
explorer (noun, person)
exploration (noun, idea)

2 CHECK.

This section provides short comprehension questions about the reading.

- Have students complete the activity individually before checking their answers with a partner.
- For higher-level students or early finishers, write additional questions on the board to complete, or have them write their own additional questions.

3 DISCOVER.

These section activities guide students from noticing the target structure in the reading to identifying information about the structure. Exercise **A** generally provides a noticing exercise, and exercise **B** elicits rules or shows students important level-appropriate aspects of the form or function of the grammar.

- Have students complete exercise **A** alone or for more interactivity and support, in pairs.
- Have students complete exercise **B** individually. This will help them learn to notice patterns and infer rules. Then, provide an opportunity for peer or class discussion to clarify the usage of the grammar and explain or elicit rules.
- See the Unit-Specific Teaching Tips for ideas to help bridge the *Explore* section to the grammar charts in *Learn*.

FLIP IT!

Have students do the *Explore* section of a lesson at home.

1. Preview the reading in class and ask students to look at the photo and title and make predictions about the content.
2. Pre-teach unfamiliar vocabulary.
3. Students read and complete the *Explore* exercises at home.
4. Students compare their answers to exercises **2** and **3** with a partner as soon as they get to class.
5. Allow students to discuss any questions they have about the grammar. Encourage other students to explain the rule.

LEARN

Grammar Charts

- See the Unit-Specific Teaching Tips for information specific to the grammar in a unit and for ideas for presenting the grammar in class.

Presentation of Model Structures

Option 1: Read the sentences in the chart and have students repeat. If the chart poses questions and answers, call on students and ask the questions, eliciting the appropriate responses.

Option 2: Call on students to read the sentences in the chart. Ask questions to check comprehension (e.g., *What form of* be *do we use with* he? *What form of the main verb do we use in a question? What part of speech is this word/phrase?*).

Practice of Model Structures

Option 1: Write the parts of the sentence on different cards or sentence strips and have students come to the board and put them in order.

Option 2: Draw the outline of the grammar chart on the board or project the customizable chart in the Teacher's eResource. Include the grammar labels (e.g., *Noun, Verb, . . .*), but do not include the example sentences. Have students provide new examples sentences of their own.

Option 3: As in Option 2, provide the model structure, but with a new example filled in and the grammar labels missing. Have students choose or tell you the correct label for each part of the sentence.

Presentation of the Notes/Rules Chart

Option 1: Have students read the notes silently (or at home). Ask them to tell a partner another example sentence. Then, have some students write more examples sentences on the board. Answer any questions.

Option 2: With partners, ask students to cover the rule/note side of the notes chart and first read the examples, noticing the bold words. See if students can tell you the rule. Then, read the rule together and check.

Practice of the Notes/Rules Chart

Option 1: Either to review or as a follow up to home study, project the notes on the board and have students write examples of their own.

Option 2: Provide examples and have students identify the rule from their chart in their book.

BE A GRAMMAR EXPLORER!

Let students know that language and its rules are always changing. They may hear examples of language that there are no rules for, and they may find that native speakers often disagree on what is "correct." Encourage them to notice the language and explore it outside of their textbooks. Try the following.

- Have a grammar *Show and Tell.* Tell students to find examples of the grammar they are studying and bring it to class. Let students figure out the grammar rule, if there is one. Guide them when necessary to a relevant chart. This can bring to light many unusual usages that they will not find rules for.
- Have students keep a grammar journal, noting examples that they find in the real world.

General Tips for Controlled Activities

- Have students compare their answers in pairs before asking for the answers from individual students. This will help reduce anxiety and give students the confidence to speak.
- Use the Teacher's eResource to project the exercise with answers on the board and let students check their own work. You can also write answers as students say them, or ask students to come up and write the answers.
- When calling on students to check answers or demonstrate the language, be sure to surprise them by calling names randomly. This will keep them more focused on the task since they are never sure who will be next.
- Avoid letting stronger or more talkative students dominate the class. Check names as you call on them, so you are sure that everyone has a chance to participate.

PRACTICE

LISTEN Activities

- Set the context, provide background and cultural notes, and pre-teach essential vocabulary. You may want to write the vocabulary on the board. Instead of pre-teaching, elicit possible meanings of the words after students listen once.

- Play the audio once from beginning to end so that students have a chance to listen for overall comprehension. They should be able to get the gist of the input in one listening. If you are reading the script, read with expression and at a natural pace. Do not slow down or overarticulate. You can also photocopy the audio script and have students read along chorally.
- Play the audio again as students complete the task. You may want to stop at intervals to give students time to answer questions.

General Listening Activity Tips

- Before any listening, have students read through the items so that they know what to listen for.
- In many exercises, you can have students predict correct answers before they listen and check.
- The audio provides another kind of language input for students. Many students are intimidated by listening, so you may need to provide extra scaffolding. Allow students to listen to the audio first to achieve a more authentic experience. Then, if students have difficulty, let them read the audio script.

SPEAK Activities

- After students work with a partner and you monitor their work, call on a few students to model for the class, addressing any common errors.
- With free speaking that asks students to offer their own ideas, allow them to work with a partner. After a set amount of time (5–8 minutes), call on two or three pairs of students to share their ideas and/or tell the class about their partners.

General Speaking Activity Tips

- Model any controlled speaking activity. Ask a student to be your partner and demonstrate the first item to the class. Have students repeat any language they may need before they begin.
- Walk around and monitor students during any group activity. Help individual students with pronunciation or other aspects of their speaking as you walk around.

WRITE Activities

- If students completed the activity for homework, put them in pairs to exchange work and provide feedback.
- As with freer speaking activities, call on students to share their ideas and/or tell the class about their partner's ideas.
- You may want to collect writing samples to use as an informal assessment. To help, have students exchange papers with a partner and provide feedback.

FLIP IT!

Have students complete the writing tasks at home. If you have a class website, blog, or LMS, let students post their work. Ask students to read each other's work and leave at least one positive comment and one comment that suggests an improvement.

EDIT Activities

- Display the corrected sentences on the board or with a projector, using the Teacher's eResource. Give students the opportunity to ask questions and discuss the corrections.
- You may want to display the EDIT activity without the answers and correct the errors as students say them or let students correct them on their own.

General Tip for Error Correction

If a student makes an error either in writing on the board or in a spoken exercise, be sure to give them a chance to correct themselves. Indicate that it is wrong with a facial expression or gesture of some kind. Give the student or her classmates a chance to identify and correct the error.

APPLY Activities

- To make the activity more interactive or to provide extra scaffolding for students, have them work in pairs or small groups to generate ideas and/or gather information.
- Students produce language in spoken or written form. After students have completed this part, provide an opportunity for them to share their work by speaking or reading to the class, a small group, or a new partner.
- Facilitate any interaction by encouraging students to get up and talk to five new classmates.

General Tips for Grouping

- To assure that students do not only talk to their friends, try assigning them to a different partner each time by using different techniques:
- Prepare cards from a deck with two of each type of card, e.g., aces, ones, twos, . . . (depending on the number of students). Hand them out and have students find their match.
- Try pairing lower-level students with higher-level students. Read their names and indicate where they should sit.
- For small groups (three to four students are best), tell students to count off in threes or fours (for classes of 12–21 students). Then, ask all number ones to raise their hands; then twos, threes, etc. Point to a part of the room and tell each group where to sit.

Review the Grammar

This section always includes an activity that combines the grammar from the lessons in a unit, a listening activity, and an editing activity. It can be used for assessment purposes by you or as a self-assessment for the students.

FLIP IT!

Have students do the controlled activities, EDIT, and LISTEN as an out-of-class assignment to allow them time to go back and review the unit as necessary.

Note: Students need the audio in order to complete the LISTEN exercise. They can find this on the Student Companion Site at NGL.Cengage.com/GrammarExplorer.

Connect the Grammar to Writing

Students first read and identify the grammar in a model. Then, they analyze the organization/content of the model text. After they brainstorm and organize their ideas, they write their own piece of writing. Students focus both on accurate usage of the target grammar and a new writing strategy or skill. The Writing Focus boxes are designed to build on each other throughout each book, giving students a toolbox for writing by the end of the series.

1 READ & NOTICE THE GRAMMAR.

> ### FLIP IT!
> Students can do the READ & NOTICE THE GRAMMAR activities at home. Then, let them check answers with a partner and brainstorm ideas for their own writing when they come to class.

- If you do this activity in class, have students preview the three parts of the activity.
- Have students read the text silently or follow along as you read it aloud. Put students in pairs to discuss answers to the grammar noticing activity.
- Have students read the Grammar Focus box and complete the task in exercise **B**.
- Have students compare the information in the graphic organizers in exercise **C** with a partner.
- Or project the graphic organizers, using the Teacher's eResource, and have students fill it in together. Discuss as a class, eliciting any corrections from students.

2 BEFORE YOU WRITE.

- After explaining the activity, provide students with enough time to generate ideas. Don't rush this part of the writing process. **Option:** Have students share their ideas in pairs or small groups. Encourage them to ask each other questions to clarify and get more information.
- Walk around the room to provide help as needed. **Option:** Have students generate ideas as an out-of-class assignment, and then share their ideas in the next class.
- See the Unit-Specific Teaching Tips for an alternative writing option that can be used for additional in-class writing or homework.

3 WRITE.

- Go over the instructions and the Writing Focus box. Have students complete the assignment in class or at home.
- See the Unit-Specific Teaching Tips for more activity ideas for practicing the Writing Focus box in class.

4 SELF ASSESS.

- Go over the checklist. Have students use the checklist to edit their own work. You may want to have students exchange their writing and use the checklist to edit each other's work and provide feedback.

> ### FLIP IT!
> Have students complete WRITE at home. If you have a class website, blog, or LMS, let students post their work. Ask students to read each other's work and leave at least one positive comment and one comment that suggests an improvement, or use the checklist and have students evaluate their own or each other's work in class.

Assessment

Grammar Explorer provides four different types of assessment:

1. **Formative Assessment within the Unit**

   Formative assessment is used to determine how learning is going and whether or not more explanation, practice, and general help are needed before continuing. The LEARN activities after the charts, the final exercises before the APPLY, and the Review the Grammar activities can serve as the formative assessment.

2. **Review the Grammar**

   By monitoring student success in these end-of-unit activities, instructors can determine if students are prepared to go on to the writing section; they can determine how much students have learned and what their problem areas might be.

3. **Connect the Grammar to Writing**

   This end-of-unit writing is another type of assessment. It will show your students' progress with the grammar of the current unit and all previous units. A rubric is a good way to evaluate students' work. Share the rubric with students before they write. You may want to start with a simple rubric, and then with each new unit add a writing focus and/or grammar review point from a previous unit or units. See page 8 for an example rubric.

4. **Assessment CD-ROM with ExamView®**

   - Create custom tests and quizzes. Teachers can choose the test questions they want and/or add their own items.
   - Can be used to create tests for various purposes that include:
     - creating a unit pretest to see what students already know;
     - creating a summative final test;
     - creating additional practice activities in the form of a quiz.

Rubric to Assess Writing

Standard	3	2	1	0
Student writing is clear and easy to understand.	Writing is clear and requires little or no inferences.	Writing is somewhat clear and requires some inferences.	Writing is more unclear than clear and requires many inferences.	Writing does not relate to the assignment or is completely unclear.
Student uses [grammar points here] correctly.	90–100 percent of the time.	70–89 percent of the time.	Less than 70 percent but more than once or twice.	Rarely if ever.
[Writing Focus for the unit; add each new writing focus as you progress through the book.]	90–100 percent of the time.	70–89 percent of the time.	Less than 70 percent, but more than once or twice.	Rarely if ever.
[Add your own focus.]	90–100 percent of the time.	70–89 percent of the time.	Less than 70 percent, but more than once or twice.	Rarely if ever.

The Present

Unit Opener

Photo: Have students look at the photo and read the caption. Ask, *What is happening in the photo?*

Location: Donje Ljubinje is a village in the Shar Mountains of Kosovo on the border of Macedonia. Ask a student to locate Kosovo and Macedonia on a map.

Theme: This unit is about customs and traditions around the world. Have students look at the photos on pages 4, 5, and 12. Ask, *Where do these people live? What are they celebrating?*

Page	Lesson	Grammar	Examples
4	1	Simple Present: Statements and Questions	She **eats** a lot. They **eat** a lot. I **don't eat** a lot. He **doesn't eat** a lot. **Does** he **sing**? **Do** they **sing**?
12	2	Present Progressive and Simple Present	She **is working**. *vs.* She **works**. They **are not working**. *vs.* They **don't work**. What **is happening**? *vs.* What **happens**?
20	**Review the Grammar**		
22	**Connect the Grammar to Writing**		

Unit Grammar Terms

action verb: a verb that shows an action.
 ➢ He **drives** every day.
 ➢ They **left** yesterday morning.

base form: the form of the verb without *to* or any endings such as *-ing, -s,* or *-ed.*
 ➢ *eat, sleep, go, walk*

frequency adverb: an adverb that tells how often something happens. Some common adverbs of frequency are *never, rarely, sometimes, often, usually,* and *always.*
 ➢ I **always** drink coffee in the morning.
 ➢ He **usually** leaves work at six.

non-action verb: a verb that does not describe an action. Non-action verbs indicate states, senses, feelings, or ownership.
 ➢ I **love** my grandparents.
 ➢ I **see** Marta. She's across the street.
 ➢ They **have** a new car.

singular noun: a noun that names only one person, place, or thing.
 ➢ They have **a son** and **a daughter**.

subject: the noun or pronoun that is the topic of a sentence.
 ➢ **Patricia** is a doctor.
 ➢ **They** are from Iceland.

***Wh-* question:** a question that asks for specific information, not "*Yes*" or "*No.*"
 ➢ **Where do they live?**
 ➢ **What do you usually do on weekends?**

***Wh-* word:** a word such as *who, what, where, when, why,* or *how* that is used to begin a *Wh-* question.
 ➢ **Why** are you crying?

***Yes/No* question:** a question that can be answered with "*Yes*" or "*No.*"
 ➢ **Do you live in Dublin?** Yes, I do./No, I don't.
 ➢ **Can you ski?** Yes, I can./No, I can't.

Student Learning Outcomes	• **Read** an article about Afar wedding traditions. • **Ask** and **answer** questions about weddings in different cultures. • **Find** and **edit** errors with the simple present and frequency adverbs. • **Write** sentences using frequency adverbs and the simple present. • **Listen** to and **complete** a conversation about birthdays in Ghana. • **Listen** to an interview and **write** the answers to questions. • **Discuss** rites of passage in different cultures.
Lesson Vocabulary	(n.) argument (v.) celebrate (n.) groom (n.) meal (n.) vacation (n.) bride (n.) culture (v.) invite (adj.) traditional (n.) wedding

EXPLORE

1 READ, page 4   10 min.

- Have students look at the photos and read the captions. Ask a student to locate Djibouti on a map.
- Explain *jewelry* by pointing out different types of jewelry worn by students. Ask, *Why is the girl in the photo wearing jewelry? What do people wear to weddings in your culture?*

Be the Expert

- The Afar people live in the East African countries of Ethiopia, Eritrea, Somalia, and Djibouti. In Djibouti, there are approximately 416,000 Afar people living on the Ethiopia-Somalia coast or in the Danakil Desert, one of the world's hottest and driest climates.
- Islam is the primary religion among Djibouti's Afar population. While Muslim men in other cultural groups are permitted to have four wives, Afar marriages are generally monogamous. Marriages between first cousins are preferred in Afar culture, and girls may be married by the age of ten.

2 CHECK, page 5   5 min.

    1. F   2. T   3. T   4. T   5. F

- **Tip:** Ask higher-level students to correct the false sentences to make them true.

3 DISCOVER, page 5   5 min.

A   1. S   2. S   3. P   4. P   5. S

B   The verbs with a singular subject end in -s, while the verbs with a plural subject do not.

- **Tip:** On one side of the board, write:

  The bride _____ a dress.
  The groom _____ for the wedding rings.
  The guests _____ presents.

  Then, on the other side of the board, write the verbs *wear*, *pay*, and *give*. Ask students to complete the sentences by using the simple present form of the correct verb. Then have students rewrite the statements in the negative.

LEARN

Chart 1.1, page 6   5 min.

- **Note 2:** Many students have trouble with the third-person singular -s ending when using the simple present. Because they have already learned that plural nouns end in -s, students often assume that the verb following a plural noun ends in -s as well. On the board, write: *The dog runs. The dogs run.* Write the number 1 above *dog* and circle the s in *runs*. Then write the number 2 above *dogs* and circle the space after *run* to show there is no s. Tell students that if they see an s at the end of the verb, they should make sure that the subject is in the third-person singular.

4 page 6   5 min.

1. eat	5. do not/don't pay
2. does not/doesn't attend	6. does not/doesn't end
3. dance	7. provides
4. invite	8. do not/don't live

Explain to students that contractions are an important part of speaking English. Without contractions, people can sound like robots. Demonstrate this by reading the following sentences with a short pause after each word: *He does not watch TV. We do not like pizza.* Then repeat the same sentences naturally with contractions, bringing your hands together to indicate when a contraction is used. Encourage students to use contractions during exercise **5**.

5 SPEAK, page 6   5 min.

Answers will vary.

- **Expansion Tip:** Write the parts of the sentences in exercise **5** on a piece of paper (e.g., *the bride/ dance*). Cut apart the pairs of subjects and verbs and distribute the pieces of paper among groups of 3–4 students. Have each group write 1–2 affirmative and negative statements using the subject and verb. Ask volunteers to share their sentences with the class.

Chart 1.2, page 7   5 min.

- **Note:** Question formation can be challenging for students because it may be very different from how questions are formed in their native languages. In many languages, questions are formed differently than in English.

- **Notes 1 & 2:** Remind students that the auxiliary *do* or *does* is needed when forming *Yes/No* and *Wh-* questions unless the question is about the subject (e.g., *Who used the toothbrush?*). Explain that when questions include *do* or *does*, the base form of the verb is used. Direct students to the glossary for the definition of *base form*.

6 page 7   10 min.

1. Do all brides wear
2. What do people give
3. Does the bride's mother cut
4. Do the bride and groom have
5. Who does the bride dance
6. What do the bride and groom do
7. What do the guests do
8. Who pays

- **Tip:** Ask students to read the questions and answers in pairs.

7 SPEAK, page 8   5 min.

Answers will vary.

- **Tip:** Ask students to think of words related to weddings (e.g., *honeymoon, reception, bridesmaids*). List these words on the board before beginning the activity.

- **Expansion Tip:** Form small groups with 2–3 pairs of students and have the class compare weddings in their cultures. Ask a volunteer from each group tell the class about the similarities and differences.

Chart 1.3, page 8   5 min.

- **Tip:** Write or type the following sentences several times on a piece of paper: *I am usually happy. Juanita sometimes forgets her homework.* Cut apart the words in each sentence and distribute the sets of words among groups of 2–3 students. Have each group form sentences by arranging the words according to the rules in the chart. Point out that there may be more than one correct way to form each sentence.

8 page 8   10 min.

1. [Usually] I am [usually] with friends on my birthday.
2. Marco is hardly ever on time for parties.
3. My parents never forget my birthday.
4. Children aren't always happy at birthday parties.
5. Does your sister send you photos often?
6. [Sometimes] Jackie [sometimes] buys unusual presents for her family [sometimes].
7. In the United States, brides rarely wear red dresses.
8. I [frequently] go back to my hometown [frequently].
9. Carlos seldom talks to his brother on the phone.
10. Do you ever visit your cousin in Spain?

PRACTICE

9 page 9   5 min.

1. do people usually celebrate
2. do not/don't celebrate
3. always wait
4. does *krada* start
5. never begins
6. always starts
7. do you usually do
8. often prepare
9. usually make
10. always fry
11. usually eat

10 SPEAK, page 9

Answers will vary.

- **Tip:** Brainstorm different topics related to birthdays on the board before you begin. Ask, *How can you celebrate a birthday?* Categories could include food, clothes, presents, party, and time of day.

- **Expansion Tip:** Encourage higher-level students to ask follow-up questions about their birthday celebrations (e.g., A: *My mother always bakes a cake for my birthday.* B: *What kind of cake does she bake?* A: *She usually bakes a chocolate cake.*).

11 page 10

A *Answers will vary. Possible answers:*

1. We don't usually give each other expensive presents.
2. I always send my parents a card on their wedding anniversary.
3. We hardly ever get together as a family.
4. I am never late for family parties.
5. My family frequently has big celebrations.
6. My parents are always happy to see me.
7. People in my family aren't often quiet during meals.
8. We rarely spend weekends together.

B *Answers will vary.*

- **Expansion Tip:** Ask students to write a question about their classmates' habits using an adverb of frequency (e.g., *When do you usually study English?*). Review the questions for appropriateness and accuracy. Then have students take turns asking their questions to different people and answering using adverbs of frequency.

12 EDIT, page 10

Kenji: How often does your family ~~does~~ get together?

Raoul: We get together about two or three times a year, but it's not always easy. My brother lives on the West Coast, and my sister is often ~~is~~ away on business trips.

Kenji: So, where do you meet when you get together?

Raoul: Well, we usually go ~~usually~~ to my parents' house. We ~~tries~~ try to get home to celebrate their wedding anniversary every year. Sometimes, my brother and I visit each other on our birthdays. Once every two or three years we take a vacation together. I'd like to do it every year, but it costs a lot of money.

Kenji: ~~Have~~ Do you have a good time with your brother and sister?

Raoul: Oh, yes, most of the time. ~~We have sometimes~~ We sometimes have/ Sometimes we have a few arguments, just like any family.

13 LISTEN, WRITE & SPEAK, page 11

A 1. Ukraine; Pentecost, Vanuatu
2. bungee jumping; land diving
3. *Answers will vary.*

B 1. Why do the boys climb the tower?
2. How do the boys jump off the tower?
3. Who digs the ground below the tower?
4. Why do the boys rarely get killed?

C 1. It is a popular vacation activity.
2. They attach themselves to a bungee cord.
3. Men dig the ground below the tower.
4. Because the ground is soft.

14 APPLY, page 11

Answers will vary.

Student Learning Outcomes	• **Read** an article about Diwali, an annual Hindu celebration. • **Complete** a conversation about a New Zealand rugby team. • **Ask** and **answer** questions about celebrations and everyday plans. • **Write** about an annual event in your home country. • **Talk** about what you are doing this week, month, semester, or year.
Lesson Vocabulary	(v.) attract (n.) costume (adj.) expensive (v.) hope (n.) parade (n.) competition (n.) design (v.) happen (v.) light (n.) prize

EXPLORE

1 READ, page 12   10 min.

• Have students look at the photos and read the captions. Ask, *Where do these women live? What are they doing?* Ask a student to find India on a map.

• Explain that *wealth* means being rich. *Goddess* is the word for a female god.

• Ask, *Do you have any celebrations in your culture that involve light?* (e.g., *fireworks, birthday candles, the sun*)

Be the Expert

• This reading is about Diwali, a Hindu festival that celebrates light over darkness and good over evil. Hindus celebrate Diwali in autumn every year by lighting oil-wick lamps and decorating their homes with colorful electric lights. Light symbolizes knowledge and consciousness in Hindu culture and serves as a reminder of the importance of education and self-improvement. By lighting lamps during Diwali, Hindus are reminded to embrace knowledge and goodness and to eliminate darkness from their hearts and minds.

2 CHECK, page 13   5 min.

1. the Festival of Lights
2. (late) October or (early) November
3. saris/a(n) (new) sari
4. on the floor
5. the goddess of wealth and success
6. a happy future for the family

3 DISCOVER, page 13   5 min.

A 1. happening now
2. generally true
3. happening now
4. happening now
5. generally true
6. generally true

B The verb form includes a helping (or auxiliary) verb, and the main verb ends in *-ing*.

• **Tip:** Write the chart below on the board. Ask students to fill in the blanks with their ideas.

Habit	Happening Now
This class meets _____. (e.g., *on Wednesdays*)	Today, we are studying _____. (e.g., *the present progressive*)
I usually eat _____ for breakfast. (e.g., *toast*)	The teacher is wearing _____ this morning. (e.g., *a green skirt*)

LEARN

Chart 1.4, page 14   5 min.

• **Note 1:** Students often have difficulty understanding the present progressive for actions that happen for an extended period of time. Explain that when a speaker uses the present progressive, they mean that the action is temporary and will not always be true. On the board, write: *Luan lives in Albania. Redona is living in Tokyo right now.* Ask students what the difference is. Elicit that in the second sentence, the speaker does not think Redona will live in Tokyo for a long time.

- **Tip:** Students often can't hear the contraction *'m* in natural speech and think the speaker is saying *I not*. On the board, write: *I am writing on the board. I'm not swimming.* Ask students to offer other suggestions for what you are not doing right now and write 3–4 additional sentences on the board. Have students repeat these sentences to practice using the contraction. Emphasize the *m* in *I'm* when demonstrating the correct pronunciation.

4 page 14   5 min.

1. are lighting
2. are/'re drawing
3. is not/'s not/isn't celebrating
4. is/'s studying
5. am not/'m not preparing
6. is/'s helping
7. is/'s washing
8. are/'re getting

5 page 14   5 min.

1. are attending
2. celebrate
3. organizes
4. marks
5. am making
6. makes
7. have
8. is dancing

Chart 1.5, page 15   5 min.

- **Note:** Compare question forms in the simple present and the present progressive. Ask, *Do you speak Spanish* (or another language spoken by students)*? (Yes, I do. / No, I don't.)* Then ask, *Are you speaking Chinese* (or another language) *right now? (No, I'm not.)* Ask, *Am I speaking English right now? (Yes, you are.)* Write these questions on the board (if possible, use different colors for the auxiliaries and the verbs) and explain that simple present questions use the auxiliary *do* and the base form of the verb, while present progressive questions use the auxiliary *be* and the base form of the verb + -*ing*.

6 page 15   10 min.

1. What are you doing
2. am/'m buying
3. Where are you living
4. am/'m renting
5. Why is your computer making
6. It is not/'s not/isn't working
7. Is your phone ringing
8. brother is/'s calling

- **Expansion Tip:** Write a list of actions on the board: *brushing your teeth, sleeping, eating breakfast, dancing, taking a shower.* Model one of the actions and ask, *What am I doing?* Have students respond in question form (e.g., *Are you dancing?*). Repeat the exercise by having students volunteer to act out the rest of the actions and ask the class what they are doing.

7 SPEAK, page 16   5 min.

Answers will vary.

Chart 1.6, page 16   5 min.

- **Note:** The difference between non-action and action verbs can be confusing for students, because many languages do not convey these differences through verb tenses.

- **Notes 3 & 4:** Non-action verbs can sometimes be used in the present progressive to emphasize the temporary nature of the verb (e.g., *I'm missing my family a lot right now.*). Explain to students that at this level, they should try to avoid using non-action verbs in the present progressive. On the board, make a chart with two columns labeled *Use the Present Progressive* and *Don't Use the Present Progressive.* In the first column, write the following sentences: *They are watching TV. She is talking to her mother.* In the second column, write: *I'm not understanding her. He's owning a red car.* Have students correct the statements in the second column to use the simple present.

8 page 16   10 min.

1. Do; like
2. love
3. think
4. do; miss
5. is/'s tasting
6. wants
7. does not/doesn't belong
8. Do; have
9. do not/don't own
10. Are; having
11. have

- **Tip:** Reassure students that this is a difficult grammar point. The difference between when the simple present and present progressive tenses are used is subtle, but with practice and exposure, students will be able to understand the difference better.

- **Expansion Tip:** After students have completed this exercise, have them read the conversations in pairs.

PRACTICE

9 page 17   10 min.

1. what are you doing

2. I am/I'm reading

3. They look

4. What are they doing

5. Are they dancing

6. They are/They're performing

7. Do they do

8. It helps

9. they believe

10. Does it work

11. it never surprises

12. The other team usually pays

13. the fans love

14. the *haka* always provides

- **Expansion Tip:** The All Blacks (the team pictured on page 17) are a famous rugby team from New Zealand, which is home to the Maori. Rugby is a sport that is similar to American football, but the players do not have padding or helmets. Ask students what they know about New Zealand and the game of rugby. Then have a student locate New Zealand on a map or globe.

10 WRITE & SPEAK, page 17   5 min.

A 1. What holidays do you enjoy?

2. What are your classmates doing right now?

3. What do you want for your birthday?

4. Are you doing anything interesting these days?

5. Do you and your friends like soccer?

6. Do you often work on weekends?

7. What is your class studying this week?

8. Where do you usually have lunch?

B *Answers will vary.*

11 page 18   10 min.

1. are; doing	7. do not/don't feel
2. hate	8. do not/don't want
3. think	9. do not/don't look
4. don't believe	10. need
5. am/'m having	11. are talking
6. tastes	

- **Expansion Tip:** In some languages, the ends of words are not pronounced as clearly as they are in English. When students learn about contractions, they may think that they can contract the ends of the words as well (e.g., *I am talking* becomes *I am talk*). Explain that in English, the *-ing* at the end of present progressive verbs should be pronounced. Have students take turns reading the conversations in groups of 3–4. Be sure to call their attention to the pronunciation of *-ing* endings.

12 READ & WRITE, page 19   20 min.

A   I <u>come</u> from Venice, Italy, and I really <u>love</u> my city. My favorite time of year <u>is</u> Carnival. People <u>wear</u> masks and beautiful costumes and <u>parade</u> through the streets. My family and I ⟨always⟩ <u>have</u> a little competition to see who <u>has</u> the best costume. My sister <u>is</u> in art school, so she ⟨usually⟩ <u>wins</u>. The rest of us <u>compete</u> for second prize!

B *Answers will vary.*

- **Tip:** Students can write their own paragraphs for homework.

- **Expansion Tip:** When students first learn the present progressive, they tend to add the auxiliary *be* before verbs in the simple present as well. Explain that if they have written *am/is/are* + a verb, the verb needs to end in *-ing*. Have students check to make sure that they have included *-ing* where necessary. Then ask them to read a partner's paragraph and circle any verbs that need to be corrected.

13 APPLY, page 19   20 min.

Answers will vary.

- **Expansion Tip:** Students can stand up and walk around the room, asking different classmates questions. After 2–3 minutes, have students find a new partner to ask questions. Repeat the activity several times.

1 page 20   10 min.

  1. Why are you sitting

  2. am/'m working

  3. have

  4. always celebrate

  5. usually visit

  6. have

  7. what are they doing

  8. is/'s taking

  9. is/'s working

 10. works

 11. am/'m not doing

 12. Do you want

 13. hear

 14. Do you like

 15. love

2 EDIT, page 20   10 min.

    In my town, Buñol, Spain, the local people ~~are organizing~~ organize a festival called *La Tomatina* every year. It always ~~is starting~~ starts on the last Wednesday in August, and it lasts for a week. *La Tomatina* is a food fight. Every summer, thousands of local people and visitors get~~s~~ together to throw tomatoes at each other. Yes, that's right—tomatoes! And I'm not talking about just a few tomatoes. *La Tomatina* ~~is using~~ uses around a hundred tons of tomatoes every year. These days the festival is becoming so popular that other countries are starting to organize their own events similar to *La Tomatina*.

3 LISTEN, page 21   10 min.

  1. I am talking about

  2. He's standing

  3. Someone's throwing

  4. I don't think

  5. do you think

  6. he's not trying

  7. He's having

  8. you're telling

  9. people like

 10. include

 11. needs

4 SPEAK, page 21   15 min.

Answers will vary.

1 READ & NOTICE THE GRAMMAR,
page 22   25 min.

A *Answers will vary.*

B   In February, my family and I usually go to
the Kila Raipur Sports Festival. Kila Raipur is a
town near my home in India. It's January now, and
we are planning our trip. We are looking forward
to this tradition. Each year, thousands of people
attend the festival.

     At the festival, people race huge tractors. Men
lift bicycles with their teeth. In this photo, men
are racing carts pulled by oxen. This is everyone's
favorite event.

C When: every year

Where: Kila Raipur, India

Who: writer and family, thousands of people

What: bicycle lifting with teeth, oxen racing,
tractor racing

• **Tip:** Use the photo to explain the word *oxen*.
  If possible, bring in a picture of a tractor to show
  the class.

2 BEFORE YOU WRITE, page 23   10 min.

Answers will vary.

• **Expansion Tip:** Before students write, it may
  be helpful for them to talk through what they are
  going to write with a partner. Ask students to use
  the web organizer to explain their story.

3 WRITE, page 23   25 min.

> **WRITING FOCUS, page 23**
>
> Ask students to provide the address of the
> building, the date the class began, the
> names of the teacher and two students, and
> a holiday when school is canceled. Write all
> of this on the board in lower-case letters. Ask
> students to tell you what to capitalize and
> make the changes as necessary.

• **Alternative Writing:** Ask students to bring in a
  photo of a special event in their cultures. Using
  the web organizer in exercise **1C** as a model, have
  them take turns describing their photos with the
  simple present and present progressive tenses.

2 Survival

The Past

Unit Opener

Photo: Have students look at the photo and read the caption. Ask, *Where are these buildings? Why are they famous?*

Location: The Parthenon is on the Acropolis in Athens, Greece. Ask a student to locate Greece on a map.

Theme: This unit talks about different types of survival. Have students look at the photos on pages 26, 33, and 39. Ask, *Which story do you think will be about the survival of animals? Languages? A person in the wild?*

Page	Lesson	Grammar	Examples
26	1	Simple Past	I **helped** the animals. They **went** to Africa. He **didn't help** us. We **didn't go** to China.
33	2	Past Progressive and Simple Past	I **was working**. They **were working**. He **wasn't sleeping**. We **weren't sleeping**.
39	3	Past Time Clauses	I was driving home **when the storm began**. It started to rain **while we were walking in the park**.
46	4	Repeated Past Actions: *Used To* and *Would*	She **used to study** history. They **didn't use to love** math. As a child, I **wouldn't study** but I **would get** good grades.
53	**Review the Grammar**		
56	**Connect the Grammar to Writing**		

Unit Grammar Terms

auxiliary verb: (also called *helping verb*.) a verb used with the main verb. *Be, do, have,* and *will* are common auxiliary verbs when they are followed by another verb.
➢ *I **am** working.*
➢ *He **won't** be in class tomorrow.*
➢ *She **can** speak Korean.*

information question: a question that asks for specific information, not "*Yes*" or "*No*."
➢ ***Where do you live?***
➢ ***When is the game?***

irregular verb: a verb with forms that do not follow the rules for regular verbs.
➢ *swim → swam*
➢ *have → had*

time clause: a clause that answers the question *When?* Time clauses are introduced by conjunctions such as *when, after, before, while,* and *since*.
➢ *I have lived here **since I was a child**.*
➢ ***While I was walking home**, it started to rain.*
➢ *I'm going to call my parents **after I eat dinner**.*

Student Learning Outcomes	• **Read** an article about the Lion Guardians in Kenya. • **Complete** a chart with regular and irregular simple past forms. • **Listen** to an interview with a filmmaker. • **Find** and **edit** errors with the simple past. • **Interview** a classmate about a recent assignment or project.
Lesson Vocabulary	(adj.) basic (adj.) local (n.) organization (v.) protect (n.) technology (v.) hunt (adj.) modern (v.) persuade (n.) saying (n.) threat

EXPLORE

1 READ, page 26   10 min.

- Have students look at the photos and read the captions. Ask, *Where does the man live?* Ask a student to find Kenya on a map.

- Explain the difference between *persuade* (*This is a good idea; do it.*) and *warn* (*This is a bad idea; don't do it.*). Ask students to give examples of something parents warn their children about and something they try to persuade their children to do.

Be the Expert

- Africa's lion population has dropped significantly in recent years. According to the Living with Lions website, there are currently approximately 30,000 lions living primarily in protected areas of eastern and southern Africa, but wild lions outside national parks are in danger of being killed off.

- With approximately 20 million cell phone subscribers, mobile devices have been becoming more common in Kenya. The Kenyan government has provided cellular technology to Maasai herders to allow them to receive information about watering holes and grazing lands, to contact doctors from remote locations, and to find deals when selling or trading cattle.

2 CHECK, page 27   5 min.

   1. F   2. T   3. F   4. T   5. T

- **Tip:** Ask higher-level students to correct the false sentences to make them true.

3 DISCOVER, page 27   5 min.

A

Group A		Group B	
killed	learned	had	became
died	persuaded	sent	taught
wanted		got	

B Group A verbs add *-ed* to form the simple past and Group B verbs do not.

- **Tip:** On the board, write the following sentences: *Last night, I studied / didn't study _____. I ate _____. I was _____.* Read the sentences to the class, filling in the blanks with information about yourself. Explain that these verb forms are used to talk about the past. Then ask students to finish the sentences with their own information.

LEARN

Chart 2.1, page 28   5 min.

- **Note 4:** Explain that the auxiliary *did + not* is used in negative simple past statements and that the auxiliary carries the tense information. The only exception to this is the verb *be*. On the board write: *Tad was sick yesterday. He had a fever. Tad e-mailed the teacher.* Ask students to make these sentences negative.

4 page 28   10 min.

1. were not/weren't	6. gave
2. killed	7. saw; called
3. sent	8. did not/didn't change; took
4. started	
5. were not/ weren't	9. studied
	10. did not/didn't save

- **Tip:** Direct students to the list of irregular verbs on page A4 in the appendix. Encourage students to use this list to check their written work.

- **Expansion Tip:** Ask students to choose three useful verbs from the list of irregular verbs in the appendix. On the board, write a simple sentence with each verb in the simple past and ask students to find the base form of each verb.

- **Note 2:** Students are often confused about subjects in sentences. On one side of the board, write the following pair of questions: *Who called you? Who did you call?* On the other side, write the following pair of answers: *I called my mother. Rita called me.* Write *S* for (*subject*) above *Who* in question 1 and above *you* in question 2. Ask students to find the subject in each response and match the questions to the answers.

5 page 29   10 min.

1. A: Did your phone ring	B: it did
2. A: Did your parents give	B: they didn't
3. A: Did the teacher send	B: s/he didn't
4. A: Did your friend pay	B: s/he did
5. A: Did you do	B: I didn't
6. A: Did I disturb	B: you didn't
7. A: Did it rain	B: it did
8. A: Did we have	B: we did

> **REAL ENGLISH, page 29**
>
> Have students think of events that happened in the past and write them on the board (e.g., *the first day of class, last Christmas*). Then ask students to write a sentence using each event and one of the time phrases (e.g., *The first day of class was two weeks ago.*).

6 SPEAK, page 30   5 min.

Answers will vary.

- **Expansion Tip:** If some students finish earlier than others, pair them with another student to ask follow-up information questions about the topic. Model this with a student (e.g., A: *Did you do anything fun last night?* B: *Yes, I did.* A: *What did you do?*). Explain that follow-up questions are part of many conversations.

7 page 30   10 min.

1. did you go
2. did you see
3. did the camera belong to
4. Did Katya write
5. gave
6. did the plane arrive

- **Expansion Tip:** Ask students to imagine that they are interviewing someone who has been to Kenya. In pairs, have them create more questions. Then ask students to interview a new partner using the questions they have written.

PRACTICE

8 page 30   10 min.

1. Did you read	6. took
2. What did she say	7. did she take
3. came	8. she took
4. found	9. She sent
5. Did it survive	

9 LISTEN & WRITE, page 31   15 min.

- **Tip:** To create interest in the topic, have students look at the photo on page 31 and read the caption. Ask, *What do you know about penguins?*

A
1. did it take	4. did they walk
2. did you choose	5. did the females return
3. did you see	

C
1. climbed	6. crowded
2. walked	7. fell
3. laid	8. survived
4. returned	9. came
5. kept	10. began

10 EDIT, page 32   10 min.

Rolf: Hi, Jun. Did you finish~~ed~~ your assignment about animal survival yesterday?

Jun: Hi, Rolf. Yes, I did. I ~~write~~ wrote about giant pandas in China.

Rolf: That's an interesting choice. How did it go?

Jun: Oh, it didn't ~~went~~ go very well.

Rolf: What ~~did go~~ went wrong?

Jun: Well, I did a lot of research, but I didn't ~~found~~ find much new information. Everyone else's assignments were at least five pages, but my assignment was only two pages.

Rolf: What did Professor Blake ~~said~~ say?

Jun: She didn't say anything—she just looked at me.

Rolf: Well, don't worry too much. I gave her the shortest assignment last week and got the highest grade in the class. She ~~sayed~~ said it was excellent!

11 APPLY, page 32   25 min.

Answers will vary.

- **Tip:** Allow lower-level students to work in pairs to create questions. Pair them with a new partner to ask and answer the questions they have written.

Student Learning Outcomes	• **Read** an interview about languages that are in danger of being lost. • **Write** and **speak** about situations in the past. • **Ask** and **answer** questions using the past progressive. • **Complete** sentences with correct verb tenses. • **Find** and **edit** errors with the simple past and past progressive. • **Write** interview questions and role-play with a partner.
Lesson Vocabulary	(adj.) alive (n.) danger (n.) musician (v.) preserve (v.) survive (n.) band (v.) encourage (v.) present (n.) recording (n.) village

EXPLORE

1 READ, page 33   10 min.

• Ask a student to locate Guatemala on a map. Explain that while Spanish is the country's official language, it is not universally spoken by the indigenous population. Over 20 Mayan languages are also spoken in Guatemala.

• Ask, *What does it mean for a language to be in danger? Do you know of any languages that are in danger?*

Be the Expert

• The term *Maya* refers to population groups in northern Central America and southern Mexico with a common linguistic and cultural heritage. Approximately 6 million Maya people live in Central America. With 21 different Maya groups composing 51 percent of Guatemala's national population, Guatemala is the only Central American republic with an indigenous culture constituting a majority of the population.

• **Expansion Tip:** Search for *Dance of the Deer* on YouTube and show students 2–3 minutes of video of this traditional Maya dance. Ask, *What is happening in this video? Why is it important for traditions to survive?*

2 CHECK, page 34   5 min.

1. b   2. c   3. a   4. c

3 DISCOVER, page 34   5 min.

A 1. b   2. a   3. a

B *be* + verb + *-ing*

• **Expansion Tip:** Play a short, simple radio commercial for the class. Allow students to listen to the commercial twice, and then write the following questions on the board: *What was this commercial advertising? Who was talking? What happened in the commercial?* Have students answer with sentences using the past progressive and write them on the board.

LEARN

Chart 2.3, page 35   5 min.

• **Notes 1 & 2:** Explain that the past progressive usually includes more information than the simple past. Write the following pair of sentences on the board: *I was eating dinner. I ate dinner.* In sentence 1, the emphasis is on the action of eating, and we want to know more: What happened when you were eating dinner? In sentence 2, the emphasis is on the completed act of eating dinner.

4 page 35   10 min.

1. was teaching
2. were listening
3. was playing
4. were talking; was not/wasn't listening
5. was looking
6. were living
7. were speaking
8. was sitting; was not/wasn't studying; was reading

REAL ENGLISH, page 35

Have students imagine that they were at the café. Ask them to use the past progressive to describe the scene in more detail.

5 WRITE & SPEAK, page 36   10 min.

Answers will vary.

- **Tip:** If students finish early, ask them to continue the conversation with follow-up questions (e.g., A: *Last night at 9:00 I was watching TV.* B: *What show were you watching?*).

Chart 2.4, page 36   5 min.

- **Expansion Tip:** Write different times on the board (e.g., *last night, Monday at 9:00 a.m., Saturday afternoon*). Ask students to write a *yes/ no* question using one of these times and the past progressive (e.g., *Were you eating dinner at 7:00 p.m. last night?*). Make sure that students have written these questions correctly. Then have students ask different classmates their question, keeping track of who says yes and no. Remind students to answer with short answers (e.g., *No, I wasn't.*). Ask volunteers to report their answers to the class.

6 page 36   10 min.

1. A. was Berta doing   B. She was teaching
2. A. Were they speaking   B. they weren't
3. A. Were you waiting   B. I was
4. A. were you going   B. I was going
5. A. was Jane talking   B. She was talking
6. A. were those people cheering   B. their team was playing
7. A. were you doing   B. I was cooking
8. A. Was it snowing   B. it wasn't

7 SPEAK, page 37   5 min.

Answers will vary.

PRACTICE

8 page 37   5 min.

1. were listening
2. played
3. stopped
4. wanted
5. left
6. asked
7. broke
8. fell
9. was walking
10. stepped
11. bought
12. was sitting
13. were studying
14. were using
15. saw
16. was eating
17. went
18. sat

- **Expansion Tip:** Ask students to read their answers aloud in pairs. Pay attention to the pronunciation of the past tenses and correct any errors.

9 page 37   10 min.

1. was dying
2. was walking
3. owned
4. thought
5. arrived
6. saw
7. was sleeping
8. opened

10 EDIT, page 38   10 min.

Dr. Anderson and his team made some interesting discoveries during a trip to Siberia in Russia. They were studying Xyzyl (*hizzle*), a local language there. They ~~were visiting~~ visited five villages during their trip, and they found that 50 to 60 people in those communities spoke Xyzyl in their daily lives. In one village, they ~~were talking~~ talked to an eleven-year-old girl called Kristina. She ~~was knowing~~ knew how to speak Xyzyl. Her grandmother was teaching her. Kristina was the youngest Xyzyl speaker in the village. Most of the other Xyzyl speakers ~~got~~ were getting old. It was clear that the Xyzyl language ~~died~~ was dying. Dr. Anderson and his team studied the language, and they ~~were making~~ made recordings to help it survive.

11 APPLY, page 38   25 min.

A 1. Where did your team go?

2. How many villages did you visit?

3. Who did you talk to in the village?

4. What were you doing in the village?

5. *Answers will vary.*

B *Answers will vary.*

- **Expansion Tip:** Ask students to write a paragraph using the information from the interview. Remind them to pay attention to simple past and past progressive verbs.

- **Alternative Writing & Speaking:** Ask students to bring in a personal photo or a picture from a magazine representing a major life event. Put students in pairs and ask them to exchange pictures. Have each student write questions about his or her partner's event (e.g., *How did you feel? What were you doing? Why were you dancing?*). Then have students interview each other. For homework, ask students to write about their partner's event using the simple past and past progressive.

Student Learning Outcomes	• **Read** an article about a mountain climber who survived an avalanche. • **Use** past time clauses to talk about interrupted events. • **Talk** about the events that occurred during the day. • **Complete** sentences based on a timeline. • **Listen** to a conversation about an Antarctic explorer. • **Write** about an accident that happened to you or someone you know.
Lesson Vocabulary	(n.) accident (v.) bury (v.) discover (v.) rescue (v.) sink (n.) bottom (n.) disaster (n.) mine (adj.) safe (n.) surface

EXPLORE

1 READ, page 39   10 min.

• Have students look at the photo and read the caption. Ask, *What is an avalanche? Why is an avalanche dangerous?*

• Use gestures or draw on the board to explain the meaning of the words *buried*, *snapping*, and *rolling*. Explain the meaning of the phrases *tons of snow* and *to take a month off*.

Be the Expert

• Jimmy Chin is a professional mountain climber, skier, filmmaker, and National Geographic photographer. Chin has climbed Mount Everest three times, and in 2006 became the first American to successfully complete a ski descent from the summit.

• **Expansion Tip:** Provide students with a hard copy of the below excerpt from Jimmy Chin's journal in which he describes his experience being caught in an avalanche. Ask students to circle the verbs and rewrite the paragraph using the simple past.

"Then the world shifts, something feels unfamiliar and I hear someone yell. I look up over my shoulder to the right and see the whole mountain moving. At first it looks like slow motion footage, then, snap! Suddenly everything moves into fast forward as I watch the mountain begin to fall apart into huge slabs. It's an ocean of snow and I am being pulled downward. Faster and faster. I am part of something too big to comprehend."

2 CHECK, page 40   5 min.

1. F (A Class 4 avalanche can destroy buildings.)

2. F (Chin was skiing with friends.)

3. T

4. F (Chin's friends did not have to dig him out.)

5. T

3 DISCOVER, page 40   5 min.

A 1. In 2011, while <u>he was skiing in the Teton Mountains</u> [1], <u>an avalanche started behind him</u>.

2. When <u>he looked up</u>, <u>trees were snapping all around him</u> [1].

B 1. past progressive

2. simple past

LEARN

Chart 2.5, page 41   5 min.

• **Note 2:** To explain interrupted events, walk across the classroom and pretend to fall down. Then ask the students what happened. On the board, draw a time line. Write *I was walking* on the bottom of the time line and draw a wavy horizontal line above this sentence. Then make an *X* at a specific point under the wavy line and write *I fell down* above the *X*. Explain that the past progressive is used in sentence 1 to show that the action was interrupted and that the simple past is used in sentence 2 to show that this second action interrupted the first action. Then combine the sentences using both *when* and *while* (i.e., *I was walking when I fell down. / While I was walking, I fell down.*).

• **Notes 3 & 4:** Explain that *while* is only used before the past progressive, whereas *when* can be used with the simple past or past progressive.

4 page 41   10 min.

1. was skiing; began
2. reached; was lying
3. lost; was swimming
4. sank; were fishing
5. cut; was cooking
6. was shopping; went off
7. found; was walking
8. was preparing; felt
9. broke; was taking
10. heard; was hiking

Chart 2.6, page 42   5 min.

- **Note 3:** Explain that a comma comes after the time clause (the clause that begins with *when*) when it comes first in a sentence. Remind students of this rule as they work on exercise **5**.

5 page 42   10 min.

1. When <u>the storm ended</u> [1], <u>the workers began to clean up</u> [2].
2. When <u>Tuan got out of the hospital</u> [1], <u>he made plans for a vacation</u> [2].
3. <u>We looked out the window</u> [2] when <u>we heard the noise</u> [1].
4. When <u>she saw the fire in her kitchen</u> [1], <u>Michelle screamed for help</u> [2].
5. <u>My son called me</u> [2] when <u>his plane landed</u> [1].
6. <u>The music started</u> [2] when <u>the bride and groom walked into the room</u> [1].
7. When <u>the phone rang</u> [1], <u>Isabelle turned the TV off</u> [2].
8. <u>I called my parents</u> [2] when <u>I received my exam results</u> [1].

- **Expansion Tip:** Write the sentences from exercise **5** on strips of paper and cut them each into two clauses. Ask students to combine the clauses to make statements and compare their answers. Remind students to pay attention to the use of commas in the sentences.

6 page 42   10 min.

1. got
2. put
3. walked
4. told
5. heard
6. bought
7. started
8. went

7 SPEAK, page 43   5 min.

Answers will vary.

- **Expansion Tip:** Have students ask their partners what happened next after each of their sentences. Students should respond using a time clause (e.g., *When I woke up this morning, I called my parents. When my mother answered the phone, I asked her a question.*).

PRACTICE

8 page 43   10 min.

1. fell
2. waited
3. began
4. arrived
5. attached
6. read
7. completed
8. watched

- **Tip:** Ask students if they have heard about this news story. Explain that a mine is a place under the ground where workers (*miners*) dig for minerals such as coal and salt. Ask students what dangers miners could face.

9 LISTEN, page 44   15 min.

A 1. 27   2. 1915   3. yes

B 1. was approaching; became
2. froze; surrounded
3. stayed; made
4. waited; did not/didn't release
5. were arranging; began
6. started; decided
7. were trying; spent
8. arrived; received

- **Tip:** Before students listen to the conversation again in exercise **B**, have them look at the photo and read the caption. Ask, *Where are the men?* Use gestures or draw on the board to explain the meaning of the verbs *approach*, *surround*, and *release*.

10 APPLY, page 45   25 min.

A   You won't believe what happened to me tonight! <u>While I was crossing Newton Street</u>, a truck went through a red light. The driver was texting <u>when the light changed</u>. He wasn't looking at the road. <u>When I jumped out of the way</u>, I fell onto the sidewalk and cut my knee. I was wearing my new jeans, too! <u>When I got home</u>, I took care of my knee and then called the police. Fortunately, I got the truck's license number <u>while I was lying in the street</u>.

B *Answers will vary.*

C *Answers will vary.*

D *Answers will vary.*

- **Alternative Writing & Speaking:** Choose a news event that has meaning for everyone in the class such as a presidential election or the death of a dignitary. Ask students where they were when they heard this news. Then have them follow the same steps as in exercise **C** and **D**.

Student Learning Outcomes	• **Read** a conversation about Lord Elgin's collection of stone carvings. • **Ask** and **answer** questions about childhood. • **Complete** an article about the Iceman with *used to* and *would*. • **Write** about the lives of people 5000 years ago and people today. • **Discuss** changes you and a partner have made in your own lives.				
Lesson Vocabulary	(n.) archaeologist (n.) arrow	(n.) complaint (n.) display	(v.) explore (n.) flour	(n.) object (n.) site	(n.) statue (n.) treasure

EXPLORE

1 READ, page 46　　　　　　　10 min.

• Have students look at the photos and read the captions. Ask, *What are some national treasures in your home country? Where are they?*

• Explain the meaning of *treasures* and *site* in the context of the conversation. Ask students to name some examples of treasure and some important historic sites.

Be the Expert

• In the early nineteenth century, the Earl of Elgin took many of the sculptures from the Acropolis and brought them to England. The sculptures are on display at the British Museum in London, but many people think they should be returned to Greece.

• **Expansion Tip:** After students have read the conversation, direct them to the last sentence. Ask, *What does Cho think is wrong?* Have students read again the previous statements by Noriko to find the answer. Then ask the class whether they agree with Cho and leave enough time for students to share their opinions.

2 CHECK, page 47　　　　　　　5 min.

　1. F　　　2. F　　　3. T　　　4. T　　　5. F

• **Tip:** Have students correct the false statements to make them true.

3 DISCOVER, page 47　　　　　　　5 min.

A 1. S　　　2. S　　　3. R　　　4. R　　　5. R

B *used to* and *would*

• **Tip:** Ask students to think of ways that the world has changed in the last 50 years. Write topics such as technology and travel on the board. Then write a pair of sentences about changes involving one of

these categories (e.g., *Fifty years ago, people used to write letters more often. Today, many people text.*). Have pairs of students discuss other changes.

LEARN

Chart 2.7, page 48　　　　　　　10 min.

• **Note 2:** Call students' attention to *used to* and *didn't use to*. Explain that *use* is the base form of the verb; when it is used in the negative, *use* does not need the past tense.

• **Expansion Tip:** Have students complete the following pair of sentences: *When I was a child, I used to. . . .* and *I didn't use to. . . .* Ask students to share their sentences.

> **REAL ENGLISH, page 48**
>
> Ask students to write sentences about how their lives have changed in the past ten years (e.g., *I used to watch TV. Now I spend that time on my homework.*). Explain that we do not use *used to* if the situation is ongoing.

4 page 48　　　　　　　10 min.

1. Archaeologists **used to remove** objects from historic sites.

2. I **used to go** to museums every weekend when I lived in Berlin.

3. My cousin **used to live** across the street, but I didn't see him much.

4. Jim **didn't use to like** math when he was in school.

5. There **used to be** a supermarket near my home until last year.

6. Carole **used to play** in a band in college.

7. I **didn't use to drive** much when I lived downtown.

8. Mike **used to work** in a bank before he got his new job.

- **Note:** Remind students that questions with *use to* follow the same rules as other simple past verbs. Even though *used to* is never used in the present tense, *use to* is still the base form.

- **Expansion Tip:** If students wrote sentences for the expansion tips above, have them write these as questions for their classmates.

> **REAL ENGLISH, page 49**
>
> Explain to students that there is no pause in informal spoken English between *used to* and the following word (e.g., *used to go* = /yustəgo/). Ask students to practice reading their sentences from exercise **4** first by whispering to themselves, and then by reading them aloud to a partner.

5 page 49   5 min.

1. Did you use to ride
2. did you use to do
3. Did your family use to live
4. did your mother use to work
5. did your family use to do
6. used to be
7. Did you use to visit
8. did you use to go

6 SPEAK, page 49   5 min.

Answers will vary.

- **Expansion Tip:** Have students write answers to the questions from exercise **5** for homework. Cross out each student's name and then distribute the papers randomly to the class. Instruct students to read the answers and guess whose paper they have.

Chart 2.9, page 50   10 min.

- **Notes 1 & 2:** To show the difference between past actions or habits and past situations or states, direct students back to exercise **5**.

7 page 50   10 min.

1. would take
2. would not/wouldn't start
3. would/'d play
4. would/'d eat
5. would not/wouldn't go
6. would/'d relax
7. would study
8. would/'d sit
9. would/'d run
10. would/'d go

- **Tip:** Students sometimes have difficulty pronouncing the word *would*. Demonstrate the correct pronunciation to the class, and then have students practice saying the word aloud a few times. Demonstrate the correct pronunciation again to correct any errors during the speaking activities.

- **Expansion Tip:** Have students read again the sentences in exercise **7**. Then ask them to write 3–4 similar sentences about their own childhood by using *would* (e.g., *When I was a child, my grandmother would take me to the ballet once a year.*). Ask students to volunteer to write sentences on the board.

PRACTICE

8 page 51   10 min.

1. discovered	6. killed
2. used to think	7. didn't spend
3. used to hunt	8. didn't grow
4. would go	9. found
5. wouldn't come	10. used

9 WRITE, page 52   15 min.

Answers will vary.

- **Expansion Tip:** Ask students who finish first to write their sentences on the board.

10 APPLY, page 52   25 min.

Answers will vary.

- **Alternative Writing & Speaking:** Write different time periods on the board (e.g., *ancient Greece, the 1700s, 1950, 1980*). Have students write 1–2 sentences about each time period with *used to*, *would*, and *didn't use to*. Ask students to volunteer to read their sentences to the class and correct errors as necessary.

1 page 53 10 min.

1. used to believe
2. put; was talking
3. landed; started
4. would walk
5. did Malik write
6. used to live; moved
7. Did you use to go; were living
8. was driving; broke down
9. wanted
10. Were you playing; hurt

2 page 53 10 min.

1. was sitting; saw
2. used to write
3. tried; happened
4. were; used to play
5. Did you have; were learning
6. went
7. was working; called; did not/didn't answer
8. used to visit

3 EDIT, page 54 10 min.

   Northern India is very hot. The area gets a lot of rain, but the water disappears very quickly because of the heat. Around 1500 years ago, the people of northern India ~~used to begin~~ began to build stepped wells to provide water for the population. They dug deep holes to reach water underground, and they ~~were making~~ made rock walls for the wells. In each well, they ~~builded~~ built stone steps and passages to help people reach the water easily. They often ~~were decorating~~ decorated the walls of the passages with beautiful designs.

   The stepped wells were long and narrow. They were cool, dark places, and they ~~were~~ often ~~having~~ had special rooms away from the heat. While people were collecting water, they would ~~took~~ take some time out of their busy day and talk with their neighbors. The wells ~~becomed~~ became important social centers.

4 LISTEN & WRITE, page 54 15 min.

A

	Eric Nerhus	Ben Nyaumbe	Kootoo Shaw	James Morrow
Activity	diving	working on a farm	sleeping	swimming
Animal	shark	python	polar bear	alligator
Place	Australia	Kenya	Canada	Florida
Reason for Survival	the shark bit his belt	he bit the python's tail	a hunter shot the polar bear	his facemask protected him

B *Answers will vary.*

5 SPEAK, page 55 15 min.

Answers will vary.

- **Expansion Tip:** After students have told their stories, have their partners ask questions. Students should use these questions to find ways to make their stories more detailed. Then pair up students with a different partner to tell their story again. Students can write their stories for homework.

Connect the Grammar to Writing

1 READ & NOTICE THE GRAMMAR,
page 56   25 min.

A *Answers will vary. Possible answers:*

A river near her house flooded.

She waited for help on the roof with her family.

B   When I was a young girl, we lived near a river.
Every spring when the snow melted, it caused the
river to rise a few feet. Then the level of the river
would fall again. One spring, however, the river
kept rising.

    One day that spring, I looked out my window.
The river was rising very quickly. My parents came
and got me. While the water was rising higher,
we climbed onto the roof of our house. From the
roof, I looked down at the river. It was covering
everything in its path. My family and I waited on
our roof for help. I was losing hope when we were
finally rescued.

C *Answers will vary. Possible answers:*

Event 3: We climbed onto the roof of our house.

Event 4: We waited and finally we were rescued.

- **Expansion Tip:** If students finish early, point out
that some information is missing from the story
(e.g., we do not know who rescued the writer
or how she was rescued). Ask students to write
questions for the writer to find out the missing
information. Then have students interview each
other in pairs with one student asking questions
and the other answering as if he or she were the
writer.

2 BEFORE YOU WRITE, page 57   10 min.

Answers will vary.

3 WRITE, page 57   25 min.

> ### WRITING FOCUS, page 57
>
> Prepare 3–4 sentences before class, one
> of which is a fragment. Write these sentences
> on the board and ask students to decide
> which one is a fragment. Then ask them to
> rewrite the fragment so it is grammatically
> correct.

- **Alternative Writing:** Have students fill out a
chain-of-events chart about an exciting event in
their life (e.g., a wedding, a party, or a vacation).
Then have them use the chart to write a paragraph
about the event.

Health and Fitness

Nouns

Unit Opener

Photo: Have students look at the photo and read the caption. Ask, *Where are the people in this photo? What are they doing?*

Location: With a population of over 24 million, Shanghai is the most populated city in China. Ask a student to locate Shanghai on a map.

Theme: This unit talks about ways that people stay healthy and fit around the world. Have students look at the photos on pages 60–61, 68, and 74–75. Ask, *What is happening in these photos? What can we learn from these stories?*

Page	Lesson	Grammar	Examples
60	1	Plural and Possessive Nouns; *Another* and *Other*	apples, classes, parties, potatoes, leaves, beliefs The **child's** room is messy. The **girls'** bicycle is blue. This pen doesn't work. I need **another** pen. Some people like to talk. **Other** people prefer to listen.
68	2	Count and Non-Count Nouns	A **doctor** is coming. Many **doctors** are coming. **Health** is important. The **coffee** tastes good.
74	3	Quantity and Measurement Words	We need **some** bananas. Give the plants **a little** water. He drank a **bottle of juice**. I bought three **loaves of bread**.
81	**Review the Grammar**		
84	**Connect the Grammar to Writing**		

Unit Grammar Terms

count noun: a noun that names something you can count. Count nouns are singular or plural.
➢ *I ate an **egg** for breakfast.*
➢ *I have **six apples** in my bag.*

measurement word: a word that is used to talk about a specific amount or quantity of a non-count noun.
➢ *We need to buy a **box** of pasta and a **gallon** of milk.*

non-count noun: a noun that names something that cannot be counted.
➢ *Carlos drinks a lot of **coffee**.*
➢ *I need some **salt** for the recipe.*

noun: a word that names a person, place, or thing.
➢ *They're **students**.*
➢ *He's a **teacher**.*

plural noun: the form of a noun that indicates more than one person, place, or thing.
➢ *He put three **boxes** on the table.*
➢ *Argentina and Mexico are **countries**.*

possessive noun: a noun that shows ownership or a relationship.
➢ ***Leo's** apartment is large.*
➢ *The **girls'** books are on the table.*

quantifier: a word used to describe the amount of a noun.
➢ *We need **some** potatoes for the recipe.*
➢ *I usually put **a little** milk in my coffee.*

Student Learning Outcomes	• **Read** an article about traditional healers in southern Africa. • **Complete** sentences with *another, other,* or *the other* and with *one* or *ones.* • **Ask** and **answer** questions about belongings. • **Complete** a pronunciation chart with different plural endings. • **Find** and **edit** errors with plural nouns and possessive nouns. • **Write** sentences about items that belong to different people.
Lesson Vocabulary	(v.) breathe (n.) height (adv.) instead (n.) patient (n.) pill (n.) diet (v.) ignore (n.) limit (n.) pattern (n.) temperature

EXPLORE

1 READ, page 60   10 min.

• Have students look at the photo and read the caption. Ask, *What is the man's job? How is he different from a western doctor?*

• Explain *drumming* through mime.

• Explain the meaning of *shells* and *ignore.*

Be the Expert

• Sangomas are well respected in African cultures. Their belief in ancestral spirits and their knowledge of traditional medicine guide their practices. Sangomas go through extensive training and can be men or women. Some estimates say that approximately 60% of people in South Africa consult a sangoma.

• Many cultures use both modern and traditional medicine. Remind students to be respectful of other cultures' practices.

2 CHECK, page 61   5 min.

   1. F   2. T   3. F   4. T   5. F

• **Tip:** Ask higher-level students to correct the false sentences.

3 DISCOVER, page 61   5 min.

A   1. healers   6. patients
     2. dances   7. ceremonies
     3. people   8. drinks
     4. women   9. bones
     5. babies   10. scientists

B Most plural nouns are formed by adding an *-s* to the singular form (e.g., *plants, dances*). The plural forms of nouns ending in *-y* (e.g., *baby*) are formed by changing the *-y* to an *-i* and adding *-es* (e.g., *babies*). Some nouns have irregular plural forms (e.g., *people, women*).

• **Expansion Tip:** Ask students to think of nouns related to health and medicine (e.g., *pill, hospital*). Put the words in two categories: singular and plural nouns.

LEARN

Chart 3.1, page 62   5 min.

• **Tip:** Write *girl* on the board and ask students which rule from the chart determines the spelling of the plural form. Then elicit the plural form and write *girls (#1)* next to the singular form. Repeat the exercise with the following nouns: *text (texts [#1]), berry (berries [#3]), wish (wishes [#2]), key (keys [#1]), tomato (tomatoes [#4]), baby (babies [#3]), bench (benches [#2]).*

4 page 62   10 min

   1. Scientists   6. teeth
   2. stories   7. bananas
   3. babies   8. potatoes
   4. children   9. lunches
   5. lives   10. beliefs

Ask students if they can think of other nouns that are only used in the plural form (e.g., *binoculars, scissors, braces, goggles, pajamas, tights, pants, shorts*). Write the nouns on the board as they are elicited and supplement the list if necessary. Then ask students to volunteer to write a sentence on the board using one of the words. Correct any errors in plural formation or subject-verb agreement.

5 page 62   10 min.

Answers will vary.

- **Expansion Tip:** Have students choose a plural noun from chart 3.1 and write it on a piece of paper. Have students ask each other the spelling of their word. When each pair has spelled the word correctly, they should switch papers and find a new partner. Have students repeat the activity until they have spelled at least ten words.

Chart 3.2, page 63   5 min.

- **Note:** Many languages show possession through different word order (e.g., *the house of the girl* vs. *the girl's house*). Because the possessive *s* looks similar to the plural *s* and the third-person *s*, it is understandable that students get confused. Remind students that possessives have an apostrophe either before or after the *s*, and that they are used with nouns rather than verbs.

6 page 63   5 min.

1. Maria's
2. nurse's
3. students'
4. children's
5. doctors'
6. baby's
7. People's
8. parents'

7 page 63   10 min.

1. dentist's
2. building's
3. Mrs. Achebe's
4. doctors'
5. Amy's
6. city's
7. women's
8. Mark and Sam's

8 page 64   10 min.

Answers will vary.

- **Expansion Tip:** Have groups of 3–4 students write sentences about things that belong to their classmates, or that they can see in the classroom. Ask students to volunteer to read one of their sentences to the class.

Chart 3.3, page 64   5 min.

- **Note:** Explain that the words *another* and *the other* refer to something that has already been mentioned. On the board, write: *I ate one chocolate bar. Now I want another one.* Circle *another* and ask students what this refers to. Draw an arrow back to *chocolate bar*. Explain that this could also be written without *one*. Then write: *Our team won the game 4–2. Jorge scored one goal, and I scored the others.* Circle *the others* and ask students what this refers to. Draw an arrow to *goal*. Explain that this could also say *the other goals* or *the other ones*.

9 page 64   10 min.

1. another
2. Other
3. The other
4. other
5. another
6. The other
7. the other
8. another

- **Tip:** Ask students to circle the noun that *another, other,* or *the other* refers to in each sentence. Ask them to write *S* for *singular* or *P* for *plural* above the nouns (e.g., circle *pill* in sentence 1, and show that this is singular by writing *S* above the circled word).

10 page 65   10 min.

1. one
2. ones
3. one
4. one
5. ones
6. one
7. ones
8. ones

- **Tip:** Ask students to circle the noun that *one* or *ones* refers to in each sentence. Ask them to write *S* for *singular* or *P* for *plural* above the nouns (e.g., circle *vitamin* in sentence 1, and show that this is singular by writing *S* above the circled word).

PRACTICE

11 page 65   5 min.

1. doctor's
2. baby's
3. patients
4. man's
5. teachers
6. people
7. children's
8. feet

12 PRONUNCIATION, page 65   15 min.

A 1. /əz/
2. /s/
3. /z/
4. /s/
5. /s/
6. /z/
7. /z/
8. /z/
9. /z/
10. /əz/
11. /əz/
12. /əz/

- **Tip:** On the board, make a chart with each of the plural ending pronunciations as the column headings and number the columns 1–3. Have students give the column number along with the answers.
- **Expansion Tip:** Tell students that they are going to get moving. Say, *If the word is in group 1, stand up. If the word is in group 2, raise one hand. If it is in group 3, raise two hands.* Model this first few times to be sure that students understand the rules. Call out the words from the list one at a time in random order.

13 page 66   10 min.

1. the other doctor
2. another bottle of vitamins
3. The other oranges
4. another error
5. The other people
6. Other weeks
7. another coat
8. Other students

14 EDIT, page 67   25 min.

The human body is amazing, but it has limits. Do you know your ~~bodies~~ body's limits in these extreme situations? Here are some helpful facts:

HEAT: When a person's body temperature reaches 107.6 degrees Fahrenheit (42 degrees Celsius), he or she can die. In a burning building, ~~adultes~~ adults can breathe air at 300 degrees F (149 degrees C) for ten minutes. Children's ~~bodys~~ bodies are not as strong.

COLD: Low ~~temperature's~~ temperatures are also very dangerous. In cold water, the human body loses heat very quickly. People usually don't survive for more than 30 minutes in water that's 40 degrees Fahrenheit (4.4 degrees Celsius).

ALTITUDE: *Altitude* is the measurement of height above the level of the sea. Many people find it difficult to breathe at 15,000 ~~foot~~ feet (4572 meters). Mountain ~~climber's~~ climbers sometimes have serious health ~~problemes~~ problems at very high altitudes.

15 APPLY, page 67   25 min.

Answers will vary.

- **Tip:** Have students make a list of 3–4 people to write about before doing exercise **A**.
- **Alternative Writing & Speaking:** Have students work in groups of 3–4 to plan an imaginary trip camping in the wild, hiking on a tropical island, or mountain climbing. Each group can only bring ten items. Have students make lists of ten items individually and then decide on the best ten items to bring. Monitor the activity to make sure that students are using plural and possessive nouns correctly. At the end of the activity, have students write their lists on the board and compare what the different groups decided to bring.

LESSON 2 | Count and Non-Count Nouns

Student Learning Outcomes	• **Read** an article about superfoods in different parts of the world.
	• **Complete** a conversation using count and non-count nouns.
	• **Ask** and **answer** questions about food.
	• **Listen** to an interview with a doctor.
	• **Write** sentences about healthy foods.

Lesson Vocabulary	(n.) bone	(n.) flavor	(adj.) popular	(v.) produce	(v.) treat
	(n.) clothing	(n.) furniture	(v.) prevent	(adj.) scientific	(n.) vitamin

EXPLORE

1 READ, page 68   10 min.

- Have students look at the photos and read the caption. Ask, *Have you tried any of these superfoods? What foods do you eat to be healthy?*

- Explain that the word *disease* means a bad sickness that lasts for a long time.

Be the Expert

- Argan nuts grow in the southwest part of Morocco. The trees are thorny, but goats still climb the trees. The nuts have a green outer layer that the goats eat. Inside is a hard shell with 1–3 kernels. It can take up to 20 hours to make one liter of oil from argan nuts.

- Acai palms are tall, thin trees that can grow to be 82 feet tall with leaves at least 9.8 feet long. The acai palm tree mainly grows in wet areas such as swamps.

- Ginseng root (the part of the plant that is underground) is most commonly used for medicinal purposes. It is usually ground into a powder and can be found in tea and energy drinks.

2 CHECK, page 69   5 min.

1. b   2. a   3. c   4. a   5. b   6. c

3 DISCOVER, page 69   5 min.

A 1. The oil from argan (nuts) is very important to the (people) of southwestern Morocco.

2. It adds flavor to food, prevents dry skin, and keeps hair soft.

3. Now some (companies) say that acai helps people lose weight.

B *Answers will vary.*

- **Tip:** Have students circle other count and non-count nouns in the reading. Then have them compare their answers in pairs.

LEARN

Chart 3.4, page 70   5 min.

- **Notes 1 & 2:** The distinction between count and non-count nouns can be difficult for students because this varies among languages.

- **Note 3:** Remind students that non-count nouns are used with singular pronouns and verb forms. If students ask how to specify amounts with non-count nouns, assure them that this will be discussed in Lesson 3.

4 page 70   10 min.

1. hair	7. time
2. say	8. times
3. is	9. information is
4. is; it	10. was
5. stores	11. is; it
6. An apartment	12. experiences

- **Tip:** On the board, create a chart with count nouns on one side and non-count nouns on the other. Add the nouns from exercise **4** to the chart as you review the answers.

REAL ENGLISH, page 70

Explain that it is helpful to classify words as being *usually* count or *usually* non-count, because there might be some occasions where the word can be used in a different way. The non-count uses are abstract ideas or a large quantity, rather than individual amounts or pieces.

- **Expansion Tip:** Direct students' attention to #12 of exercise **4** and explain that some nouns have both a count and non-count form. Write the following pairs of sentences on the board and ask students to fill in the blanks with either the count or non-count form of the words in parentheses:

  1. *The teacher has _____ teaching grammar.*

     Cindy told us about her _____ in Africa.

     (experience)

  2. *Sophie loves _____. At the restaurant, she ordered a plate with four different _____.*

     (cheese)

  3. *Did you cut your _____? I found two _____ in my soup. (hair)*

Chart 3.5, page 71   5 min.

- **Note:** On the board, make a chart with a column for each of the four categories: 1 = a category of related items, 2 = something that does not have separate parts, 3 = an abstract noun, 4 = a subject of study. Ask students to close their books. Call out a non-count noun that fits in one of the categories (e.g., *sugar*) and elicit the category (2) from the class. Write *sugar* in column 2. Continue the activity until you have elicited two words in each category. Then ask students to think of more words for each category.

5 page 71   10 min.

1. biology (4)	7. experience (3)
2. homework (1)	8. advice (3)
3. food (1)	9. money (1)
4. cheese (2)	10. energy (3)
5. fruit (1)	11. mail (1)
6. coffee (2)	

PRACTICE

6 page 72   10 min.

1. fruit is	7. homework
2. it smells	8. help
3. isn't	9. it's
4. times	10. time
5. look	11. exercise
6. They do	12. aren't

7 page 72   10 min.

1. time	7. exercise
2. homework	8. time
3. classes	9. times
4. assignment	10. energy
5. fun	11. health
6. advice	

- **Expansion Tip:** Have students write similar conversations using information about themselves. Model this by replacing details from the dialog with your own information (e.g., A: *Hey Anna, do you want to go to the movies tonight?* B: *Yes! I have time. I don't have a lot of homework tonight.*).

8 LISTEN, WRITE & SPEAK, page 73   10 min.

A squash, green vegetables, lettuce, cabbage, oranges

B
1. squash	5. green vegetables, lettuce, cabbage
2. squash	
3. oranges	6. green vegetables, lettuce, cabbage
4. oranges	

C *Answers will vary.*

D *Answers will vary.*

- **Expansion Tip:** Have students work in groups of 3–4 to create a menu for a healthy meal. Then ask for a volunteer from each group to present their ideas to the class. Correct any errors with count and non-count nouns.

9 APPLY, page 73   10 min.

Answers will vary.

Student Learning Outcomes	• **Read** an article about sports science. • **Give advice** about healthy eating. • **Listen** to a conversation about different kinds of diets. • **Write** sentences about different diets. • **Find** and **edit** errors in a paragraph about a fitness program. • **Discuss** healthy and unhealthy habits.
Lesson Vocabulary	(v.) analyze (n.) calorie (n.) effort (adj.) obvious (n.) practice (v.) avoid (n.) container (adv.) especially (n.) performance (n.) success

EXPLORE

1 READ, page 74   5 min.

- Have students look at the photo and read the caption. Ask, *What are they celebrating? What makes someone a good soccer player?*
- Explain that *star players* are the best players, the *head coach* is the person who manages and trains a sports team, and *frequently* means very often.

Be the Expert

- There are two soccer teams in the northern English city of Manchester: Manchester City and Manchester United. For a long time, Manchester United was the more successful team. This made Manchester City's 2012 win even more exciting.
- Winning the English Premier League title is the top honor for English soccer teams. In England, the game of soccer is referred to as *football*.
- Have students do an Internet search for *Manchester City FC* to find pictures and videos of the team.

2 CHECK, page 75   5 min.

1. b   2. c   3. a   4. b

3 DISCOVER, page 75   10 min.

A 1. reasons   4. playing time
2. money   5. money
3. teams

B 1. C   2. NC   3. C   4. NC   5. NC
C 1. b   2. a   3. b   4. b

LEARN

Chart 3.6, page 76   5 min.

- **Note 3:** There is a distinction between *a few* and *few: few* implies that there is a lack of something. On the board, write the following sentences: *I have a few friends. I have few friends.* Explain that both sentences mean that you have approximately 3 friends, but that sentence 2 implies that you wish you had more friends.

4 page 76   10 min.

1. some	5. much	9. many
2. Many	6. A lot of	10. many
3. a few	7. some	11. a little
4. any	8. some	12. much

Chart 3.7, page 77   5 min.

- **Note:** Explain that nouns that are usually non-count can be used with an indefinite article or a number when referring to the noun as a single unit or to a serving size of the noun (e.g., *a coffee, two pastas*).

5 page 77   10 min.

1. slices	5. sticks	9. pieces
2. tube	6. loaves	10. gallons
3. sheet	7. bar	11. piece
4. piece	8. bowl	12. quart

- **Tip:** Explain that chart 3.7 includes examples of measurement words but that some of the non-count nouns in the chart can be used with more than one measurement word (e.g., *a pint/bowl of ice cream, a bottle/glass of juice*). Students should refer to the examples in the chart to complete exercise **5**.

6 SPEAK, page 77   5 min.

Answers will vary.

- **Expansion Tip:** Have students write a shopping list with additional non-count nouns and the measurement words from chart 3.7. Have them compare their lists in groups.

PRACTICE

7 page 78   10 min.

1. a lot of	7. slice
2. glasses	8. much
3. some	9. can
4. any	10. teaspoons
5. some	11. bottle
6. not many	

- **Expansion Tip:** Before this activity, ask, *Do you have any advice for healthy eating?* On the board, write:

Eat some _____.

Don't eat a lot of _____.

Eat a little _____.

Have students work in pairs to complete the sentences with their own ideas. Then ask for volunteers to share their answers with the class.

8 SPEAK, page 78   5 min.

Answers will vary.

9 page 78   5 min.

1. a lot of	4. much; some
2. jar; pound	5. bar; a little
3. any; bowl; piece	

- **Tip:** Explain that for most of the answers in exercise **9**, other options besides the words and phrases in the box are possible. Have students think of additional answers with a partner. Then ask students to volunteer to share their answers with the class.

10 LISTEN, WRITE & SPEAK, page 79   15 min.

A *Answers will vary.*

B

Diet Comparisons	Low-Fat Diet	Vegetarian Diet	Vegan Diet	Paleo Diet
vegetables	✓	✓	✓	✓
fruit	?	✓	✓	✓
grain	✓	✓	✓	✗
meat/protein	✓	?	✗	✓
dairy	✓	✓	✗	?
sugar	?	✓	✓	✗

C *Answers will vary.*

D *Answers will vary.*

E *Answers will vary.*

11 EDIT & SPEAK, page 80   10 min.

A   I wasn't always fit. I used to eat ~~many~~ a lot of fast food, such as hamburgers and pizza, and I didn't get ~~many~~ much exercise. I wasn't very happy. I wanted to lose ~~any~~ some weight and feel fit and healthy. I didn't want to go on a special diet. ~~Much~~ Many diets have a lot of rules, and I want to enjoy a ~~sheet~~ slice of pizza or a ~~jar~~ bowl of ice cream sometimes. Then, a ~~little~~ few months ago, I found a great new fitness plan online. The plan lets me eat different kinds of food. I even have dessert a ~~little~~ few times a week. I take a walk or ride my bike every morning. Now I'm fit and healthy, and I feel great!

B *Answers will vary.*

12 APPLY, page 80   20 min.

Answers will vary.

- **Tip:** Have students switch papers and read their partner's charts. Then ask them to write 3–4 questions for their partner, using the example in exercise **B** as a guide. Have students interview each other with the questions they have written. Have higher-level students ask follow-up questions as well.

- **Expansion Tip:** For homework, have students write a paragraph of 5–6 sentences about their partner's eating habits. Have them pay attention to count and non-count nouns and measurement and quantity words. After students have written the paragraphs, ask them to switch papers and read about themselves.

1 page 81   10 min.

1. a
2. a
3. some
4. some
5. a

6. a
7. some
8. a
9. some
10. an

2 page 81   10 min.

1. machines
2. equipment
3. fruit
4. apples

5. fact
6. information
7. suggestions
8. advice

3 page 81   10 min.

1. many
2. a few
3. Many
4. any
5. a lot of

6. a few
7. some
8. a little
9. some
10. many

4 EDIT, page 82   10 min.

~~Much~~ Many species of wild animals are dying out. This is a huge problem. The ~~healths~~ health of one group of living things often depends on another group of living things. This is true for humans, too.

~~An~~ A good example of this is in Cambodia. In 2000, scientist Jenny Daltry took a team of scientists into Cambodia's Cardamom Mountains. She wanted to make a list of the different kinds of animals there. Daltry's team discovered ~~much~~ many Siamese crocodiles there. There were 150!

The crocodiles live in marshes. Marshes are soft wet areas of land with ~~much~~ many plants. The crocodiles help keep the marsh areas wet and alive. They dig mud out of the marshes and help keep ~~a~~ water there, even during the dry season. As a result, other animals have a good source of ~~waters~~ water. This is also helpful to humans.

5 LISTEN & SPEAK, page 83   20 min.

A **Speaker 1:** c, e   **Speaker 4:** b

     Speaker 2: a, g   **Speaker 5:** d, f

     Speaker 3: h

B *Answers will vary.*

C *Answers will vary.*

- **Tip:** Elicit nouns that are related to the sports listed in exercise **C** and write them on the board (e.g., *running: laps, sneakers, distance, sprints, marathon*).

- **Expansion Tip:** Ask students to write 5–6 sentences about their partner's answers to exercise **C**.

Connect the Grammar to Writing

1 READ & NOTICE THE GRAMMAR, page 84   25 min.

A *Answers will vary.*

B

Nouns	(Adjective) + Noun (with or without *a/an*)	Quantity Word + (Adjective) + Noun
Count	your body a long walk comfortable shoes 30 minutes an hour a safe way a week Other people your mind	any shoes any fancy machines Some people several miles a lot of drills
Non-Count	The best exercise appropriate clothing additional pain	little time a lot of expensive clothing little money a lot of stress

C *Answers may vary. Possible answers:*

Reason 1: It's easy and inexpensive.

Supporting Facts:

1. You only need a comfortable pair of shoes and some appropriate clothing.

2. It only takes 30 minutes to an hour.

Reason 2: It's a safe way to stay fit.

Supporting Facts:

1. It doesn't put a lot of stress on your body.

2. It doesn't cause additional pain.

- **Tip:** If students have difficulty understanding reasons and supporting facts, write the following sentence on the board: *This is the best English class in the school.* Explain that this is your opinion, or a statement that you believe is true. Then elicit the reasons why you think this is true (e.g., *The students learn a lot.*). Ask, *What is a fact that supports your reason for thinking this?* (e.g., *Students are able to improve their grammar and remember the rules.*) Explain that a supporting fact gives more specific information about this reason. Supporting facts are different from opinions.

2 BEFORE YOU WRITE, page 85   25 min.

Answers will vary.

- **Tip:** As a class, think of some ways to stay fit. Make a list on the board.

3 WRITE, page 85   25 min.

> **WRITING FOCUS, page 85**
>
> On the board, write six sentences with errors in subject-verb agreement with count and non-count nouns using the list from exercise **2** (e.g., *Yoga classes is a good way to exercise and improve mental health.*). Have students volunteer to correct the errors by using the proper form of the verb.

- **Alternative Writing:** Have students choose one of the diets from exercise **10** on page 79 and complete a chart like the one in exercise **1C** with their opinion about the diet. Then ask students to write three paragraphs discussing their opinion about the diet and giving at least two reasons for their opinion.

Going Places

Pronouns, Prepositions, and Articles

Unit Opener

Photo: Have students examine the photo and read the caption. Ask, *What do you think the lines of light represent?*

Location: Farms cover 90 percent of North Dakota, located in the Midwest. Ask a student to locate North Dakota on a map.

Theme: This unit is about traveling around the world. Ask students to look at the photos throughout the unit. Ask, *Where would you like to visit? Why?*

Page	Lesson	Grammar	Examples
88	1	Personal Pronouns and Possessive Adjectives	**We** arrived late. John visited **us**. **Her** coat is black. This coat is **hers**. I hurt **myself**.
96	2	Prepositions of Time, Place, and Direction	Our train leaves **in the morning**. The teacher is standing **near** the window.
103	3	Articles	She needs **a** coat. We looked at **the** map.
110	4	Articles with Place Names	Baghdad is on **the** Tigris River. **The** Eiffel Tower is in Paris.
116	**Review the Grammar**		
118	**Connect the Grammar to Writing**		

Unit Grammar Terms

article: a word used before a noun: *a, an, the.*
➢ I looked up at **the** moon.
➢ Lucy had **a** sandwich and **an** apple for lunch.

object pronoun: a pronoun that takes the place of a noun as the object of the sentence: *me, you, him, her, it, us, them.*
➢ *Rita* is my neighbor. I see **her** every day.
➢ Can you help **us**?

possessive adjective: an adjective that shows ownership or relationship: *my, your, his, her, its, our, their.* Possessive pronouns are used in place of a possessive adjective + noun.
➢ **My** car is green.
➢ **Your** keys are on the table.

possessive pronoun: a pronoun that shows ownership or relationship: *mine, yours, his, hers, ours, theirs.*
➢ My sister's eyes are blue. **Mine** are brown. What color are **yours**?

preposition: a word that describes the relationships between nouns. Prepositions show space, time, direction, cause, and effect.
➢ I live **on** Center Street.
➢ We left **at** noon.

pronoun: a word that takes the place of a noun or refers to a noun.
➢ *The teacher* is sick today. **He** has a cold.

reflexive pronoun: a pronoun that refers back to the subject of the sentence: *myself, yourself, himself, herself, itself, ourselves, yourselves, themselves.*
➢ She saw **herself** in the mirror.

Student Learning Outcomes	• **Read** a conversation about bike riding in Mexico City. • **Complete** conversations with possessive pronouns, possessive adjectives, and reflexive pronouns. • **Identify** the correct pronouns or possessive adjectives required to complete sentences. • **Listen** to a man describing his experiences on a Mediterranean cruise. • **Tell** classmates about travel experiences. • **Write** sentences about classmates' travel stories.
Lesson Vocabulary	(n.) airline (v.) commute (n.) cruise (n.) flight (n.) passport (v.) arrange (n.) coworker (n.) environment (ph. v.) get around (n.) solution

EXPLORE

1 READ, page 88   5 min.

• Have students look at the photos and read the captions. Ask, *Why do you think bike riding is a good idea for the city? Why do you think some people don't like the idea?*

Be the Expert

• The metropolitan area of Mexico City is one of the largest in the world, with a population of approximately 19 million.

• In 2011, residents of Mexico City had possibly the worst commute in the world, with approximately 4 million cars on the road. In 2012, the city tried to change this. They put in new bus routes, banned cars from some narrow streets, and added 1200 bicycles to a bike-sharing program.

• Many cities now have bike-sharing programs. Cyclists can use their smartphone to reserve a bike, then return it to a different docking station (area for bikes) in the city. However, some critics complain that cities need to make bike lanes so that cycling is safe as well as simple.

2 CHECK, page 89   5 min.

  1. c   2. b   3. d; a   4. c

3 DISCOVER, page 89   10 min.

A 1. Peter and Kate   4. Bikes
   2. Peter and Kate's flight   5. People in Mexico City
   3. Peter

B

Position in Sentence		
Subject	**Object**	**Possessive Adjective**
It I	them	your their

• **Tip:** Have students work in pairs to add to the chart above. Have them write as many pronouns as possible, and then compare their answers with other pairs or direct them to charts 4.1 and 4.2 to check their answers.

LEARN

Chart 4.1, page 90   5 min.

• **Note:** Students whose native languages have formal and informal words for *you* may be hesitant to use the same pronoun for both formal and informal use. Explain that in English, intonation can convey a more formal tone.

• **Note 1:** Students sometimes include both a noun and a pronoun as the subject of a sentence. Remind students that pronouns *replace* nouns. Write the following sentences on the board and have students correct the errors: 1. *My sister she is younger than me.* 2. *The cat it is in the tree.* Students should note that they need to delete either the nouns or the pronouns.

• **Note 2:** Some students have a tendency to omit the object pronoun *it*. Write the following sentences on the board and have students correct the errors: 1. *I like the book. Did you read?* 2. *My home is far away. I miss very much.* Show students they should add *it* after *read* and *miss*.

4 page 90   5 min.

1. He   5. They

2. them   6. He; it

3. it   7. us

4. She, it

- **Tip:** Have students circle the noun that the pronoun is replacing in each sentence. Explain that sometimes the noun can be in an earlier sentence. For example, *them* in sentence 2, replaces a noun in sentence 1 (*friends*). Have students work in pairs, and then compare their answers with other pairs. If students are having trouble with this, repeat the same activity for exercise **5**.

5 page 90   10 min.

1. It   5. me

2. them   6. It; it

3. her   7. you

4. him   8. us

Chart 4.2, page 91   5 min.

- **Note 1:** In some other languages, the possessive adjective agrees with the object, not the owner. Explain that in English, the possessive always relates to the gender of the owner (e.g., *She loves her brother. He misses his mother.*).

- **Note 1:** Note that in some instances, other languages may use definite articles instead of possessives. For example, in Spanish, body parts are not possessions, but in English, they are (e.g., English: *He shook my hand.* Spanish: *He shook the hand.*).

- **Note 2:** Students sometimes use possessive pronouns in place of possessive adjectives when the noun is plural. This may be because they see the final *s*. Explain that a noun will not directly follow a pronoun. Write sentences on the board and have students correct the errors. Sample sentences: *This bike is my. Hers shoes are green.*

- **Note 5:** To demonstrate the difference between *their, they're,* and *there,* dictate three sentences to the class. Have students write exactly what they hear. Then have them compare with a partner and have volunteers write the sentences on the board. Possible sentences: *The kids rode their bikes. They're on vacation. There are three bikes for sale.* Have students discuss why the spelling they chose is correct.

6 page 91   5 min.

1. your; mine   5. yours; mine

2. His; him; hers   6. Ours

3. Our   7. his

4. theirs

7 page 92   10 min.

1. There   4. its   7. their   9. Its

2. it's   5. they're   8. It's   10. it's

3. there   6. their

- **Expansion Tip:** Have students work in pairs to write a similar conversation. Tell them to try to use at least four examples of *it's, its, their, there,* and *they're.* Then ask volunteers to perform their conversations for the class. Write a chart on the board with one column for each set of words and ask the other students to put a check in the correct column when *its/it's* and *they're/there/their* are used.

Chart 4.3, page 92   5 min.

- **Note:** Students sometimes see the pattern of *my = myself,* etc., and assume that *he = hisself* and *they = theirselves.* If students make these errors, point out that they should use *him* and *them* as the base word for the reflexive pronouns.

- **Note 3:** Reflexive pronouns can be used to emphasize that this person did the action, not someone else, e.g., *I did it myself.*

8 page 92   10 min.

1. yourself   4. themselves   7. itself

2. himself   5. myself   8. herself

3. yourselves   6. ourselves

- **Tip:** Explain that *take care of yourself* is a common salutation. *Feeling sorry for someone* means that you pity them. *To feel sorry for yourself* usually means to be sadder than necessary about something that has happened to you.

- **Expansion Tip:** Have students work in pairs to read the sentences in exercise **8** again, and add another sentence as a reply, e.g., sentence 1: *I enjoyed myself a lot!* sentence 2: *I hope he didn't hurt himself very badly.* Encourage students to use reflexive pronouns whenever appropriate.

PRACTICE

9 page 93   10 min.

1. yours	5. my	9. Their
2. Your	6. me	10. It's
3. mine	7. myself	11. them
4. it	8. your	12. ourselves

10 page 93   10 min.

1. his; he; himself	5. itself; its
2. I; myself; me	6. our; ourselves
3. yours/his/hers/theirs; mine	7. I; my; it; his
4. their; they; her	8. yourself; She; hers

11 page 94   10 min.

1. my	4. our	7. us
2. I	5. them	8. we
3. We	6. It	

12 LISTEN, page 94   15 min.

- **Tip:** To stimulate interest in the activity, ask students what often happens to passengers on a cruise. Elicit the answer *seasickness*, as this is mentioned in the listening. Explain that students will complete exercise **11**, which is told from Eva's point of view, and then they will listen to Aaron talking about the cruise in exercise **12**.

A 1. Ricardo   3. Eva

   2. Lara   4. Aaron

B

Name	What happened? Why?
1. Ricardo	He was seasick. He forgot his medicine.
2. Lara	She cut herself on a piece of broken glass.
3. Eva	She lost her balance and fell down. She hurt her shoulder.
4. Aaron	He dropped his phone into the sea.

13 APPLY, page 95   20 min.

Answers will vary.

- **Tip:** Before filling out the chart, on the board brainstorm types of trips and problems (e.g., *car trips: traffic, bad weather; airplane trips: flight delays, lost luggage.*).

- **Expansion Tip:** For homework, have students write their own story about an eventful trip they have taken. Then have students share their stories in class.

- **Alternative Apply:** Have students create a brochure to promote a restaurant, hotel, or tourist attraction. Encourage students to use possessive adjectives and pronouns and reflexive pronouns (e.g., *Try our delicious desserts and pamper yourself by the pool.*).

Student Learning Outcomes	• **Read** a website page about diving in the Bahamas. • **Talk** about yourself using prepositions of time and place. • **Ask** and **answer** questions with prepositions about your country. • **Find** and **edit** errors in an article about vacation tours on the Honey Road. • **Listen** to a description of a creative-writing vacation and **answer** questions. • **Write** about trips that classmates have taken.
Lesson Vocabulary	(n.) diver (v.) earn (n.) island (n.) route (adj.) unusual (v.) differ (n.) entrance (n.) region (n.) season (n.) variety

EXPLORE

1 READ, page 96   5 min.

- Have students look at the photos and read the captions. Ask, *What do you notice? Would you like to go to this place? Why, or why not?*

- If possible, show students an image of a mahi-mahi and a manta ray.

Be the Expert

- The Bahamas are a group of 700 islands, but people live on only 30 of them. Tourism is a major industry, with approximately 4 million tourists visiting the Bahamas each year. English and Creole are spoken in the Bahamas, and literacy is 96 percent.

- The blue holes can provide valuable information for scientists about oxygen-free environments on other planets. They are extremely dangerous for divers, however, and are considered as challenging as climbing Mt. Everest is for mountain climbers. Below the freshwater surface, there is a gas called *swamp gas*, which is hydrogen sulfide. It can be deadly in high concentrations.

- Do an Internet image search for *Bahamas Blue Holes* for pictures to show the class.

2 CHECK, page 97   5 min.

1. c   2. b   3. c

3 DISCOVER, page 97   10 min.

A

Phrases about Time	Phrases about Place
for many years; from season to season; In October; In the winter	in the Atlantic; from many countries; in the islands' clear waters; from above; to underwater caves; in the Bahamas; on Earth; at the surface; below that; to the sea

B In both columns: *from, in, to*
In one column: *for, on, at, below*

- **Tip:** Explain to students that the words at the beginning of these expressions are called prepositions, and they can be used in different ways for place and time. Write sentence frames that include prepositional phrases on the board, and have students complete in pairs.
  For many years, I have _____ by myself.
  My favorite place on earth is _____.
  In the winter, my family _____.

LEARN

Chart 4.4, page 98   5 min.

- **Tip:** Because prepositions are such short words, students may not pay attention to their use. To practice the prepositions, have pairs of students write sentences for: *at, in, on, for, from . . . until,* and *during.* On the board, make columns with each preposition. Have students read their sentences aloud to the class. Then have the other students check to make sure that the sentence is correct. If the sentence is correct, write the prepositional phrase in the correct column. Repeat the activity until there are at least two phrases in each column.

4 page 98 — 10 min.

1. for	4. on; until	7. for
2. in	5. on; at	8. at
3. in	6. at; in	

5 SPEAK, page 98 — 10 min.

Answers will vary.

- **Expansion Tip:** Have students work in pairs. Each student should answer items 1 and 2 about a friend or relative. Their partners should ask follow-up questions that the first student answers. Encourage students to use as many prepositions of time as possible.

Chart 4.5, page 99 — 5 min.

- **Notes 1, 2 & 3:** Students often find it useful to visualize what each preposition of place means. Draw stick figures on the board to represent each preposition of place. Have students label the figures with an appropriate prepositional phrase.

- **Notes 2, 3 & 4:** To show the difference between the prepositions, draw a stick figure on the board. Ask, *Where does this person live?* Write the least to the most detailed answers on the board: *He lives in London/on Baker Street/at 221b Baker Street.* Then ask students to do the same for the address of the language school.

- **Tip:** Use hand gestures or mime actions (e.g., walk toward the window) to represent *near, behind, next to, in, on, toward, over,* and *through.* Then have students take turns choosing prepositions to mime, and have their partners guess the preposition.

6 page 99 — 10 min.

1. in	3. at	5. in	7. in
2. on	4. on	6. at	8. at

- **Expansion Tip:** Bring in a map of the area in which your language class is located. Ask each student to pick a location some distance from your class, and keep it secret. Then have students work in pairs and give their partners directions to their secret locations. Listeners should try to find the location on the map based on the directions. Model an example with the class to illustrate how they can give directions using *in, near, on,* etc.

REAL ENGLISH, page 99

Have students work in pairs to create a short conversation using 3–4 of the prepositional phrases: *in class, at school, on vacation, at home, at work.* Students can begin their conversation with *Where is Henri? I have to talk to him,* or create their own opener. Have students read their conversations in small groups or to the class.

7 page 99 — 5 min.

1. behind	4. between	7. outside
2. under	5. toward	8. near
3. across	6. from	

REAL ENGLISH, page 100

Elicit times and places from the students and write them on the board (e.g., time: *July/Monday;* place: *beach/supermarket*). Then have students create sentences with times and places. Model an example such as: *(In July) I went to the beach (in July).* Have volunteers share their sentences with the class.

PRACTICE

8 SPEAK, page 100 — 15 min.

A

1. to	5. in	9. to	13. between
2. for	6. at	10. on	14. on
3. from	7. for	11. across	15. toward
4. until	8. from	12. at	

B *Answers will vary.*

- **Expansion Tip:** Ask students to read the conversation again, and discuss whether the place they grew up is more similar to the United States or Indonesia. Ask, *What advice would you have for tourists who need to cross the street in your city?* Have students write tips, using as many prepositional phrases as possible.

9 page 101 — 5 min.

1. on May 3rd	5. at night
2. at the airport	6. on Monday
3. at three o'clock	7. to/into a new house
4. in the morning	8. at 24 Oak Road

- **Expansion Tip:** Have students read the conversations in exercises **8** and **9** in pairs. Encourage them to speak with correct question intonation and express emotions.

10 EDIT, page 101   10 min.

Balyolu (pronounced bal-yoll-oo) is Turkish for "honey road." It is also the name of an unusual tour ~~on~~ in northeast Turkey.

Catherine Jaffee is a woman from Colorado in the United States. ~~At~~ In 2008, she went to Turkey and traveled for two years. When she reached Kars, a historic region ~~on~~ in Turkey, she thought of an idea for a tour. About 900 years ago, Kars was ~~in~~ on the Silk Road, an important trading route ~~from~~ between Europe and China. Kars was an important trading center ~~in~~ during/at that time. Jaffee became fascinated by the way people in Kars earn their living: beekeeping and making honey.

Jaffee created a travel experience for visitors that also helped local people. On a Balyolu tour, travelers walked several miles a day ~~at~~ for seven days. They passed ~~under~~ through many areas with beautiful scenery. Along the way, the walkers met beekeepers and their families and tasted different kinds of honey. It was the perfect trip for anyone with a sweet tooth!

- **Tip:** Explain that when something occurs a certain amount of times every day, the expression "a day" is often used (e.g., *I do homework for two hours a day.*). Explain that a person who has a *sweet tooth* is someone who likes desserts and sweet items.

11 LISTEN, page 102   15 min.

1. in Paris

2. on July 6th

3. for one month

4. in the Latin Quarter

5. at (about) 8 o'clock in the evening

6. outside a bookstore/beside the river

7. in a café/in cafés

8. before the trip

- **Tip:** This listening activity may be challenging for many students. Have students listen with their books closed and ask, *Where did the course take place? Where did the students come from?* Then have students open their books, read the questions, and discuss what else they remember. Play the audio one or two more times and have students write the answers. Ask volunteers to write their answers on the board, and play the audio again to check answers as a class. For lower-level students, print a copy of the audio script for them to read.

12 APPLY, page 102   25 min.

Answers will vary.

- **Tip:** Give students enough time to think of their answers either by assigning the first column for homework, or allowing five minutes to think of an interesting trip. Remind students that, although they have read about very exotic vacations in this chapter, their answers can be about any trip that they have taken outside of their city.

- **Alternative Apply:** Have students work in groups of 2–3 to create a list of tips for tourists who might visit their city or town. They should answer questions such as: *What is the best time of year to visit? Where should the tourists stay? What should they see? What advice would you give?* (Remind students about the earlier listening about crossing the street.) Have students present their information in groups, while the other students take notes.

Student Learning Outcomes	• **Read** an article about an adventure in Alaska and Yukon, Canada. • **Complete** conversations with *a, an, some, the,* or Ø. • **Read** an informational chart to **complete** sentences about a balloon flight. • **Listen** to a radio broadcast about a balloon flight. • **Discuss** your opinion of a balloon flight. • **Describe** a vacation activity to a partner. • **Write** about an interesting adventure.				
Lesson Vocabulary	(n.) adventure (adj.) amazing	(n.) equipment (n.) journey	(n.) limit (adj.) lonely	(v.) manage (n.) sight	(n.) speed (n.) supplies

EXPLORE

1 READ, page 103   5 min.

• Have students look at the photos and read the captions. Ask students what they already know about Alaska. Then ask, *Would you like to go on an expedition like this? Why, or why not?*

Be the Expert

• Andrew Skurka is an extreme trekker, writer, speaker, and guide. He has written a book, *The Ultimate Hiker's Gear Guide,* and he offers guided trips with names such as "Southwest Adventure" and "Backpacking Essentials." According to his website, he has traveled over 30,000 miles through the wilderness.

• Alaska has the largest area of all the states in the United States. It has a population of approximately 648,000 and Juneau, the capital, has a population of approximately 31,000 people. More than a third of the state is forested, and about a quarter of the land is designated wilderness and parkland.

• Search for *Andrew Skurka* for more information about the adventurer, or *Alaska photos* for images.

2 CHECK, page 104   5 min.

1. F	3. T	5. T
2. F	4. F	6. F

• **Tip:** Ask higher-level students to rewrite false sentences so that they are correct.

3 DISCOVER, page 104   5 min.

The second sentence of each pair is about a specific thing.

• **Tip:** Write the following pairs of sentences on the board:

1. (a) *I love the camera.*
   (b) *My sister gave me a camera for my birthday.*
2. (a) *The company designed a new type of raft.*
   (b) *John works for an interesting company.*
3. (a) *Alex bought a new backpack for his trip.*
   (b) *The backpack is very light.*

Have students decide which ones come first, and which are second. Have students explain how they made their choices. Note that the article should be *a* in the first sentence and *the* in the second.

LEARN

Chart 4.6, page 105   5 min.

• **Note:** Because articles are such short words, students may not notice how they are used in English. Try to help students pay attention to how these are used by writing *a* and *the* on the board in big letters, and circling these words. As students answer questions and speak in class, tap the circles to call attention to the articles.

• **Note:** Some languages do not use articles at all. Because non-count nouns and plural nouns do not always need an article, students may not realize that singular count nouns always need an article. The only exceptions are proper nouns. Write the following sentences on the board and have students correct the mistake in each pair of sentences: 1. *She has brother. Her brother paints houses.* 2. *They liked movie last night. They ate popcorn.* Explain that *houses* is plural and *popcorn* is non-count, so they do not need articles.

4 page 105   10 min.

1. the	3. The	5. The	7. The
2. a	4. some	6. the	8. a

- **Tip:** Have students discuss why they chose their answers for each article in exercise **4**. Discuss sentence 1 as a class. Have students write the number of the rule they applied next to each sentence. Ask, *Why is the answer* the snow? If necessary, explain that it is because snow is uncountable, and the listener knows that *snow* refers to only the snow that was there during Skurka's trip. This is similar to rule 4. Point out that on page 104, the caption talks about *the ice,* which is a similar use of the definite article.

Chart 4.7, page 106   5 min.

- **Note 1:** When the gender is unknown or if someone is speaking generally, *they/them/their/theirs* is often used to avoid saying *he or she, him or her,* etc. For example, it is more common to say, *Hikers need to carry their supplies on their backs* than *A hiker needs to carry his or her supplies on his back.*

5 page 106   10 min.

1. National parks are interesting places to visit.
2. Bikes are fast and cheap.
3. Boats are a slow way to travel.
4. Cruises are expensive.
5. Taxis are hard to find at night.
6. Cars are convenient, but they cost a lot.
7. Backpacks are useful items.
8. Explorers have interesting jobs.

- **Expansion Tip:** As a class, write several abstract topics on the board (e.g., *money, love, health*). Have students work in groups to write generalizations about the topics (e.g., *An apple a day keeps the doctor away. Love is more important than money.*). Have groups switch papers and discuss whether they agree. Have them write an additional sentence for each topic, and then read the sentences to the class.

6 page 106   5 min.

1. G	3. S	5. G	7. G
2. G	4. S	6. S	8. S

PRACTICE

7 page 107   5 min.

1. A	4. The	7. some	9. Ø
2. a	5. Some	8. an	10. The
3. some	6. A		

8 page 107   10 min.

1. the	4. the	7. the /Ø	10. a
2. a/the	5. The	8. the	11. a
3. a	6. some	9. the	12. Ø

- **Expansion Tip:** Have students create their own conversation about an errand that they need to do in the next few days. Encourage students to pay close attention to definite and indefinite articles. Have volunteers read their conversations to the class.

9 READ, LISTEN & SPEAK, page 108   25 min.

A

1. a	3. some; the	5. The; a	7. The
2. the	4. Ø; the	6. a	8. The; Ø

- **Tip:** Use the photo to explain *lawn chair* and *balloon.* Ask students what the dangers of this type of flight could be.

B

1. an	3. Ø	5. a	7. The
2. a	4. a	6. The	8. a

C
1. F (Kent Couch owns a gas station.)
2. T
3. T
4. F (They expected to fly at a height of 15,000–18,000 feet.)
5. F (Each man had a small gun.)
6. F (The weather in the north was bad.)
7. T
8: F (Their journey was not a success.)

- **Tip:** The audio is separated into three tracks: before, during, and after the flight. Explain that students will only be able to answer questions 1–5 with the first track, 6–7 with the second, and 8 with the third.

D *Answers will vary.*

10 APPLY, page 109   15 min.

Answers will vary.

- **Alternative Apply:** Have students choose the location of one of the activities or adventures in this unit, and describe it to a group of 3–4, leaving out the name of the place. Then have other students guess the location (e.g., *Breathing is hard here, but it is very beautiful. I like this because I love the water. Where do I want to go?* Answer: *Diving in the Bahamas.*). Then have students choose one place and write an e-mail home, as if they were on vacation in this place. They should write five sentences and use articles appropriately.

Student Learning Outcomes	• **Read** posts from two travel blogs. • **Talk** about geographic places. • **Complete** sentences with *the* or Ø. • **Ask** and **answer** questions about geographic places. • **Write** sentences about famous places and their locations. • **Find** and **edit** errors in a travel blog. • **Ask** and **answer** questions about cities or towns that you have visited.

Lesson Vocabulary	(n.) blog (n.) business trip	(n.) client (v.) decide	(n.) desert (n.) fall	(n.) meeting (n.) photography	(v.) post (adj.) wonderful

EXPLORE

1 READ, page 110 — 5 min.

• Have students look at the photos and ask, *Which would you rather visit? Why?* Explain that they are going to read two travel blogs, or online journals.

Be the Expert

• All the places Greg describes in his blog except for Portsmouth, his hometown, are famous American landmarks. The places Maya mentions are significant sites in New York City.

• Mount Rushmore National Memorial is a sculpture carved into the face of a mountain. It depicts four US presidents: Thomas Jefferson, George Washington, Theodore Roosevelt, and Abraham Lincoln. Approximately 3 million people visit it every year.

• Central Park in New York City covers 843 acres in the middle of Manhattan. It is free to the public. Since it opened in 1858, the park has been a place where New Yorkers can enjoy nature in the middle of a city.

• Search for images of the specific sites and ask students which ones they like the best.

2 CHECK, page 111 — 5 min.

1. Portsmouth, New Hampshire
2. all over the United States and Canada
3. the Mojave Desert
4. the Museum of Modern Art
5. the Plaza Hotel

3 DISCOVER, page 111 — 10 min.

A

Place Names with *The*	Place Names without *The*
the United States	Canada
the Rocky Mountains	Portsmouth, New
the Mojave Desert	Hampshire
the Mississippi River	New England
the Museum of	Mount Rushmore
Modern Art	San Diego
the Plaza Hotel	New York City
the Empire State	Grand Central Station
Building	Fifth Avenue
the Brooklyn Bridge	Central Park

B We use *the* before names of mountain ranges, some countries, deserts, rivers, buildings, and bridges.

• **Tip:** Have students add to the list of places on the board. Notice which places have *the,* and which do not.

LEARN

Chart 4.8, page 112 — 5 min.

• **Note:** Explain to students that the rules for using articles with geographic names are outlined in this chart. It may be helpful to have students arrange the information in a chart form with types of geographic places and examples that are meaningful to them. For example:

Country: Poland

Country with of/kingdom/republic: The Czech Republic.

River: The Vistula.

4 page 112   10 min.

1. the   6. The; Ø; the; the
2. Ø; the   7. The
3. Ø; Ø   8. the
4. Ø; the   9. Ø; Ø
5. Ø   10. Ø; the

- **Tip:** Have students write the number of the applicable rule in the chart next to each sentence. Ask, *Why is the answer to item 1* the Rocky Mountains? Note that it is because this is a plural geographic name—rule 3 on the chart. Have students compare their answers in pairs.

5 SPEAK, page 113   5 min.

Answers will vary.

- **Expansion Tip:** If possible, bring in a map of the world for the class. Have students work in groups of 2–3 to prepare 8–10 quiz questions (e.g., *Where are the Hawaiian Islands? Is the Mojave Desert in Asia?*). Encourage students to use the chart to make sure that they have used *the* and *no article* correctly. Have the groups give the questions to another team to answer. Then have the first group correct the quiz.

Chart 4.9, page 113   5 min.

- **Note:** To help students practice these rules, write the names of the places in chart 4.9 on a sheet of paper and cut each one out separately. Do not include *the* in any of the place names. Make enough copies for each group of 3–4 students and add the correct number of papers with only the word *the*. Have students close their books and add *the* to the correct places. Then have them open their books and check their answers.

6 page 113   10 min.

1. the   5. Ø   9. Ø
2. Ø   6. the   10. the
3. The   7. the   11. Ø
4. The   8. the   12. the

- **Expansion Tip:** Have students work in groups of 3–4 to make a list of places in the city or town where the school is located. This should include parks, hotels, airports, etc., but not street names. Have each team take turns naming six places. If they use *the* or *no article* correctly, they get a point. Write the place names on the board and keep a tally of points earned. The team with the most points wins.

PRACTICE

7 SPEAK & WRITE page 114   15 min.

A

Famous Places	Locations
1. the Burj Al Arab Hotel d	a. Ø Japan
2. the Great Pyramid of Giza e	b. the Himalayas
3. the Sydney Opera House f	c. Ø Rio de Janeiro
4. Ø Mount Everest b	d. Ø Dubai
5. Ø Copacabana Beach c	e. Ø Egypt
6. the Louvre Museum g	f. Ø Australia
7. Ø Haneda Airport a	g. Ø Paris

B *Answers will vary.*

C *Answers will vary.*

- **Tip:** Depending on students' general level of world knowledge, you may want to assign exercise **C** for homework. Students can also use material from this textbook for ideas of places to write about.

8 EDIT, page 115   10 min.

    I just got back from a great business trip to ~~the~~ South America. The trip started in Peru with two sales meetings in ~~the~~ Lima. Then, I flew to Venezuela for a meeting with clients in ~~the~~ Valencia. They also have an office in the Philippines. I want to go there someday! The second week I was in Chile. I had some free time, so I went skiing in the Andes. The scenery was amazing!

    I arrived at ~~the~~ Logan Airport in Boston last night. I like to travel, but it's nice to be home— ~~the~~ New England is really beautiful this time of year.

9 APPLY, page 115   25 min.

Answers will vary.

- **Alternative Apply:** Have students use an English travel website such as *TripAdvisor* to research a place that they would like to visit. Have students read what other people have said about hotels, museums, sights, etc., and then create their own itinerary. If the Internet is not available, have students use a world map to plan their perfect trip. Encourage students to write sentences using pronouns and articles appropriately.

1 page 116   10 min.

1. your   4. Ø   7. Ø   10. by

2. she's   5. in   8. some   11. a

3. for   6. from   9. her   12. an

2 EDIT, page 116   10 min.

Last year, I took a vacation to ~~the~~ Singapore with my sister Ana. We went ~~at~~ in September and had a great time. We stayed at a nice hotel, and the food there was delicious. We visited all of ~~a~~ the popular tourist places. We also went shopping ~~in~~ on Orchard Road, one of the main shopping areas. ~~At~~ In the evenings, we would sit at an outdoor café and talk until late ~~in~~ at night. It was a wonderful vacation. I want to go back there someday!

3 LISTEN & SPEAK, page 117   15 min.

A 1. b   2. b

B *Answers will vary. Possible answers:*

The Public Garden	Newbury Street	Faneuil Hall Marketplace
beautiful in the spring and summer; has a lot of flowers; a nice place to go for a walk, sit on a park bench to read and relax, or have a picnic; very peaceful; ice skating in the winter	a beautiful street; popular shopping area; has expensive shops; a nice place to meet friends and window shop; good restaurants in the area; restaurants have tables outside in the summer	near the waterfront; easy to get to by public transportation; good place to meet up with friends; has fantastic seafood; a popular tourist spot; an important part of the city's history; a good place to take out-of-town visitors

• **Tip:** Students may need to listen to the audio more than once. Explain that "to window shop" means that you look in the windows at the items without buying anything. An area that is near an ocean, lake, etc., is called *the waterfront*.

C *Answers will vary.*

4 page 117   10 min.

Answers will vary.

• **Expansion Tip:** If students are from different countries, have them prepare a 1–2 minute presentation about their hometown. If students are from the same area, have them research somewhere that they would like to go, and give a presentation about a new city. Have students take notes as they listen to the presentations. Then have students work in groups of 4–5 to discuss where they would like to go, and why.

1 READ & NOTICE THE GRAMMAR, page 118 — 15 min.

B   Last summer I went <u>to</u> Italy with my friends Maria and Beth. One day we woke up early <u>in</u> the morning and drove <u>to</u> a town <u>on</u> the coast. <u>From</u> there, we took a boat <u>to</u> a small island. This island is now my favorite place <u>in</u> the world!

I loved the colorful fishing boats <u>on</u> the beach and the pretty pink houses. The weather was perfect and the people were friendly. In fact, while we were looking <u>at</u> the boats, a fisherman waved <u>to</u> us. He and his wife invited us to have lunch with them. We had a picnic lunch <u>by</u> the sea. <u>In</u> the afternoon, we walked <u>along</u> the beach and had coffee <u>at</u> an outdoor café. When it was time to leave, I didn't want to go!

C

Where did she go?	to an island; to Italy
When did she visit this place?	last summer
Who was there?	the writer, her friends, a fisherman and his wife
What did she do?	drove to a town on the coast; took a boat to a small island; had a picnic lunch by the sea; walked along the beach; had coffee at an outdoor café
What did she see?	colorful fishing boats; the beach; pretty pink houses; an outdoor café

• **Expansion Tip:** Have students close their books, and ask them to try to remember as much of the story as they can. Have students work in pairs to tell the story using as many prepositions of time, place, and direction as possible.

2 BEFORE YOU WRITE, page 119 — 10 min.

Answers will vary.

3 WRITE, page 119 — 25 min.

WRITING FOCUS, page 119

Copy several sentences from page 118 onto slips of paper. Cut each sentence up into short phrases. Give each group of three students the phrases for two sentences. Have them close their books and put the phrases in the correct order. When they have finished, have them open their books to check their answers.

| One day | we woke up | early in the morning |
| and drove | to a town | on the coast |

• **Tip:** Often a favorite place will be somewhere that the person has been more than once. Reassure students that they can write about the first time they went to a specific place, or the first time that they brought someone else to this place.

• **Alternative Writing:** Have students write about a place where something special happened in their lives. It could be the place they met their spouse, a park where they saw a celebrity, etc. Ask, *What happened? When did it happen? Where is this place? Who was there? What made the moment so special?* Have students write two paragraphs about this place.

• **Alternative Writing:** Have students write about their bedroom, the position of the room in the house, on the street, and in the larger world. They should also describe where the furniture is in the room, and when they use each piece. Have students write two paragraphs about their rooms. Encourage them to use as many prepositions of time, place, and direction as possible.

5 A Changing World

The Present Perfect

Unit Opener

Photo: Have students look at the photo and read the caption. Ask, *How is this photo related to the theme of the unit? How has the penguins' environment changed?*

Location: The penguins are pictured on an iceberg near Antarctica. Ask a student to locate Antarctica on a map.

Theme: This unit is about changes to the world around us. Ask, *What about the world is changing?* Have students look at the photos throughout the unit for ideas.

Page	Lesson	Grammar	Examples
122	1	Present Perfect: Statements and Questions	I **have washed** the dishes. John **hasn't called** today. What **have** they **found**? Who **has been** to Italy?
130	2	Present Perfect with *For* and *Since*	I haven't seen Molly **for a long time**. She has lived in Mexico **since she was 21**.
136	3	Present Perfect and Simple Past	**Have** you **seen** that movie? Yes, I **saw** it yesterday.
144	4	Present Perfect Progressive	I've **been getting up** early lately. **Have** you **been waiting** for a long time?
151	**Review the Grammar**		
154	**Connect the Grammar to Writing**		

Unit Grammar Terms

time clause: a clause that tells when an action or event happened or will happen. Time clauses are introduced by conjunctions such as *when, after, before, while,* and *since.*
  ➤ I have lived here **since I was a child**.
  ➤ **While I was walking home,** it began to rain.
  ➤ I'm going to call my parents **after I eat dinner**.

present perfect: a verb form that connects the past to the present.
  ➤ I **have washed** the dishes.
  ➤ John **hasn't called** today.

present perfect progressive: a verb form used

for a situation or habit that began in the past and continues up to the present or an action in progress that is not yet completed.
  ➤ I've **been getting** up early.
  ➤ **Have** you **been waiting** for a long time?

Student Learning Outcomes	• **Read** an excerpt from a lecture about Asia's Aral Sea. • **Complete** a chart with different forms of irregular verbs. • **Complete** sentences using adverbs and the present perfect. • **Write** facts about climate change using the present perfect. • **Ask** and **answer** questions about activities and life experiences.		
Lesson Vocabulary	(v.) affect (adj.) agricultural	(adj.) average (n.) border	(n.) level (v.) melt	(adj.) original (n.) population	(v.) return (n.) situation

EXPLORE

1 READ, page 122   10 min.

- Before reading, read the captions and use the photos to guess what the reading is about.

- Explain that *species of fish* means kinds of fish. Use hand gestures to explain *rise* and *go down*.

- Elicit the meaning of *used up* (e.g., *When something is used up, there is no more of that thing.*).

Be the Expert

- The Aral Sea was once the fourth largest salt lake in the world. The Amu Darya and Syr Darya Rivers flow into the Aral Sea. In the 1960s, these rivers were diverted to supply water to the desert for agriculture (mainly cotton).

- In 2010, Ban Ki-moon, the Secretary-General of the United Nations, called the shrinking sea "one of the worst . . . environmental disasters in the world."

- Pollutants from the water have contaminated the surrounding soil. The lack of water has led to hotter summers and colder winters. It has also caused serious health problems for many people.

2 CHECK, page 122   5 min.

1. b   2. b   3. a

3 DISCOVER, page 123   5 min.

A 1. a   2. b

B *Answers will vary.*

LEARN

Chart 5.1, page 124   5 min.

- **Note 2:** Point out that the auxiliary verb *have/has* signals the present perfect.

- **Note 3:** This may be the first time that students encounter the past participle form, or third form of a verb. Direct students to the list of common irregular

verb forms on page **A4** and explain that they will use this third form for all present perfect verbs.

- **Expansion Tip:** Dictate the following sentences to students: *Anna went to Asia in 1996. Juan has gone to Asia three times.* Have students write exactly what they hear. Repeat the sentences three times each, and then have students dictate the sentences as you write them on the board. Ask, *When did Anna go to Asia? When did Juan go to Asia?* Ask students to identify the two tenses (simple past and present perfect). Then ask students what verb is used in sentence 2 (*go*). Explain that *gone* is the past participle of *go*.

4 page 124   10 min.

1. has/'s become
2. has not/hasn't helped
3. has/'s been
4. have not/haven't heard
5. has/'s gone
6. has not/hasn't read
7. have not/haven't spoken
8. have/'ve done
9. has/'s called
10. has/'s seen
11. has/'s returned
12. have not/haven't eaten

5 page 125   10 min.

A

Base Form	Simple Past	Past Participle
be	was/were	been
become	became	become
hear	heard	heard
go	went	gone
do	did	done
speak	spoke	spoken
see	saw	seen
read	read	read

- **Expansion Tip:** On the board, make a tic-tac-toe grid and write the base form of the eight verbs from the chart in exercise **A** plus one additional verb in the squares. Model a game of tic-tac-toe with a student. Explain that in order to get an *X* or an *O* in a box, students must create a sentence in the present perfect using the word in the box (e.g., see: *I have seen that movie five times.*). Have students work in teams of 2–3 to create sentences. Then have one team play opposite another. Explain that they will judge whether the sentences formed by their opponents are correct. If the sentence is correct, the team can put their symbol in the square. If not, they lose their turn. Play until one team has won.
- **Expansion Tip:** If time allows, write sentences with errors from the tic-tac-toe game on the board and correct them as a class.

6 WRITE & SPEAK, page 125   5 min.

Answers will vary.

- **Tip:** Allow students a good amount of time to think about their answers. They may need additional time to decide what they want to share about themselves.
- **Expansion Tip:** Ask higher-level students to continue the conversation with follow-up questions.

Chart 5.2, page 126   5 min.

- **Note:** Point out that present perfect questions follow the same pattern as present simple questions: auxiliary + subject + verb, but with *have/has* rather than *do/does* and the past participle rather than the base form of the verb. Explaining these connections can help students see the logic behind the grammar.
- **Note:** The verb *be* follows the same pattern as all other verbs in the present perfect (e.g., *Have you been to Paris? Yes, I have.*).

7 page 126   10 min.

1. Have you visited South America?
2. What have you learned this week?
3. Has Bill started his new job?
4. Have you read the news today?
5. Where (in Europe) have you been (in Europe)?
6. What have you eaten today?
7. Who has been absent this week?
8. Who has she called today?

8 page 126   5 min.

1. Have you and Scott visited
2. Has he read
3. have you done
4. has she gone
5. Has it stopped
6. have they decided
7. Has she finished
8. has had

- **Expansion Tip:** To show that these questions can be used in the real world, ask students to make up answers to each of the questions (e.g., in item 4, elicit answers such as *She's gone home. / She's traveling in Peru right now.*). Students will soon understand that they can use their imaginations.

Chart 5.3, page 127   5 min.

- **Notes 1 & 6:** *Already* and *yet* can both be used in questions, but they have different meanings. *Already* can show surprise that an event has happened so early (e.g., *Has everyone arrived already? = They are here and I am surprised.*), while *yet* can convey that the speaker expects this to happen, but doesn't know if it has happened at the time of speaking (e.g., *Has everyone arrived yet? = They aren't here, but they should arrive soon.*).

9 page 127   5 min.

1. yet	5. just
2. never	6. still
3. already	7. yet
4. lately	8. lately

- **Expansion Tip:** To help students understand adverb placement, copy and cut up the sentence parts below. Have students form sentences using adverbs with the present perfect. Have several students volunteer to write their sentences on the board. Then ask follow-up questions to make sure that students understand the meaning of each sentence (e.g., *I have just moved to a new house.* Ask, *Have you unpacked all your boxes already?*).

I	have	already	moved	to a new house
They	still	haven't	heard	the news
ever	never	just	yet	recently

10 SPEAK, page 127   10 min.

Answers will vary.

- **Tip:** As a class, form the questions orally before beginning the activity.

- **Expansion Tip:** Ask students to report what they have learned to the class using full sentences (e.g., *Marie has run in a race.*).

11 WRITE & SPEAK, page 128   15 min.

A 1. the population of the Earth has grown to over seven billion

2. human activity has caused changes in the climate

3. Average temperatures have risen

4. Most of this increase has happened recently

5. Temperatures in the Arctic have increased

6. The ice has begun to melt

7. Sea levels have risen

8. Climate change has already affected many groups of people

B *Answers will vary.*

12 LISTEN, page 129   10 min.

1. He's just found
2. I've just changed
3. We've eaten
4. Where have you been
5. Who's finished
6. Has she ever been
7. I've never flown
8. Have they sold; yet

13 APPLY, page 129   20 min.

Answers will vary.

- **Tip:** Writing the questions for exercise **A** can be assigned for homework. Then start the following class opening with the interviews. Alternatively, exercise **C** can be assigned for homework.

Student Learning Outcomes	• **Read** an article about Paro, the robot seal.
	• **Talk** about your experiences with technology.
	• **Listen** to conversations from a help line at an electronics company.
	• **Find** and **edit** errors in conversations with the present perfect.
	• **Write** facts about yourself that are true at the present time.

Lesson Vocabulary	(adj.) calm	(adj.) elderly	(n.) pet	(v.) respond	(adj.) similar
	(n.) connection	(n.) factory	(v.) replace	(n.) robot	(n.) therapy

EXPLORE

1 READ, page 130   5 min.

• Have students look at the photos and read the captions. Ask, *What do you notice about these seals? How can they help elderly people?*

Be the Expert

• Paro, the robot seal is more than just a stuffed animal. The robot responds to people's voices and can remember what its owner likes and dislikes. If it gets a pat after it does something, it will do the same action again. If its owner hits it after it does something, it will not repeat the action. The robot also responds to the name that the owner gives it.

• Many elderly people live in nursing homes. According to one website (the CDC) there are approximately 16,000 nursing homes in the United States, and 1.7 million beds.

• Use key words *Paro robot seal video* to watch footage of the robot seals moving and interacting.

2 CHECK, page 130   5 min.

    1. F   2. T   3. T   4. F   5. T

• **Tip:** Ask higher-level students to correct the false statements.

3 DISCOVER, page 131   5 min.

A 1. for many years

    2. for a long time

    3. Since Paro first appeared in 2005

    4. since 2008

B 1. a   2. b

• **Tip:** Write the following sentences on the board and ask students to fill in the blanks: *We have been in this class for _____ minutes. We have studied the present perfect tense since _____.*

Compare answers as a class. Remind students that *for* is used with an amount of time, while *since* is used with a point in time.

LEARN

Chart 5.4, page 132   5 min.

• **Note 1:** Explain that *for* or *since* can be used for the same information. For example, in December, the following sentences mean the same thing: *I've known the teacher **for** 3 months. I've known the teacher **since** September.*

• **Note 4:** Students sometimes add *for* to questions asking *how long*. You may want to point out that *for* is not needed in these questions (e.g., *~~For h~~ How long have you known the teacher?*).

4 page 132   10 min.

    1. since 2009   5. for many years

    2. for a long time   6. Since April

    3. since the 1990s   7. for two years

    4. for several years   8. For five years

• **Expansion Tip:** Have students work in pairs to rewrite the answers to exercise **4** that use *for* as *since* time periods and the answers that use *since* as *for* time periods. Instruct students to consider the current date when rewriting the time periods (e.g., in 2015, *since 2009* could be rewritten as *for six years*).

Chart 5.5, page 133   5 min.

• **Note:** On the board, write: *We've been in the same room since we started class.* Underline *since we started class* and ask, *How long have we been in the room?* Elicit the amount of time (e.g., *for one hour/since 2:00 p.m.*) and write this under the time clause. Explain that time clauses may not give a specific number, but they are another way to show an amount of time that has passed.

5 page 133 — 10 min.

1. Life has changed a lot since
2. Since his cell phone broke,
3. we have not/haven't spoken to her
4. I have not/haven't seen Alicia
5. Since I got a smartphone,
6. Jack has been to Australia twice
7. the students have enjoyed all of the classes
8. I have not/haven't had any problems with it

- **Expansion Tip:** On the board, make a list of past time clauses (e.g., *Since this class started, Since I was ten years old, Since I got a new cell phone, Since the president was elected, Since my friend started jogging, Since I got a puppy*). Have students choose two past time clauses and finish the sentences with their own ideas (e.g., *Since this class started, I have learned a lot of English.*).

PRACTICE

6 WRITE & SPEAK, page 134 — 10 min.

A 1. have been; since
2. have enjoyed; for
3. have/'ve used; for
4. has/'s had; since
5. have not/haven't bought; for
6. has taken; since
7. have not/haven't received; since
8. has sent; since

B *Answers will vary.*

- **Expansion Tip:** Ask students to choose one of the items in the box. Tell them to use past time clauses to convince their partner to buy the same product (e.g., *I've had this phone for 6 months. The battery lasts for a long time. I haven't charged it since the day before yesterday, but it still works.*). Emphasize that students should use the present perfect where appropriate.

7 LISTEN, page 134 — 15 min.

A phone: 2

Internet connection: 3

MP3 player: 1

B 1. have you had   8. since
2. had   9. 's been
3. for   10. I've been
4. for   11. for
5. has been   12. We've had
6. I've had   13. hasn't worked
7. recently   14. we lost

- **Expansion Tip:** Have students role-play the conversations in pairs. If time allows, ask students to continue the conversations orally.

8 EDIT, page 135 — 10 min.

1. A: That's a nice watch, Paulo. I don't think I've ~~saw~~ seen it before.

   B: I've only had it ~~since~~ for two weeks. It was a birthday present from my parents.

2. A: I've been on a diet for two months ~~ago~~.

   B: Oh, how much weight have you lost?

   A: Not much, but I have felt so much better since I started my diet.

3. A: How long ~~are~~ have you been interested in music, Anna?

   B: Oh, I've loved music since I ~~am~~ was a child. My mother used to sing to me all the time.

4. A: Kazu, you speak French! I didn't know that.

   B: Yeah, I took it in high school. But I ~~don't speak~~ haven't spoken French for several years. I've forgotten a lot.

9 APPLY, page 135 — 20 min.

Answers will vary.

- **Tip:** Write example sentences about yourself on the board. Ask students to form *How long* questions about each sentence using the present perfect. Use *for* or *since* in your responses (e.g., A: *I want to travel around the world.* B: *How long have you wanted to do this?* A: *Since I took my first plane trip when I was eight.*).

- **Alternative Writing & Speaking:** After completing exercise **B**, ask students to write three true statements and one false statement about their partner using the information they have learned and the present perfect. Have other students guess which statement is false.

<table>
<tr><td rowspan="1">Student Learning Outcomes</td><td>
<ul>
<li>Read a conversation about a program that makes drawings of characters from literature.</li>
<li>Complete conversations with the present perfect and simple past.</li>
<li>Read about science fiction movies and how they have predicted the future.</li>
<li>Write true sentences about yourself and answer follow-up questions.</li>
<li>Find and edit errors in an article about a software developer in Uganda.</li>
<li>Ask and answer questions about activities you have done.</li>
</ul>
</td></tr>
</table>

Lesson Vocabulary	(n.) app	(v.) create	(n.) description	(n.) novel	(n.) science fiction
	(n.) character	(n.) crime	(adj.) disappointed	(adj.) proud	(n.) training

EXPLORE

1 READ, page 136   10 min.

- Have students look at the pictures and read the captions. Ask, *Who is the person in these pictures? How are the pictures similar? How are they different?*

- Direct students to the definitions of *fictional* and *composite*. Explain that the pictures on Brian Davis's website are composite drawings of fictional characters based on different descriptions in literature. Ask, *Which fictional character would you like to see a composite drawing of? Why?*

Be the Expert

- For a long time, artists and (more recently) computer programs have helped law enforcement officers identify and catch criminals. These programs compile information about the criminal from different eyewitnesses to create a single picture called a *composite*.

- Brian Davis's composites website uses the same computer program along with authors' descriptions of characters from literature to create pictures of fictional characters. These descriptions of the characters appear below the corresponding pictures on the website. To find Davis's composites website, type *the composites* into an Internet search engine.

2 CHECK, page 137   5 min.

1. b   2. c   3. c   4. a

3 DISCOVER, page 137   5 min.

A 1. indefinite time   3. indefinite time

2. definite time   4. definite time

B the present perfect

LEARN

Chart 5.6, page 138   5 min.

- **Notes 1 & 2:** Many students have trouble deciding when to use the present perfect and the simple past because both tenses can refer to the same time period (e.g., someone who ate sushi for the first time two days ago could say either *I have eaten sushi.* or *I ate sushi two days ago.*). To show the difference between the tenses, draw a time line on the board with an arrow pointing to a specific point near the right side of the timeline. Then draw a second timeline and write *???* over a large area to the left of the arrow. Explain that the arrow means we know when something happened in the past, while the question marks mean that we don't know the exact time something happened. Then write the following pair of sentences on the board: *I have eaten sushi. I ate sushi two days ago.* Ask students to match the sentences to the timelines. Explain, *In the first sentence, you don't know when I ate sushi. In the second, you know the exact time.*

4 page 138   10 min.

1. Have you ever visited	6. I started
2. I looked	7. have read
3. did you think	8. watched
4. I haven't seen	9. surprised
5. I found	10. looked

5 page 138   10 min.

1. Have you seen	6. liked
2. watched	7. Have you seen
3. have not/haven't seen	8. have not/haven't watched
4. Did you enjoy	
5. were	

- **Expansion Tip:** Have students read the dialog aloud in pairs. Walk around and correct any errors with the present perfect or simple present. If students finish early, ask them to discuss other TV shows that they have seen recently.

Chart 5.7, page 139   5 min.

- **Note 1:** Explain that the present perfect or the simple past can convey very different meanings. Draw timelines on the board to show that the present perfect sentences continue to the present, while the simple past sentences have already ended. Write these examples on the board: (A) *I have had a terrible cough for two days.* (B) *I had a terrible cough for two days.* Ask, *In which of these sentences do I want to stay away from you?* (A) *In which sentence are you feeling better now?* (B) *How do you know?*

- **Notes 1 & 2:** Remind students that the adverbs they learned in Lesson 1 of this unit (e.g., *recently, lately*) signal the present perfect, while more exact time words signal the simple past (e.g., *yesterday, last week*).

- **Note 2:** Students may be confused about what time period *this morning* or *this afternoon* refers to. Explain that *this* refers to the present day. If it is afternoon, *this afternoon* refers to now. If it is evening, *this afternoon* is in the past.

6 page 139   10 min.

1. has/'s been	5. lived
2. was	6. have lived
3. used	7. has/'s taught
4. have/'ve used	8. taught

7 page 140   10 min.

1. have not/haven't seen	5. has/'s answered
2. did not/didn't see	6. answered
3. Did you talk	7. ate
4. Have you talked	8. have/'ve eaten

- **Expansion Tip:** Have students write two sentences using *this morning* or *this afternoon* and the sentences in exercise **7** as a model. Ask them to use the present perfect in one sentence and the simple past in the other. Remind students to use the present perfect or simple past based on the time of writing (e.g., at 2 p.m.: *I didn't eat breakfast this morning. I haven't eaten anything this afternoon.*). Then ask the class to share their sentences in groups of three. Pay attention to students' use of the tenses.

PRACTICE

8 READ & WRITE, page 140   15 min.

1. has increased	6. built
2. was	7. appeared
3. has grown	8. came
4. spoke	9. have become
5. have designed	10. have allowed

- **Tip:** To create interest in the topic before beginning the exercise, ask students to name and describe some popular science fiction movies or TV shows they have seen.

9 page 142   10 min.

1. I finished
2. Have you read
3. I have/I've read
4. did you read
5. I read
6. did you think
7. I found
8. You enjoyed
9. you have not/haven't read
10. I have not/haven't had
11. I have/I've spent
12. I borrowed
13. I have not/haven't started

10 WRITE & SPEAK, page 142   15 min.

Answers will vary.

- **Tip:** As a class, think of some possible topics to write about (e.g., *friends, sports, technology, jobs*). Make a list of topics on the board. Allow students enough time to write sentences based on these topics when completing the exercise.

- **Expansion Tip:** On the board, make a timeline starting ten years ago with markings representing each year until the present. Draw an arrow from the beginning of the current year until the present and write a sample sentence about yourself using the present perfect (e.g., *I have taught this class since the beginning of the year.*). Then write a sentence about an event that happened during a previous year above an *X* to show that the event began and ended in the past (e.g., *I moved to New York in 2010.*). Ask students to create their own timelines with at least three present perfect and three simple past sentences. When they are finished, have students compare their timelines with a partner.

- **Tip:** To create interest in the topic, ask, *What is an app? What are some examples of apps? Who creates these apps?* Tell students to read the article to find the answers.

    Abdu Sakalala is a 22-year-old student in Uganda. His life ~~has~~ changed when a phone company ~~has run~~ ran a training course for software developers in Uganda last year. Sakalala attended the course and then he ~~has~~ started creating his own apps (programs) for mobile phones. Since then, Sakalala ~~wrote~~ has written several successful apps for cell phones. For example, he has produced a dictionary app, a translation app, and a sports app for soccer fans. Some of these apps have received international attention, and Sakalala has already made almost $400,000 from his work.

    But Sakalala is most proud of *Uganda Theme*. This is an app that changes the display on cell phones with pictures and sounds from his country. When it ~~has~~ appeared on the Internet, it immediately ~~has become~~ became one of the most popular downloads in the world that week.

A   **Janice:**   <u>Have</u> you ever <u>visited</u> Europe?

    Logan: Yes <u>I've been</u> there several times.

    Janice: Oh really? Where <u>have</u> you <u>been</u>?

    Logan: <u>I've been</u> to Italy, France, and Spain.

    Janice: When <u>did</u> you <u>go</u> to Spain?

    Logan: I <u>went</u> last summer with some friends.

B   *Answers will vary.*

- **Expansion Tip:** Have students choose one of the activities in the box. Using the conversation in exercise **A** as a model, have students write a conversation about the new activity. Remind the class to pay attention to their use of the present perfect and simple past. Have students practice reading their conversations with a partner, and then act them out in front of the class.

- **Alternative Writing & Speaking:** Have students write a commercial for a type of technology (e.g., a cell phone or a laptop). This should be a conversation between two people in which one person tells the other how the product has changed his or her life. Encourage students to use the present perfect and simple past in their conversations. Have students practice reading their conversations with a partner, and then act them out in front of the class.

Student Learning Outcomes	• **Read** an article about the Inuit people and climate change. • **Complete** conversations using the present perfect progressive and the present perfect. • **Ask** and **answer** questions using *How long* and the present perfect progressive. • **Listen** to a conversation with a student from Sweden and **answer** questions. • **Write** about changes that you and your family have made.
Lesson Vocabulary	(n.) attack (v.) govern (v.) improve (n.) mining (adj.) native (n.) dog sled (n.) ground (n.) independence (adj.) national (v.) run

EXPLORE

1 READ, page 144   10 min.

• Have students look at the photos and read the captions. Ask, *Where do these animals live? Why are they important?*

• Elicit the meaning of *independence* (e.g., *being free from a ruler or dictator*).

Be the Expert

• Students might be familiar with the term *Eskimo* already. This is a general term that is often used to describe all Arctic peoples. In Alaska, *Eskimo* is usually used because there are Inuit and Yupik people. However, in Canada and Greenland, where Arctic people are all Inuit, they consider the term *Eskimo* to be offensive, because people thought it meant "eater of raw meat." In Canada, the preferred term is *Inuit*; in Greenland, it is *Kalaallit* or *Greenlanders*.

• Have students search the Internet for *Inuit stone carvings* to see examples of Inuit art.

2 CHECK, page 145   10 min.

1. b, e, g
2. b, e, d, g
3. a, b, c, e, g
4. b, e, g
5. b, e, f, g

3 DISCOVER, page 145   5 min.

A 1. still happening
2. still happening
3. finished
4. still happening
5. still happening

B The verb of the actions that are still happening has an *-ing* ending.

LEARN

Chart 5.8, page 146   5 min.

• **Note 1:** When using contractions and the present perfect progressive, students often omit *-s* and *-ve*. (e.g., *I been watching TV* instead of *I've been watching TV*.). Practice pronunciation by drilling the sentences in the affirmative/negative box for chart 5.8 as a class.

4 page 146   10 min.

1. have/'ve been reading
2. have been living
3. has/'s been changing
4. have been earning
5. have not/haven't been teaching
6. have been visiting
7. have been writing
8. has been growing
9. have been using
10. have not/haven't been helping

• **Expansion Tip:** Have students work in groups of 3–4. On the board, write: *What have you been reading/studying/watching/listening to lately?* Have students discuss their answers in groups, using full sentences. Ask volunteers to report their findings to the class.

Chart 5.9, page 147   5 min.

• **Note:** Because the present perfect progressive has three separate elements, students might omit the *have/has* or *been* in speech. Use a non-verbal gesture, such as counting out the words on your fingers, to remind them to pronounce each word.

5 page 147   10 min.

1. What have you been doing recently?

2. How long has he been living here?

3. Have you been eating a healthy diet?

4. Has she been going to class?

5. Why has he been shouting?

6. Have you been playing the piano for a long time?

7. Why has Andre been working on weekends lately?

8. Who has been teaching the class this week?

9. What have you been reading lately?

10. Have you been studying a lot lately?

- **Tip:** Remind students to check their answers carefully to make sure that they include *been* in each question.

6 SPEAK, page 147   5 min.

Answers will vary.

- **Expansion Tip:** Have students mime activities based on prompts, and have other students guess what they have been doing. Model one example and ask students to guess what you have been doing, and only answer if the present perfect progressive is formed correctly (e.g., *Have you been cutting onions? Have you been lifting weights? Have you been studying all night?*).

Chart 5.10, page 148   5 min.

- **Note 1:** Show the distinction between the present perfect progressive and present perfect by writing the following sentences on the board: *I've cut my finger. I've been cutting my finger.* To elicit the difference between the two sentences, mime the action in the second sentence to show the difference in meaning between cutting your finger once and continuing to cut it repeatedly.

7 page 148   10 min.

1. have/'ve changed	5. have/'ve been using
2. have/'ve been working	6. have you been reading
3. have you owned	7. has/'s taken
4. has/'s gone	8. has/'s had

PRACTICE

8 page 148   10 min.

1. have you seen

2. you have not/haven't been exercising

3. I have not/haven't had

4. I have/I've been working

5. has/'s it been going

6. I have/I've just finished

7. you have/you've been looking

8. I have/I've already told

9. have you read

10. I have/I've been trying

- **Expansion Tip:** Have students read the dialogues aloud in pairs. Correct any errors with the present perfect or the present perfect progressive.

9 WRITE & SPEAK, page 149   10 min.

Answers will vary.

- **Tip:** For exercise **C**, place students in groups of 4, so that each partner from exercise **B** can listen to their original partner talk about them and can correct where necessary.

10 LISTEN, WRITE & SPEAK, page 149   25 min.

A 1. b   2. b

B 1. Where has Lars lived all his life?

2. What has/What's been happening to the ground under Kiruna recently?

3. What has/What's changed in Kiruna so far?

4. What have the Sami people been doing for hundreds of years?

5. How have the Sami people's lives changed?

C *Answers will vary.*

D *Answers will vary.*

11 APPLY, page 150   25 min.

Answers will vary.

- **Tip:** Have students complete exercise **C** for homework. At the beginning of the next class, pair students and ask them to edit their partner's paragraph. Remind them to focus on their partner's use of present perfect, simple past, and present perfect progressive.

1 page 151   10 min.

1. have left/have been leaving

2. have returned/have been returning

3. left

4. returned

5. has fallen/has been falling

6. left

7. was

8. have been discussing

2 page 151   10 min.

1. have known	6. hasn't been cleaning
2. since	7. saved
3. left	8. has gone
4. crossed	9. has been sending
5. settled	10. for

3 EDIT, page 152   10 min.

• **Tip:** To create interest in the topic, ask students where in the world they would most like to live and why. Then ask students to describe the photo. Ask, *Who do you think lives on this island? How do you think this island has changed?*

    Moyenne Island in the Seychelles was deserted and forgotten for fifty years. Then, in 1964, British newspaper editor Brendon Grimshaw ~~has~~ bought the island. He moved there nine years later, and ~~lived~~ has lived/has been living there ever since.

    When Grimshaw moved to Moyenne Island, it ~~has been~~ was empty. Small trees and bushes covered the land, and there weren't any paths. Grimshaw wanted to take care of the island, so he asked a local man, Rene Lafortune, to help him. Since the two men ~~have~~ started working, they ~~has~~ have planted 16,000 trees. Some of the first trees have now ~~been growing~~ grown to over 60 feet tall. The two men have also built more than three miles (5 km) of nature paths.

    Grimshaw has been working hard on his project ~~since~~ for around forty years, and today Moyenne Island is a huge success story. Since Grimshaw bought the island, it ~~have~~ has attracted about 2000 new birds. Grimshaw has also raised over 100 giant tortoises on the island.

    Since 2008, Moyenne Island ~~was~~ has been a national park. It is a beautiful example of how one person's dream can change at least a small area of the world.

4 LISTEN, page 153   15 min.

A *Answers will vary.*

B a

C 1. has changed; hasn't changed

    2. 've been using; appeared

    3. came

    4. received

    5. didn't say

    6. has been shutting

    7. has been

5 SPEAK, page 153   15 min.

Answers will vary.

• **Alternative Speaking:** Tell students that they are going to debate the following statement: *Technology has changed our lives for the better.* Split the class in half. Tell one half that they are pro (they think this is true) and the other that they are con (they think this is not true). Have students prepare their arguments in pairs, and then have them debate the question with two students from the opposing side. After 3–4 minutes, have the pairs switch and talk to a new pair of students. At the end, ask the class whether they agree or disagree with the statement.

Connect the Grammar to Writing

1 page 154   15 min.

A *Answers will vary.*

B   The sun went down three hours ago. Since then, it's gotten very dark. The moon has risen, and the stars have been appearing in the sky.

    Many birds, butterflies, and small animals have disappeared for the night. Others have become active. A raccoon is in my yard. It's been coming into my yard every night this winter. I hear an owl. I've heard it a few times before.

    Since the sun went down, it's become much colder. The temperature has already dropped six degrees. I've put on a warm sweater, socks, and slippers. I like a lot of things about winter, but not the cold!

C **Recent Event:** The sun went down.

Changes: It's gotten very dark.

The moon has risen.

The stars have been appearing in the sky.

Many birds, butterflies, and small animals have disappeared.

Others have become active.

It's become much colder.

The temperature has dropped six degrees.

I've put on a warm sweater, socks, and slippers.

2 BEFORE YOU WRITE, page 155   5 min.

Answers will vary.

3 WRITE, page 155   25 min.

> **WRITING FOCUS, page 155**
>
> Write additional sentences containing comma errors on the board for students to correct. Then ask students to write one sentence with a comma error for a partner to correct.

- **Alternative Writing:** Ask students to imagine that they are being interviewed for a job. Ask, *What job would you like? How have you been preparing for this job?* Have students make a list of some ways they have changed over the past five years using the present perfect and present perfect progressive (e.g., *I have become a student. I have been learning English.*).

- **Alternative Writing:** Have students make a list of some life events such as getting married, moving to a new city, or having a baby. Choose one of these events and have students write a story about an imaginary person who is in the middle of this event (e.g., *Basia is moving to a new city next week. She has already packed ten boxes. She has been walking around her neighborhood taking photos. She hasn't said goodbye to her neighbors yet.*).

Appearances and Behavior

Adjectives and Adverbs

Unit Opener

Photo: Have students view the photo and read the caption. Ask, *What is this animal? How would you describe it? How would you describe the place where the picture was taken?*

Location: Madagascar's stone forest is an enormous rock formation. Over millions of years, water dissolved the rock to form tall, sharp towers. Many unusual animals, including several types of lemurs, live there. Like gorillas, monkeys, and people, lemurs are part of a biological group called *primates.*

Theme: This unit is about describing appearances and behavior. Have students look at the photo on page 159. Ask, *Which sentence is more descriptive? There is a crocodile. There is a scary looking crocodile with sharp teeth.* Have students describe another photo in an interesting way.

Page	Lesson	Grammar	Examples
158	1	Adjectives	Jack told a **funny** story. The baby is **adorable**. I sat on a **park** bench. We saw some **ancient Egyptian** sculptures. He's a **kind** and **patient** person.
165	2	Adverbs	They are **slow** animals. They move **slowly**. She was the **best** player. She played **well** in the game. She was **somewhat tired**.
172	**Review the Grammar**		
174	**Connect the Grammar to Writing**		

Unit Grammar Terms

adjective: a word that describes or modifies a noun or pronoun.
➤ *She is **friendly**.*
➤ *Brazil is a **huge** country.*

adverb: a word that describes or modifies a verb, an adjective, or another adverb.
➤ *He eats **quickly**.*
➤ *She drives **carefully**.*

adverb of degree: an adverb that makes adjectives or other adverbs stronger or weaker.
➤ *He eats **somewhat** quickly.*
➤ *She drives **very** carefully.*

adverb of manner: an adverb that describes the action of the verb. Many adverbs of manner are formed by adding *-ly* to the adjective.
➤ *You sing **beautifully**.*
➤ *He speaks **slowly**.*

linking verb: a verb that connects, or links, the subject with an adjective (or in some cases a noun) that describes it. The verb *be* is the most common example. Other common linking verbs: *appear, be, become, feel, get, look, seem, smell, sound,* or *taste.*
➤ *The girl **looks** happy.*
➤ *The cake **smells** delicious.*
➤ *Rene **became** a doctor. She **is** a surgeon.*

Student Learning Outcomes	• **Read** an article about koalas in Australia. • **Listen** and **complete** a conversation about peacocks by adding adjectives. • **Put** descriptive words in the correct order. • **Write** sentences about yourself using adjectives. • **Ask** and **answer** questions using nouns as adjectives.			
Lesson Vocabulary	(ph. v.) break into (n.) claw	(n.) creature (adj.) deceptive	(n.) feather (adj.) fierce	(n.) pocket (n.) scratch	(n.) symbol (n.) thief

EXPLORE

1 READ, page 158   10 min.

Be the Expert

- Koalas can eat one eighth of their weight in eucalyptus leaves each day. A 120-pound person who ate that much would consume 15 pounds of food every day.

- Zookeepers believed that the thieves wanted to steal the animals to make money for drugs.

- While many zoos house a few koalas, Australia also has whole sanctuaries for koalas. There, visitors can see koalas in their natural habitat.

- Although tourists love to see koalas, is it healthy for the koalas? A recent study from the University of Melbourne found that koalas get very stressed when humans are noisy or come too close to them. Stress takes energy, and koalas have a very low-energy diet. They sleep 20 hours a day to conserve energy.

2 CHECK, page 159   5 min.

  1. F   2. F   3. F   4. T   5. T   6. F

- **Tip:** Make sure students understand why incorrect sentences are false. Ask higher-level students to rewrite the false sentences so that they are true.

3 DISCOVER, page 159   10 min.

A 1. cute; popular   4. harmful

    2. very fierce   5. water; high

    3. deep; sharp

B 1. ✓   2. ✗   3. ✓   4. ✓

- **Expansion Tip:** Ask students to think of more adjectives that describe personalities and looks. Make a list on the board. Have students match the adjectives to people and animals.

LEARN

Chart 6.1, page 160   5 min.

- **Notes 2 & 3:** English adjective placement can be confusing to students, because adjectives are sometimes after the noun in English. On the vboard, write: *I saw a cute koala. The koala looks cute.* Ask students why the adjective comes after the verb in sentence two. (*Looks* is a linking verb.)

- **Note 4:** On the board, write: *a car/an orange car* and *an old painting/a beautiful old painting.* Ask students what the rule is for using *a/an* with adjectives. (It depends on the first adjective in the list of adjectives, not the noun.)

4 page 160   5 min.

  1. Koalas have thick fur.

  2. Thieves didn't take the angry koala.

     They were afraid of its sharp claws.

  3. Australia is enormous, and

     Australian animals are fascinating.

  4. The zoo helps sick animals.

     The koala appeared ill, but it seems healthy now.

  5. Crocodiles have sharp teeth and powerful jaws.

     That crocodile looks hungry.

5 page 160   10 min.

  1. The bear's fur looks soft.

  2. That is an enormous crocodile.

  3. Kangaroos have strong legs.

  4. Pandas are shy animals.

  5. The zoo has a great exhibit.

  6. Australia has an interesting history.

- **Note:** On the board, write: *It was an expensive plane ticket. The girl sat on the dirty park bench.* Ask, *What two nouns are used as adjectives? What are the other adjectives? Which adjective is closest to each noun?* (The noun used as an adjective will always be directly before the noun it modifies.)

- **Note:** When pronouncing nouns modified by other nouns used as adjectives, the stress is usually on the noun (e.g., SHOE store; PLANE ticket).

6 page 161   5 min.

1. school nurse	5. car keys
2. desk drawer	6. computer store
3. furniture design	7. grocery bag
4. leather coat	8. orange juice

7 page 161   5 min.

1. shoes; shoe	5. books; book
2. car; cars	6. restaurant; restaurants
3. movie; movies	7. vegetable; vegetables
4. mountain; mountains	8. apartment; apartments

- **Expansion Tip:** Have students work in pairs to ask and answer follow-up questions to the sentences in exercise **7**. Encourage students to use nouns as adjectives as they ask and answer questions.

Chart 6.3, page 162   5 min.

- **Note 3:** The way that commas are used with a list of adjectives differs from the way they are used with nouns. Students may assume that the structure is the same, with a comma inbetween the adjectives. Explain that *and* or commas are only used when the adjectives are in the same category (e.g., *He was a polite, well-mannered boy.* OR, *I like the pink and green dress.*).

8 page 162   5 min.

1. big apartment	7. beautiful green silk
2. good Mexican	8. great old
3. round glass	9. long and sharp/ sharp and long
4. nice new winter	10. impressive and beautiful modern
5. interesting historical	
6. strange old stone	

- **Expansion Tip:** On the board, draw a table with several or all of the categories from chart 6.3. Then make a list of nouns in the right column (e.g., *purse, uniform, desk, house, etc.*). Have

students add more examples of adjectives to as many categories as possible.

- **Alternative Expansion Tip:** Bring in 3–4 objects and show them to the class for one minute. Then put them away. Ask students to describe the objects using as many adjectives as possible.

PRACTICE

9 page 163   10 min.

1. favorite	4. green	7. terrible
2. amazing	5. brown	8. nice
3. colorful	6. attractive	

- **Tip:** Have students read the conversations in pairs. Have students who finish early think of alternative adjectives that fit the conversation. Ask volunteers to read their new conversations to the class.

10 page 164   10 min.

1. common farm animals
2. long brown hair
3. an exciting and interesting city/ an exciting, interesting city/ an interesting and exciting city/ an interesting, exciting city
4. a kind and friendly person
5. small green leaves
6. a scary black spider
7. a wonderful new shoe store
8. delicious Indian food

11 APPLY, page 164   25 min.

A
1. police	5. grocery
2. TV	6. computer
3. art	7. fire
4. phone	8. train

B *Answers will vary.*

- **Alternative Apply:** Ask students to work in groups of 2–3 to write a conversation with at least eight adjectives including four nouns as adjectives. Have students start with the line: *I have to make a very important phone call . . .* Ask students to practice their conversations and present them to the class.

C *Answers will vary.*

Student Learning Outcomes	• **Read** an article about moko—the tattoo art of the Maori. • **Complete** a paragraph about a person whom the author admires. • **Find** and **edit** errors with adverbs and adjectives in an e-mail. • **Listen** to a radio show about a job interview. • **Discuss** situations in which it is important to make a good impression. • **Write** sentences with adjectives and adverbs about making a good impression.
Lesson Vocabulary	(v.) admire (adv.) appropriately (n.) method (adj.) painful (n.) tattoo (n.) advice (n.) courage (v.) mind (n.) purpose (n.) tool

EXPLORE

1 READ, page 165   10 min.

• Have students find New Zealand on a map. Ask, *What do you already know about this country?* An earlier unit features the All Blacks, a rugby team from New Zealand.

Be the Expert

• This reading is about the Maori in New Zealand. New Zealand is a group of islands near Australia. The Maori arrived here before 1300 AD, from islands in Polynesia. In 1840, the British signed a treaty with the Maori, although warfare between the groups continued for some years. The country gained its independence from Britain in 1947.

• Traditionally, Maori women had their lips and chins tattooed and men had their full faces tattooed.

• George Tamihana Nuku, a Maori Chief, explains that *moko* is part of an ancient tradition. It was considered a gift from the gods. He says that a real *moko* "defines who your parents and grandparents [were] from the beginning of time."

• Have students search for key terms and images: *George Nuku, moko,* and *Maori.*

2 CHECK, page 166   5 min.

  1. b   2. c   3. b   4. c

3 DISCOVER, page 166   5 min.

A 1. wears   2. sat

B Adverbs of manner usually come after the verb or after the verb + the object. Do not put adverbs of manner between the verb and the object.

• **Tip:** Ask students to think about their morning routine. What is something that they do quickly? What is something that they do carefully? Explain that chart 6.4 explains *how* we do things.

LEARN

Chart 6.4, page 167   5 min.

• **Note 2:** Putting an adverb between a verb and an object is a very common mistake for students. On the board, write:

Subject	Verb	Object	Adverb
She	answered	the questions	carefully.
The dog	wagged	his tail	happily.

Ask the class for more examples of sentences that fit this pattern.

• **Note 3:** Remind students of the linking verbs that they learned in Lesson 1. Have them list some linking verbs and write them on the board.

• **Note 4:** Direct students to the appendix for the spelling rules. Have students quiz each other.

4 page 167   5 min.

  1. proudly   5. clearly   9. hard

  2. quietly   6. well   10. fast

  3. bravely   7. honestly

  4. early   8. quickly

5 page 168   5 min.

  1. My brother doesn't drive safely.

  2. We worked hard last semester.

  3. Journalists write their reports quickly.

  4. Martina walked (slowly) along the beach (slowly).

  5. The professor didn't (completely) answer my question (completely).

  6. The mail arrived early.

7. The children played (happily) in the yard (happily).

8. I held the baby gently.

- **Expansion Tip:** Follow up exercise **5** by having students work in pairs to write their own sentences about a few of the situations or topics in the exercise. Model this activity with sentence 1. Ask, *What else can you say about your brother? He drives too fast/dangerously.* Or, *When I'm in the car with him, I grip my seat nervously.* Each sentence should have at least one adverb. If students have difficulty thinking of adverbs, encourage them to look back at exercises **4** and **5** for ideas. Ask volunteers to read their sentences. Write sentences with errors on the board and elicit corrections from the class.

Chart 6.5, page 168   5 min.

- **Note 1:** Adverbs of degree can also be called intensifiers because they show the intensity of the adjective or adverb that follows.

- **Note 2:** Although the word order of adverbs of degree is not usually a problem, students can be reluctant to incorporate these adverbs into their speech. Encourage students to use these adverbs in their own speech by using hand gestures that symbolize a lot or a little, and ask students to clarify using an adverb of degree.

> ### REAL ENGLISH, page 168
>
> In British English, *quite* can make an adjective or adverb weaker. In American English, *quite* makes an adjective or adverb stronger. Ask students to imagine that they are on vacation and their suitcases were lost. They are complaining about this situation. What would they say to their friend? What would they say to the people at the airline? Have students create two short conversations—one formal, the other informal. Have them use adverbs of degree and adjectives to emphasize their unhappiness at the situation.

6 page 168   10 min.

1. Steven's assignment sounds somewhat boring.

2. This song is extremely popular.

3. Elsa's shoes looked quite expensive.

4. The discussion ended pretty quickly.

5. This software doesn't seem very helpful.

6. I was so tired last night.

7. That movie was really scary.

8. Liza speaks Russian fairly well.

7 page 169   5 min.

1. weaker	5. stronger
2. stronger	6. weaker
3. stronger	7. stronger
4. weaker	8. stronger

- **Expansion Tip:** Have students read the sentences in exercise **7** aloud, with emphasis on the adverb of degree. Explain that they should use an appropriate tone when they speak, e.g., *The article was pretty interesting.* Because this makes the adjective *interesting* a little weaker, the speaker would probably not sound very excited when they said it. Then have students use a stronger/weaker adverb in its place, and change their intonation as appropriate, e.g., *The article was extremely interesting.* This time, the speaker should sound excited.

PRACTICE

8 page 169   5 min.

1. suddenly	5. proudly
2. happy	6. cheap; good
3. hard	7. quickly; clearly
4. well	8. bad; badly

9 page 170   10 min.

1. nice	7. well
2. happily	8. beautifully
3. terrific	9. curious
4. healthy	10. frequently
5. regularly	11. interesting
6. active	12. great

- **Expansion Tip:** Have students choose someone they admire to write descriptive sentences about this person. Then have them read their descriptions to a partner. Encourage students to use adverbs of manner and degree whenever possible. When they have finished their descriptions, have students write notes about their partner's person and share these notes with their partner. If possible, have students bring in a photo of the person to show their partner.

- **Tip:** Before starting, ask students to give advice to someone who has an interview. Write students' tips on the board.

A Hi, Jessica and Mark,

I need some advice. I had an interview for a job as a DJ at my local radio station, but I was ~~unsuccessfully~~ unsuccessful. I've had a lot of experience as a DJ, and I work very hard. I wore a ~~new nice~~ nice new suit to the interview, and I felt pretty ~~confidently~~ confident when I left my house.

Before the interview, I read some interview tips and techniques online. For example, one said, "Copy the interviewer's movements closely." Well, I tried that technique, but the interviewers didn't seem to like it very much. Anyway, I didn't get the job. Now I'm ~~real~~ really confused. I know I made a few mistakes in the interview, but nothing really bad. At first, I was ~~nervously~~ nervous but that was because I arrived ~~lately~~ late. When the interview started, I spoke loudly, smiled frequently, and talked a lot—well, until they asked me to stop. Also, I didn't ask any questions, but in general, I thought it went ~~good~~ well. Where did I go wrong?

Thanks,

Kevin in Ohio

C *Answers will vary.*

D

Kevin's Behaviors	Radio Expert's (Mark's) Advice
1. wore a suit	Bad choice. Dress appropriately.
2. arrived late	Bad choice. You cannot be late. Get there early.
3. copied the interviewers	Bad choice. Dangerous. They can think you are making fun of them.
4. spoke loudly	Bad choice. Speak clearly.
5. smiled frequently	Good choice.
6. didn't ask questions	Bad choice. Ask questions. Write down questions beforehand and bring them with you.

E *Answers will vary.*

Answers will vary.

- **Expansion Tip:** Have students work in groups to prepare and deliver a two-minute formal presentation on their tips to the class. Presentations should cover at least three tips, and should include an example for each. Have listeners take notes on each presentation. When all groups have finished, have students share what they learned from the other presentations.

- **Alternative Apply:** Have students write about a time in their lives when they felt an extreme emotion. Examples of possible situations include a wedding, a new baby, a move to a new place, or an accident. Have students describe the situation in 4–5 sentences using adjectives and adverbs where appropriate.

1 page 172   5 min.

1. unhappy	7. well
2. angry	8. completely
3. bad	9. very
4. hard	10. very
5. carefully	11. smart and studious
6. good	12. successful

- **TIP:** Use this conversation to give students practice in emphasizing the correct words in conversation. Have students who finish early read the conversation aloud with a partner. Encourage students to use appropriate stress.

2 EDIT, page 172   10 min.

Venus is a ~~pet famous~~ famous pet cat. She even has her own social networking page. She has also appeared on national TV.

Many people are interested in Venus because she has an unusual appearance, as you can see! One half of her face is black with ~~an~~ a green eye, and the other half has ~~stripes orange~~ orange stripes and a blue eye. How does something like this happen?

According to Leslie Lyons, a professor at the University of California, Davis, cats like Venus are extremely rare. Cats with orange and ~~blacks~~ black coats are not unusual. However, cats with different colored eyes are ~~unusually~~ unusual. This means Professor Lyons is much more interested in the real mystery about Venus: her ~~blue beautiful~~ beautiful blue eye.

3 LISTEN & SPEAK, page 173   10 min.

A 1. b   2. a   3. b   4. b   5. a

B *Answers will vary.*

- **Expansion Tip:** Have students work in pairs to talk about the bowerbirds and their habits. Then have each pair write 2–3 sentences about the bowerbirds, using as many adjectives and adverbs as possible. Have volunteers read their sentences to the class.

- **Expansion Tip:** To demonstrate how adjectives and adverbs can make writing more interesting, ask students to write a paragraph about bowerbirds. Challenge students to see who can use the most descriptive adjectives and adverbs in their paragraphs. Then have volunteers read their paragraphs aloud. Ask the class to identify the adjectives and write them on the board. Do the same with adverbs. Discuss with the class which adjectives or adverbs are the most interesting, vivid, or powerful.

4 SPEAK & WRITE, page 173   25 min.

Answers will vary.

Connect the Grammar to Writing

1 READ & NOTICE THE GRAMMAR,
page 174   25 min.

A *Answers will vary.*

B   The <u>yellow-tailed</u> <u>woolly</u> monkey is a (very) <u>rare</u> animal. It has <u>thick</u> <u>brown</u> fur and <u>white</u> hair around its mouth. The monkey is named for the <u>bright</u> <u>yellow</u> fur underneath its <u>long</u>, <u>curled</u> tail. These monkeys live in a <u>small</u> area in the <u>high</u> mountains of Peru. With their <u>long</u> arms and legs and <u>powerful</u> tail, they move (quickly) through the forests.

    Unfortunately, these monkeys have lost a lot of their <u>natural</u> habitat. Farms and cattle ranches are some of the reasons for this. People are now working (hard) to protect these <u>amazing</u> animals.

C

Appearance	yellow-tailed woolly monkey; very rare; thick brown fur; white hair; bright yellow fur; long, curled tail; long arms and legs; powerful tail
Habitat (where it lives)	small area; high mountains; natural habitat
Movements or Bahavior	move quickly

2 BEFORE YOU WRITE, page 175   10 min.

Answers will vary.

- **Expansion Tip:** If possible, have students research the animal they have chosen for exercise **2** online. Students should look for descriptions of the animal's appearance, habitat, movements, or behavior, and include words that reflect those descriptions in their charts. Make sure students are aware that they can only copy individual words, not whole phrases or sentences. Students can then use some of those adjectives and adverbs in the paragraphs they write for exercise **3**.

3 WRITE, page 175   25 min.

WRITING FOCUS, page 175

Write the paragraph below on the board. Ask students which adjectives and adverbs should be deleted. Have students work in pairs to delete at least 5–6. Then compare versions as a class.

    My beautiful shiny goldfish is named Michael. He swims very happily in his somewhat large glass fish bowl. He has attractive white and brown little fins and a very cute fat orange body. He is kind of large for a normal goldfish. He really doesn't like to share his big goldfish bowl with other fish. When my adorable little red-haired children tried to give him some nice new friends, he snapped at them very violently!

- **Alternative Writing:** Imagine that you have been transported 15 years into the future and you can see your future self. What do you look like? Where do you live? What are you doing? How do you act? Begin with: *It is the year 20____. I am _____.* Write 5–6 sentences and use as many adjectives and adverbs as possible. Be nice to yourself—imagine a great future!

UNIT 7 Tomorrow and Beyond

The Future

Unit Opener

Photo: Have students look at the photo and read the caption. Ask, *Do you want to stay in one of these pods? Why, or why not?* This pod hotel is a design for the near future. The hotel may or may not be built. Ask students where they think it is.

Location: Capsule hotels with very small rooms are popular in Japan. They provide cheap accommodation. The ones without windows can be built underground. Ask, *Why might pod hotels be popular in some areas of the world?*

Theme: This unit is about the future. It discusses space travel, the future of work, and coral reefs. Have students look at the photos on pages 178, 186–187, and 192–193. Ask, *How do these pictures relate to the theme?*

Page	Lesson	Grammar	Examples
178	1	Future with *Will* and *Be Going To*	We **will** win. **Will** they help us? I'm **not going to** stay. What **will** she need?
186	2	Using Present Forms to Express the Future	When **does** the train **leave** tomorrow? She's not **traveling** to Norway this summer.
192	3	Comparison of Future Forms; Future Time Clauses	I'**ll do** it tomorrow. I'**m going** to the beach tomorrow. When I **get** home, I'll cook dinner.
200	**Review the Grammar**		
202	**Connect the Grammar to Writing**		

Unit Grammar Terms

adverb: a word that describes or modifies a verb, an adjective, or another adverb.
  ➢ He eats **quickly**.
  ➢ She drives **carefully**.

clause: a group of words with a subject and a verb.
  ➢ We watched the game. (one clause)
  ➢ We watched the game after we ate dinner. (two clauses)

contraction: two words combined into a shorter form.
  ➢ did not → **didn't**
  ➢ she is → **she's**
  ➢ I am → **I'm**
  ➢ we will → **we'll**

main clause: a clause that can stand alone as a sentence. It has a subject and a verb.
  ➢ **I heard the news** when I was driving home.

time clause: a clause that tells when an action or event happened or will happen. Time clauses are introduced by conjunctions such as *when, after, before, while,* and *since.*
  ➢ I have lived here **since I was a child**.
  ➢ **While I was walking home**, it began to rain.
  ➢ I'm going to call my parents **after I eat dinner**.

time expression: a phrase that tells when something happened or will happen. Time expressions usually go at the end or the beginning of a sentence.
  ➢ **Last week** I went hiking.
  ➢ She's moving **next month**.

73

Student Learning Outcomes	• **Read** an article about space travel for tourists. • **Write** questions about the future using *will*. • **Ask** and **answer** questions about future plans. • **Listen** to speakers and **ask** and **answer** questions about the information. • **Find** and edit errors with *will* and *be going to*. • **Write** predictions about the future.				
Lesson Vocabulary	(n.) advance (n.) exhibit	(adj.) memorable (n.) mission	(v.) orbit (n.) passenger	(n.) planet (adj.) practical	(n.) spacecraft (adj.) spectacular

EXPLORE

1 READ, page 178   15 min.

- **Tip:** Use the photo to elicit definitions and teach vocabulary such as *spacecraft* and *orbit*. This will help students anticipate the content of the article.

- **Tip:** Have students use context cues to guess the meaning of *spectacular* and *astronaut*. Ask students to identify the parts of speech for each new word. Through discussion, elicit that *orbit* is both a verb and a noun.

Be the Expert

- Virgin Galactic was founded in 2004 by Richard Branson, the founder of Virgin Atlantic Airways and other businesses. Virgin Galactic plans to offer space flights to tourists as well as to launch satellites and space science missions. NASA is working with Virgin to carry out experiments with 3D printing in space.

- Space Adventures was founded in 1998 by Eric Anderson. In 2001, Space Adventures sent their first clients into space, including the first tourist to orbit the Earth. That person paid $20 million for the experience. The company has two paying customers for a trip around the moon, which may take place in 2017 or 2018.

2 CHECK, page 179   5 min.

1. Space Adventures
2. Virgin Galactic
3. Space Adventures
4. Space Adventures

- **Expansion Tip:** Have students write three more statements about the information in the article and exchange them with partners. Partners should then identify which company each statement describes.

3 DISCOVER, page 179   5 min.

A 1. take   3. experience
     2. have   4. cheap

B a

- **Tip:** Write the second sentence from exercise **A** on the board. Work with students to identify the parts of the sentence: subject + *will* + base form of verb + object. This will lead into the chart on page 180.

LEARN

Chart 7.1, page 180   10 min.

- **Note 1:** Write descriptions of the uses for *will* (a through d) on the board. In a different column, write the example sentences in random order. Have students match each sentence to the use. Then have them check their answers in the chart.

- **Note 2:** Write several sentences with a pronoun and *will* in their full (non-contracted) form on the board and have students rewrite using contractions (e.g., *I will leave soon. They will not have a test tomorrow.*).

4 page 180   5 min.

A 1. will get   5. won't be   9. won't want
     2. will visit   6. will open   10. will welcome
     3. will/'ll talk   7. will remain   11. won't miss
     4. will have   8. will be

B 1. When will the museum open?
     2. What will the astronauts talk about?
     3. Where will the new exhibits be?
     4. What will visitors see?
     5. Will there be activities for children?
     6. When will the exhibit close?
     7. Will there be new exhibits every year?
     8. Will the museum be open on major holidays?

- **Tip:** Have students work in pairs to role-play conversations in which they ask the questions they have written, and their partner answers the questions. Ask students to create new answers to the questions that use *will* either in its full form or as part of a contraction.
- **Expansion Tip:** Have students talk in pairs about what they would like to see in a space museum and why. Call on student pairs to share their ideas with the class. Encourage class discussion about which exhibits would be the most fun, informative, exciting, etc.

Chart 7.2, page 182   10 min.

- **Notes 1 & 2:** Write several sentences on the board with errors in form (e.g., *She's not going watch TV. Do you going to talk to the teacher?*). Have the class correct your errors.
- **Tip:** Have students work in pairs to list the ways in which the uses of *will* and *be going to* are similar or different.

5 page 182   10 min.

1. Are you going to do
2. I am/I'm going to go
3. are you going to see
4. Phil and I are going to take
5. they are/they're going to love
6. are you and Phil going to do
7. We are/We're going to attend
8. Are you going to study
9. I am/I'm not going to do
10. I am/I'm going to sleep

- **Tip:** Have students read the conversation aloud in pairs. Encourage students to alternate between saying *going to* and *gonna* as they read aloud.

6 SPEAK, page 183   5 min.

Answers will vary.

- **Tip:** Call on students to tell the class about their partner's plans, using *be going to* whenever it is appropriate.

REAL ENGLISH, page 183

Tell students to write the full form of the verbs they hear. Emphasize that the reduced form is used in informal speech only, but it is important to understand it. Then say several sentences using the reduced form *gonna* as students listen and write the sentences with full forms.

PRACTICE

7 LISTEN, page 183   5 min.

1. 'm going to buy
2. 's going to go
3. aren't going to spend
4. will be
5. 'm going to be; 'll wait
6. will open
7. won't be
8. won't like

8 WRITE & SPEAK, page 184   15 min.

A 1. Are you going to take classes here next semester?
2. What are you going to do this weekend?
3. Will you be in class on Wednesday?
4. Will people visit Mars someday?
5. How will people travel in the future?
6. When are you going to call your parents?

B *Answers will vary.*

- **Alternative Speaking:** Have students choose one of these topics: weekend plans, summer plans, future transportation, future housing. They should prepare a one-minute talk on the topic to present to a small group.

9 LISTEN, WRITE & SPEAK, page 184 · 20 min.

A

	Glenn	Sylvia	Mark
Two Years	be a pilot	finish medical school	join the Air Force
Five Years	start astronaut training	be a doctor	be a flight engineer
Ten Years	be in space	go on her first space mission	work for NASA

B *Answers will vary. Sample answers:*

1. When will Glenn be in space?

2. What is Mark going to do in two years?

3. When will Mark work for NASA?

4. When is Glenn going to start astronaut training?

5. What is Sylvia going to be in five years?

C *Answers will vary.*

- **Tip:** Call on students and ask questions about the three speakers: *What are the speakers doing now? Why does Sylvia want to be an astronaut? Why is Mark going to work hard?* To increase interest in the activity, encourage students to make up additional details about the speakers and include the details in their answers.

10 EDIT, page 185 · 5 min.

I grew up in a house with a big yard and a lot of room to play. However, I don't think that children of the future are going to be so lucky. The world's population will ~~continues~~ continue to increase, and this means all of us will live in smaller homes. I think some big cities in Asia, such as Seoul and Singapore, will ~~serves~~ serve as models for the cities of the future. People are going to live in high-rise apartment buildings. These apartment buildings are going to be cheaper, safer, and more practical than separate houses.

There are going to be more advances in electronics. Also, people will/are going to have more entertainment choices in their homes in the future. We won't ~~to~~ go out very often to watch movies or concerts. Movie theaters will go out of business in the future.

11 APPLY, page 185 · 15 min.

Answers will vary.

- **Alternative Writing:** Have students write a paragraph about what their own futures will be like in ten or twenty years. Write these questions on the board and encourage students to answer them in their paragraphs: *Where will you live? What will you be doing? What kind of transportation will people be using? How are people going to dress? What problems are people going to face?*

> **REAL ENGLISH, page 185**
>
> Have students work in pairs to create a conversation in which they use both *definitely* and *probably* with the future. Ask volunteers to present their conversations to the class. Have the class provide feedback on whether volunteers have used the adverbs correctly.

Student Learning Outcomes	• **Read** a conversation and an excerpt from a lecture about the future of work. • **Complete** sentences with present verb forms to express the future. • **Listen** to sentences to identify the correct verb form. • **Talk** about plans on a calendar. • **Write** about plans for next week.

Lesson Vocabulary	(n.) calendar	(v.) contact	(n.) future	(n.) lecture	(n.) research
	(adj.) central	(n.) figure	(v.) hire	(n.) presentation	(n.) schedule

EXPLORE

1 READ, page 186   15 min.

• Use the photos to elicit ideas about work in the future. Ask, *What are the employees doing? What kind of technology are they using? How will this change work?*

• **Tip:** After students read and listen, have them work in pairs to ask and answer questions about the content.

Be the Expert

• Experts predict the following changes in work over the next decade or two:

 – Movement toward more science- and technology-based fields

 – More freelance and part-time jobs

 – More flexible career paths and schedules

 – More collaboration as the Internet allows people around the world to work together

 – Longer working lives—as people live longer, they will work a greater number of years

• Ask students to work in small groups to make predictions about the future of work, and then compare their predictions with the list above. Elicit reasons for the changes.

2 CHECK, page 187   5 min.

   1. F   2. T   3. T   4. F   5. T

• **Tip:** Have students identify where they found the answers to the questions.

3 DISCOVER, page 187   5 min.

A

Simple Present	Present Progressive
doesn't start	are you coming
begins	'm leaving
save	's going
finishes	're giving
have	

B 1. future

   2. The simple present refers to schedules and the present progressive refers to personal plans.

• **Tip:** Point out that chart 7.3 focuses on using simple present for schedules.

LEARN

Chart 7.3, page 188   10 min.

• **Note 1:** Write a schedule on the board for the next week (yours, TV shows, special events, etc.) or display one with a projector. Ask students questions about the coming events (e.g., *When does the soccer game start?*).

• **Note 2:** Have students write questions with the verbs in the chart, and then take turns asking and answering them in pairs. Point out that they can make up answers.

4 page 188   10 min.

   1. does; begin; begins

   2. does; leave; leaves

   3. does; arrive; arrives

   4. do; start; do not/don't start

   5. do not/don't open

   6. does; get; gets

   7. closes

   8. does not/doesn't leave

   9. does; start; starts

  10. finish; has

- **Notes 1 & 2:** Write example sentences on the board that use the present progressive with no time expression, an indefinite future expression (*someday, one day, sometime*), and a specific time expression (*tomorrow, at 7 p.m., this Saturday*). Ask students which ones use an indefinite expression incorrectly (*Someday I'm learning to fly*), which use the present (no time expression), and which are future (specific time expression).

5 page 189   5 min.

1. I am/I'm working
2. When are they leaving
3. We are/We're going
4. Is Craig graduating
5. He is not/isn't having
6. I am/I'm meeting
7. Where are you going
8. What are you doing
9. Are you visiting
10. How are you getting

6 SPEAK, page 189   5 min.

Answers will vary.

PRACTICE

7 page 190   5 min.

1. are you doing	7. Are you handing
2. I'm just spending	8. I don't understand
3. she's not coming	9. starts
4. is speaking	10. are meeting
5. is talking	11. are you meeting
6. does it start	

- **Alternative Writing & Speaking:** Have students work in pairs to write their own conversations. Suggest that they use both simple present and present progressive to talk about plans. Call on pairs to volunteer to present their conversations to the class.

8 LISTEN, page 190   10 min.

1. future; tomorrow
2. future; next Thursday
3. present; every morning
4. present; right now
5. future; this afternoon
6. future; on Friday
7. present; every week
8. present; right now

- **Expansion Tip:** Have students write their own statements or questions using a present or future time expression. Ask volunteers to say the sentences aloud. Have the class identify the verb as present or future, and state which words are helpful in determining the time.

9 APPLY, page 191   25 min.

- **Expansion Tip:** Have students find new partners and tell each other about their first partners' plans.

Student Learning Outcomes	• **Read** a blog post about coral reefs. • **Write** sentences with future time clauses. • **Find** and **edit** errors with future forms. • **Speak** about plans using future time clauses. • **Write** and **speak** about schedules for tomorrow.				
Lesson Vocabulary	(n.) behavior (adj.) breathtaking	(n.) coast (v.) collect	(n.) documentary (n.) oil	(n.) percentage (adj.) serious	(n.) topic (adj.) toxic

EXPLORE

1 READ, page 192   15 min.

• Use the photo to teach the meaning of *underwater* and *coral reef*. Ask why coral reefs might be important and what threats they are facing.

• **Expansion Tip:** On the board, draw a diagram with three boxes on the left and arrows from each box pointing to a box on the right labeled *Damage to Coral Reefs*. Have students complete the diagram with information from the text, and then compare their diagrams in pairs. Ask volunteers to complete the diagram on the board.

Be the Expert

• Coral reefs are home to perhaps one quarter of all the species in the ocean, even though they cover less than one percent of the ocean bottom. The Great Barrier Reef is the largest coral reef and spans 2600 km, or 1600 miles, off the east coast of Australia. Coral grows slowly—at a rate less than 2 cm to 15 cm per year. The Great Barrier Reef began growing 20,000 years ago.

• In addition to warming, rising seas, and pollution, people who harvest the coral or damage it by fishing also threaten coral reefs.

• Suggest that students research ways to protect coral reefs and share their findings with the class.

2 CHECK, page 193   5 min.

1. a   2. b   3. a   4. b   5. b

• **Tip:** Have students write three questions about the future of coral reefs, and then take turns asking and answering their questions with a partner. Suggest that students write at least one question about the present and one about the future.

3 DISCOVER, page 193   5 min.

A 1. I have   2. you read   3. it's

B the simple present

• **Tip:** Write: *Use _____ verb forms in future time clauses that begin with* when *and* before. Ask students to complete the rule about the verb form used, and then check their answers in chart 7.6 on page 195.

LEARN

Chart 7.5, page 194   10 min.

• **Tip:** Write these categories on the board: *events on a timetable/schedule, definite plans in the near future, predictions, intentions, decisions made at the time of speaking.* Ask students which form is used in each situation.

4 page 194   5 min.

1. I'll carry	6. are going
2. I'm going to visit	7. I'm staying
3. It's going to snow	8. is going to have
4. will be	9. I'll lend
5. is going	10. I'm going to take

• **Tip:** Suggest that students make one of these changes to each sentence: make it negative, make it a question, or change the subject. Then have students share their new sentences with partners.

5 page 194   5 min.

1. b/c	5. c	9. c
2. a/c	6. b	10. a
3. b	7. b	
4. b/c	8. a/c	

- **Note 2:** Write sentences on the board using *before, after, as soon as,* and *when* to introduce a future time clause. Have students identify which events happen first in each sentence.

- **Note 4:** Have students rewrite the example sentences by switching the order of clauses. Make sure students understand that commas are not required when the order of these two sentences is reversed.

6 page 196   10 min.

1. After I finish my homework (1), I'm going to bed (2).

2. When I finish this book about coral reefs (1), I am going to write my essay (2).

3. Lulu is going to call the office (2) as soon as she receives the information (1).

4. My sister will read all the instructions (1) before she uses her new phone (2).

5. I'll start cooking dinner (2) when you get home (1).

6. My brother is going to buy a new computer (2) when he receives his next paycheck (1).

7. After I go to the gym (1), I'm going to go to the supermarket (2).

8. I'll clean the living room (1) before our guests arrive tonight (2).

9. I'll help you (2) as soon as I send this e-mail (1).

10. After she graduates from college (1), she's going to move to Toronto (2).

- **Tip:** Have students rewrite the sentences by switching the order of the clauses. Encourage them to refer back to rule 4 on page 195 to confirm that they have used the correct punctuation.

7 page 196   5 min.

1. After the rain stops, we're going to take a walk.

2. Louise will go back to work as soon as she is better.

3. I'll let you know as soon as my plane lands in Paris.

4. Andy will be surprised when I arrive at his birthday party.

5. Before I leave, I will show you that website.

6. They're going to take some photos of the Alps when they visit Switzerland.

7. When my sister saves enough money, she is going to buy a car.

8. He'll call you as soon as he finishes his homework.

9. When I see Sam, I'll invite him to the party.

10. I'll say goodbye to you before I leave tonight.

PRACTICE

8 page 196   10 min.

1. are you doing	6. ends
2. I'm going to watch	7. Are you going to go
3. are you going to	8. I'm giving
4. starts	9. I'll watch
5. does it end	10. I'll record

9 page 197   10 min.

1. After I talk to Hans, I'm going to write my assignment./I'm going to write my assignment after I talk to Hans.

2. When Rui and Fatima arrive, we're going to have dinner./We're going to have dinner when Rui and Fatima arrive.

3. Barbara is going to buy a few things before she goes home./Before she goes home, Barbara is going to buy a few things.

4. When Mary calls, I'm going to ask about the test./I'm going to ask about the test when Mary calls.

5. As soon as she finishes law school, she is going to move to Ohio./She's going to move to Ohio as soon as she finishes law school.

6. When I finish my homework, I'm going to go for a run./I'm going to go for a run when I finish my homework.

7. Before he sells his house, he's going to paint it./He's going to paint his house before he sells it.

8. After I make dinner, I'm going to watch the news./I'm going to watch the news after I make dinner.

10 SPEAK, page 198   5 min.

Answers will vary.

- **Tip:** After students have said their sentences to their partners, have them write each sentence two different ways: with the time clause at the beginning and with the time clause at the end.

- **Alternative Speaking:** Write other sentence stems on the board: *When I start a new job, Before I finish school, As soon as I have some free time, After I take the test.* Have students complete the sentences with their own ideas. Then have them write the sentences with the time clauses at the end.

- **Tip:** Have students look at the photo and describe the bear and its surroundings. Ask students to make one sentence using a time clause about what the bear will do (e.g., *When the bear sees the photographer, it will run away.*).

A Canadian company wants to build an oil pipeline in central Canada. It ~~carries~~ will carry oil from Alberta to the coast of British Columbia, over 700 miles (1120 km) away. The pipeline will ~~carrying~~ carry oil to the coast, where big ships will ~~to~~ collect the oil for the next stage of its journey. The pipeline will create a new market for Canadian oil in China and other Asian countries.

Unfortunately, the plan is going to take the pipeline through the Great Bear Rainforest. Many people do not want this to happen. The building of the pipeline will ~~threatens~~ threaten animals such as the Kermode Bear. Also, some of the local people think that the ships are going to cause problems. They are afraid that one of the ships will spill oil when it ~~will~~ travels along the coast of British Columbia.

A *Answers will vary.*

B 1. is going to answer; calls

    2. When she speaks with Frank, she is/'s going to ask/will ask him about the lion's diet.

    3. is/'s going to call; interviews

    4. is going to use/will use; talks

    5. finishes; is going to leave/will leave

    6. As soon as she leaves her office, she is going to go/will go to the store.

    7. When she goes to the store, she is going to buy/ will buy her mother's birthday present.

    8. is going to get/will get; does

C *Answers will vary.*

- **Alternative Writing:** Have students write a paragraph about their partner's schedule including their opinion of it.

D *Answers will vary.*

1 page 200   5 min.

1. I'll talk; I send

2. do you finish/will you finish; I'll call; I leave

3. does the library close; it closes

4. Are you going (to go); I'm leaving, is

2 EDIT, page 200   5 min.

• **Tip:** Have students read the title and look at the photo. Ask them to guess what the paragraph will be about, and then have them read to check their predictions.

    Counting zebras in the wild has always been difficult. However, counting zebras ~~becomes~~ will become much easier in the future thanks to a new computer program called *Stripespotter*. In the future, scientists will just take photos of zebras. After they ~~will~~ take photos of the zebras, *Stripespotter* ~~is doing~~ will do the rest of the work. It will ~~to~~ examine the stripes on each zebra. The pattern of a zebra's stripes is like the barcode on a product at the supermarket. Each one is different. After scientists ~~are going to~~ collect enough photos, they ~~are having~~ will have an accurate record of the zebra population.

3 LISTEN, WRITE & SPEAK, page 201   20 min.

A Speaker 1: Matt—learn to play the guitar

    Speaker 2: Tammy—run a marathon

B 1. Plans: take a class at a music store; practice every day; listen to music a lot

    Prediction: I won't become famous. I probably won't be very good.

    2. Plans: buy a new pair of running shoes; join a running club; enter some short races

    Prediction: It's going to be really hard. I'll get in great shape.

C *Answers will vary.*

4 WRITE & SPEAK, page 201   10 min.

Answers will vary.

• **Expansion Tip:** Have students work in small groups to share their goals and predictions, as the other group members take notes. When the groups have finished sharing, have students find a partner from another group to tell about the goals and predictions of the members of their original group.

Connect the Grammar to Writing

1 READ & NOTICE THE GRAMMAR, page 202

20 min.

A *Answers will vary.*

- **Tip:** With books closed, write the example sentences from the Grammar Focus on the board in random order. Ask students to identify which make predictions and which express intentions.

B *Answers will vary. Possible answers:*

1. more people will use them
2. they will take us places quickly and safely
3. people will want them when they are cheap
4. they will be good for the environment
5. they will use less fuel than cars
6. they will also take up less space, so we won't need as many large parking lots
7. there will be more space for parks and trees
8. there will be more personal transporters at airports and in large factories
9. workers at airports and factories will find them very helpful and convenient
10. police officers, letter carriers, and security guards will probably find them very useful in their work

C When they become cheaper; When workers at these places try them; as soon as I can

2 BEFORE YOU WRITE, page 203

15 min.

Answers will vary.

- **Tip:** For exercise **A**, you might suggest that students review the list of topics from exercise **11A** on page 185 to start their brainstorming session.

3 WRITE, page 203

15 min.

> ### WRITING FOCUS, page 203
>
> Write other gender-specific terms on the board (e.g., *waitress, foreman, mailman, chairman, headmaster*). Have students work in pairs to use their dictionaries and write sentences with gender-neutral language instead of each term on the board.

- **Expansion Tip:** Have students exchange the charts they created for exercise **2B** with a partner. Then have the partner write a possible topic sentence for a paragraph about that prediction.

- **Alternative Writing:** Brainstorm a list of occupations that students think will be popular in 20 years and write them on the board. For one of the occupations, elicit some predictions about that job (e.g., *Teachers won't come into the classroom anymore. They will teach from home, using the Internet.*). Have students work in pairs to choose a job and list their predictions. Then have students write three paragraphs on the topic.

Comparatives and Superlatives

Unit Opener

Photo: Have students look at the photo and read the caption. Elicit their ideas about the photo. Ask, *What can you see? Why are the cars piled up like this? Have you ever seen a scrap yard before?*

Location: This photo is from a scrap yard in Victoria, British Columbia, in Canada. The metal will be recycled for other products. British Columbia encourages people to recycle older cars for this purpose.

Theme: The theme of this unit is consumer society. Look at the photos on page 204–207, 213–214, and 220. Ask, *What do all these photos have in common? What do you think are the dangers or drawbacks of a consumer society?*

Page	Lesson	Grammar	Examples
206	1	Comparative Adjectives and Adverbs	The blue car is **nicer than** the gray car. Carol drives **more carefully than** Peter.
213	2	Comparisons with (*Not*) *As . . . As* and *Less*	My car is **as big as** your car. This phone is **not as good as** that one. This phone is **less expensive than** that one.
220	3	Superlative Adjectives and Adverbs	The red car is **the nicest car** in the parking lot. She runs **the fastest** of all the players on the team. This is **the least expensive** phone in the store.
227	**Review the Grammar**		
230	**Connect the Grammar to Writing**		

Unit Grammar Terms

comparative: the form of an adjective used to talk about the difference between two people, places, or things.
➢ I'm **taller** than my mother.
➢ That book is **more interesting** than this one.

irregular adjective: an adjective that does not change form in the usual way.
➢ good → **better**
➢ bad → **worse**

irregular adverb: an adverb that does not change form in the usual way.
➢ well → **better**
➢ badly → **worse**

possessive pronoun: a pronoun that shows ownership or relationship: *mine, yours, his, hers, ours, theirs*. Possessive pronouns are used in place of a possessive adjective + noun.
➢ My sister's eyes are blue. **Mine** are brown. What color are **yours**?

superlative: the form of an adjective or adverb used to compare three or more people, places, or things.
➢ Mount Everest is **the highest** mountain in the world.
➢ Evgeny is **the youngest** student in our class.

Student Learning Outcomes	• **Read** an article about consumer societies. • **Compare** three types of laptop computers. • **Listen** to six consumers who are deciding what to buy. • **Write** sentences comparing vacation choices. • **Discuss** vacation choices with a partner.
Lesson Vocabulary	(n.) consumer (v.) operate (adj.) responsible (n.) society (n.) variety (n.) market (n.) product (n.) screen (v.) tend (n.) waste

EXPLORE

1 READ, page 206   5 min.

• **Tip:** Before reading, pre-teach the word *waste* (*garbage/rubbish*). Ask, *What do you see in these photos? How do the items relate to the theme of the unit?*

Be the Expert

• In 2006, Americans threw out an average of 4.6 pounds of trash for each person every day. That totals up to 251 million tons of trash—a staggering amount.

• E-waste is a term that is used to describe electronic waste. This includes computers, cell phones, and televisions. E-waste can be very dangerous to the environment, because many of these products contain toxic substances. Interestingly, some of these toxic substances are what make products safer for us when we use them. For example, lead protects us from radiation. However, when these products are thrown into a dump, they can release the lead into the ground, and eventually it can travel into our water sources.

• **Expansion Tip:** "Green" is an adjective that is used to describe how environmentally friendly a person, city, or country is. Ask, *Is it important to be green? Why?* Then ask, *What are some ways that you try to be green?* On the board, elicit a list of green activities that students do or could do in the future (e.g., *recycle, buy fewer things, buy things used, buy items made with recycled materials, buy items that can be recycled*).

2 CHECK, page 207   5 min.

1. F   2. F   3. T   4. F

• **Tip:** Ask higher-level students to correct the false statements.

3 DISCOVER, page 207   5 min.

A 1. wider   2. more responsible

B 1. long   2. short

• **Tip:** On the board, write these questions: *What is one new product that helps you to live more comfortably? What can newer phones do that old phones can't do?* For higher-level students, ask, *Do you think that a consumer society means that people have better lives? Explain your answer.* Have students discuss these questions in small groups and share their answers with the class.

LEARN

Chart 8.1, page 208   5 min.

• **Note 1:** Students often substitute *from* for *than* or omit *than* altogether. Write *than* prominently on the board, and point to it for emphasis when reviewing the activities. Leave this on the board as a reference for speaking activities. Point to *than* if you hear students omitting the word.

• **Note 4:** The rules about *more* and *-er* can be more flexible than other grammar rules. Explain that although there is some variation, it is important to follow the typical usage pattern as they are learning the language.

• **Note:** Students often use two comparatives, e.g., *He is more quieter than his brother.* Write this example on the board and point out that each comparative sentence should have *-er* or *more*, but not both.

• **Note:** Explain that it is sometimes possible to compare nouns using the same basic pattern: *more* + noun + *than* (e.g., *I have more books than you do. This cake has more sugar than that cake.*).

Use hand gestures to show how the adverbs are used, e.g., hold your hands far apart for *a lot* and close together for *a little*. If students finish the expansion activity above, have them revise their sentences by adding the adverbs. If students don't finish the activity, write the names of four famous people on the board and four adjectives. Have students compare the people using comparative adjectives and the adverbs in the box.

4 page 208   10 min.

1. more quiet than/ quieter than
2. more important than
3. nicer than
4. bigger than
5. more efficient
6. better than
7. easier than
8. worse than
9. hotter
10. farther than

- **Expansion Tip:** On the board, draw a 3-column table. Write the names of famous people in the two outer columns and adjectives that students suggest in the center column. Ask students to compare the famous people. Model an example (e.g., *Jennifer Lopez is more beautiful than Vladimir Putin.*). Have students work in pairs and write at least three sentences. Ask volunteers to read their sentences to the class. If possible, leave this list on the board for future activities in this unit.

Chart 8.2, page 209   5 min.

- **Note 4:** *Better* is both the comparative adjective for *good* and the comparative adverb for *well*. Similarly, *bad* and *badly* both change to *worse*. On the board, write: *I sing better than my brother does. This song is better than the last one.* Ask, *What does* better *refer to in each sentence? Is* better *used as an adjective or an adverb in each?* Note that sentence 1 = *sing*, adverb and sentence 2 = *song*, adjective.

5 page 209   5 min.

1. better than; more quickly than; more often than
2. harder than; more frequently than; longer than
3. more rapidly than; more easily than; more carefully than

6 page 209   10 min.

1. works more efficiently than
2. keeps time more accurately than
3. calls more often than
4. rings more loudly than
5. shops more frequently than
6. types more quickly than
7. sings worse than
8. studies harder than

- **Expansion Tip:** Continue the Expansion Tip activity for exercise **4**, but erase the adjectives in the center column. Elicit verbs to put in this column instead, e.g., *sing, dance, mediate, act, travel, etc.* Then add a column of adverbs that students suggest, e.g., *beautifully, gracefully, fast, hard.* Have students work in pairs to create comparative sentences using the famous people, verbs, and adverbs.

Chart 8.3, page 210   5 min.

- **Note 1:** *One* or *ones* can be used in place of an object. For example: *This book is larger than that one.* On the board, write: *The chocolate cake is better than the vanilla cake. That chair is softer than this chair.* Have students rewrite these sentences to sound more natural. *The chocolate cake is better than the vanilla* one*. That chair is softer than this* one*.*

7 page 210   5 min.

1. than yours
2. than
3. than I do
4. more expensive
5. did
6. mine
7. than Kelly's did
8. than he is

8 page 210   10 min.

1. than mine (is)
2. than his father (does)
3. than Chad's (is)
4. than she (did)
5. than ours (is)
6. than yours (does)
7. than theirs (is)
8. than her sister (does)

- **Expansion Tip:** Write a chart with information about two people. Have students work in pairs to write three sentences that compare the people using the information they have learned about comparisons.

	Age	Height	Weight	Grade on test	Runs a mile in:
Joe	23	5'4"	130 lbs.	90	8 mins
Ann	25	5'1"	110 lbs.	80	6 mins

PRACTICE

9 page 211   10 min.

1. worse than
2. older than
3. more modern
4. cheaper than
5. happier/more happy

6. more often than
7. bigger
8. nicer than
9. larger
10. more frequently than

- **Expansion Tip:** Have students read the conversation aloud with a partner placing stress on the adverbs and adjectives. Explain that *than* is not usually a stressed word. Model the first sentence as an example: *My PHONE is working WORSE than EVER.*

10 page 211   10 min.

1. larger than; smaller than
2. lighter than; heavier than
3. newer than; older than
4. cheaper than; more expensive than
5. more quickly than; more slowly than
6. more reliably than
7. more quietly than
8. better than

- **Expansion tip:** Ask students which laptop

computer they would choose. Have students work in groups of 3–4 and convince their classmates to choose the same computer. Encourage them to use as many comparative adjectives and adverbs as possible.

11 LISTEN, page 212   15 min.

1. green coat; It is more comfortable.
2. family car; It is cheaper to run.
3. yellow roses; They are much fresher.
4. downtown; It is much more convenient for work.
5. black boots; The black ones will last longer.
6. small TV; The picture is clearer.

12 APPLY, page 212   35 min.

Answers will vary.

- **Tip:** Assign exercises **A–D** for homework, or have students work in pairs to create sentences.

- **Expansion Tip:** Have students work in groups of 3–4. Tell the groups to imagine that they are going to go on a vacation together, but they need to decide which one. Tell students they have eight minutes to persuade each other to vote for their vacation. As a class, find out which vacation each group chooses.

Student Learning Outcomes	• **Read** an excerpt from a discussion about online reviews. • **Complete** comparisons using *(not) as . . . as* and *less*. • **Compare** Internet movie services using a chart. • **Find** and **edit** errors in online reviews. • **Write** sentences comparing products and services. • **Talk** to a partner about how products and services compare with each other.
Lesson Vocabulary	(adj.) complicated (adj.) effective (adv.) likely (adj.) positive (adj.) stylish (n.) customer (adj.) harmful (n.) marketing (adj.) satisfied (adj.) valuable

EXPLORE

1 READ, page 213   5 min.

• **Tip:** Before reading, ask students to look at the title and ask, *What are online reviews? What do the stars represent?*

Be the Expert

In the United States, Amazon, Yelp, and TripAdvisor are three places that many people look for reviews. Amazon has reviews of books and other consumer products. Yelp has reviews of local businesses such as stores, restaurants, hair salons, and car mechanics. TripAdvisor has reviews of hotels, flights, restaurants, museums, and national parks.

• **Expansion Tip:** Ask students if they read online reviews often. If so, what websites do they like? What is useful about these sites? What is not useful? If students don't look at online reviews, how do they find information about products?

2 CHECK, page 214   5 min.

1. F	3. T	5. F
2. T	4. T	6. F

• **Tip:** Ask higher-level students to correct the false statements.

3 DISCOVER, page 214   10 min.

A
1. equal	4. not equal
2. not equal	5. equal
3. not equal	6. equal

B
1. as	2. than

• **Tip:** On the board, write the following sentences: *Clothes at _____ (name of store) are less expensive than they are at _____ (different store). The food at _____ (restaurant) is not as good as the food at _____ (different restaurant).*

Have students complete the sentences with their own ideas. Then have them discuss their ideas in groups of 3–4.

LEARN

Chart 8.4, page 215   5 min.

• **Note 1:** The most common mistake with this grammar point is forgetting to include *as* both times. Write *as* prominently on the board, and point to this if students forget to include *as*. Errors will most likely occur during speaking activities.

• **Note 3:** Explain that formal English uses a more complete sentence structure: *She's as smart as he is.* The informal spoken version uses only an object pronoun. Have students practice transforming sentences from formal to informal and vice versa.

4 page 215   10 min.

1. as effective as	5. as warm as
2. as well as	6. as comfortable as
3. as useful as	7. as fast as
4. as carefully as	8. as frequently as

5 page 215   10 min.

1. Desktop computers are as popular as laptops (are).

2. Microwave ovens work as well as regular ovens (do).

3. Motorcycles go as fast as cars (do).

4. This hotel room is as big as my apartment (is).

5. A smartphone sends messages as quickly as a laptop (does).

6. My mother speaks English as well as my father (does).

7. Gabi goes shopping as often as Linda (does).

8. Trains are as comfortable as airplanes (are).

- **Expansion Tip:** Explain that *similes* compare one object to another using *like* or *as*. Certain similes are commonly used to describe things. On the board, write two columns. Ask students to match the two words and create a simile. Model the first as an example: *as busy as a bee.*

_____	1. busy (a)	a. bee
_____	2. cool (e)	b. sheet
_____	3. easy (c)	c. pie
_____	4. sick (d)	d. dog
_____	5. white (b)	e. cucumber

Ask students to describe any similar similes that are common in their first languages.

Chart 8.5, page 216   5 min.

- **Note 3:** Students may be confused about the fact that *less* is not commonly used with shorter adjectives. On the board, draw two stick figures, where one (Fred) is taller than the other (Frank). Write: *Frank is less tall than Fred.* Ask, *Is this correct?* Elicit that it is technically correct, but the *usage* is uncommon and somewhat awkward because *tall* is a one-syllable adjective. It is possible to say: *Fred is taller than Frank. Frank is not as tall as Fred.* Or, *Frank is shorter than Fred.*

6 page 216   10 min.

1. aren't as nice as

2. less fashionable than

3. is not/isn't as stylish

4. less expensive

5. is not/isn't as fancy as

6. is not/isn't as efficient

7. does not/doesn't make coffee as quickly

8. does not/doesn't taste as good

- **Expansion Tip:** Have students look at exercise **5** again. Did they agree with these sentences? Have them change 2–3 sentences to make comparisons with *less* or *not as . . . as* (e.g., *Most cafeterias are less expensive than restaurants.*). Have students discuss their sentences in groups of 3–4.

7 page 217   10 min.

1. My watch is not/isn't as attractive as yours.

2. Sally's shoes are less fancy than Jill's.

3. Adam does not/doesn't exercise as frequently as he used to.

4. This supermarket is less expensive than the one across the street.

5. The actor's new movie is less exciting than his last one.

6. This gym is not/isn't as convenient as the one near my house.

7. This review is not/isn't ~~not~~ as positive as that one.

8. The new tablet starts up less quickly than the old one.

PRACTICE

8 page 217   5 min.

1. is not/isn't as big as

2. is not/isn't as heavy as

3. less expensive

4. did not/didn't take photos as often as

5. not as complicated as

6. less difficult

7. as nice as

8. as good as

9 EDIT, page 218   10 min.

- **Tip:** Before beginning this activity, direct students to the photo and ask them to describe what it is. Explain that often when people buy a playhouse for their backyard, it needs assembly.

***** **A Huge Success!**

Our family loves this! Our last playhouse was much less exciting than the Jolly Roger. It was also less attractive ~~as~~ than this one. And this is really an important point: it wasn't as safe ~~as~~. **–Maria**

*** Hard to Build

My kids enjoyed this, but for me, putting it together was just as hard **as** building a real pirate ship! It's true that I probably don't build things as quickly as a lot of other people do. And maybe I'm not as good with tools as they ~~do~~ **are**, but I still think this product should be less complicated than **it is**! **–Sam**

**** Fun for Younger Kids

My four-year-old son says this play structure is **as** fun as a real pirate ship! He plays in it as often as he can, but my six-year-old daughter isn't as enthusiastic as he is about it. I'm a little disappointed because she uses it less often ~~then~~ **than** I expected. **–Lin**

10 page 219   10 min.

1. is as cheap as

2. is less expensive than/is not/isn't as expensive as

3. is not/isn't as high as

4. adds new movies less frequently than/doesn't / does not add new movies as frequently as

5. is less difficult than/is not as difficult as

6. find movies as easily as

7. is as good as

8. is less helpful than/is not/isn't as helpful as

- **Tip:** Make sure that students understand that an Internet movie service allows customers to access movies through the service for a fee. These services may require an initial *membership fee* to become a member and an additional amount each month (*the monthly rate*).

- **Expansion Tip:** Ask students which movie services they would choose from the chart and why? If most students in the class either use or are familiar with movie services, ask them to discuss which ones they subscribe to. Have them compare their services in groups of 3–4, and then write 2–3 sentences using (*not*) as . . . as and *less than*.

11 APPLY, page 219   25 min.

Answers will vary.

- **Tip:** As a class, choose a type of product and have students work in groups of 3–4 to define characteristics that they could use to compare products of that type. Remind students to use the charts in exercise **10** on this page and exercise **10** on page 211 as models.

- **Expansion Tip:** Have each group present their findings to the class. After each group has presented, ask the other students in the audience to vote for which product they would choose.

- **Alternative Apply:** Have students write two online reviews. One should be for a product that they love, and the other for a product that they have been very disappointed with. Encourage students to use *less* and (*not*) as. . . as where appropriate. Ask for volunteers to read their reviews to the class.

LESSON 3 | Superlative Adjectives and Adverbs

| Student Learning Outcomes | • **Read** an article about garbage on Mount Everest.
• **Listen** to conversations with questions that include superlatives.
• **Complete** sentences with superlatives in a conversation about cell phones.
• **Speak** about people, places, and things using superlatives.
• **Find** and **edit** errors in an article about trash in the desert.
• **Write** general knowledge sentences that use superlatives. |

| Lesson Vocabulary | (n.) challenge | (v.) climb | (n.) dump | (n.) junk | (n.) threat |
| | (n.) charity | (adj.) concerned | (n.) garbage | (n.) mineral | (n.) top |

EXPLORE

1 READ, page 220   10 min.

• **Tip:** Before reading, ask students what they know about Mount Everest. Then ask them to look at the photo on page 220. Ask, *What is happening in this picture? How is it related to the photo on page 221?*

Be the Expert

• With a peak at 29,029 feet (8848 meters) above sea level, Mount Everest is the highest mountain in the world.

• In 1953, Sir Edmund Hillary, a New Zealander, and Tenzing Norgay, his Sherpa guide from Nepal, first climbed to the top of Mount Everest. Since then, approximately 3500 people have reached the top. They leave supplies on the mountain. Since 2008, the annual Eco-Everest Expedition has cleaned up 13 tons of garbage from the mountain including oxygen bottles and tents.

• Now, the Nepalese government requires a $4000 deposit from climbers to make sure that they bring back all their trash.

• 1.5 tons of garbage was collected by climbers and 15 artists. They turned this trash into 74 pieces of art. Some of the profit from the artwork goes to the Everest Summiteers Association, which helps to clean up the mountain. Search online for *Mt. Everest 8848 Art Project* for more information.

2 CHECK, page 221   5 min.

1. dirty   4. often
2. difficult   5. art
3. a popular

3 DISCOVER, page 221   10 min.

A

Adjectives with *-est*		Adjectives with *most*	
high	cold	exciting	interesting
dirty	windy	attractive	expensive
tough	big		

B a

• **Tip:** Elicit names of cities from the students and write them on the board. Ask, *Which city is the most exciting? Which is the biggest? Which is the dirtiest? Which is the most attractive?* Have students compare the cities in groups of 2–3.

LEARN

Chart 8.6, page 222   5 min.

• **Notes 1 & 2:** To illustrate the difference between comparative and superlative adjectives and adverbs, draw two mountains (triangles) of different sizes on the board. Ask, *Which mountain is higher?* Then draw another mountain. Ask, *Which mountain is the highest?* Explain that with two items, we use comparatives, but with three or more, we use a superlative.

• **Notes 3, 4, 5 & 6:** Point out to students that superlative rules follow the same pattern as comparative rules. The difference is that superlatives usually use *the + -est/most* while comparatives use *-er/more + than*. Have some students call out comparatives, and other students decide what the superlative form would be, e.g., *more difficult than = the most difficult; taller than = the tallest.*

4 page 222 — 10 min.

1. The biggest
2. the worst
3. the most difficult
4. the most experienced
5. (the) farthest
6. the easiest
7. the most quickly
8. the highest
9. the best
10. the stupidest/the most stupid

5 LISTEN & SPEAK, page 223 — 10 min.

A
1. most efficiently
2. the most beautiful
3. the worst
4. most frequently
5. the most important
6. the most interesting
7. the closest
8. the smartest

B *Answers will vary.*

> **REAL ENGLISH, page 223**
>
> Ask students to write one question for their classmates, using a superlative. Explain that they should use a possessive pronoun with their question, e.g., *Who is your oldest relative? What is your greatest quality? What was your most interesting class last semester?* Check the questions to make sure that they are appropriate and grammatically correct. Then have students ask and answer their questions in groups of 4–5. Model this to show that students should answer in full sentences, e.g., *My oldest relative is my grandfather's cousin. He's 90 years old.*

Chart 8.7, page 223 — 5 min.

- **Note 1:** Remind students about the grammar patterns for *less* with comparatives. Explain that *the least* follows similar patterns, and is rarely used with one-syllable adjectives.

- **Note 2:** Explain that superlatives never include *than*, but often include phrases such as *in the world, of all the students*, etc. to show the group in which the item belongs. On the board, write: *He is bigger than his brother. That restaurant is more expensive than this one.* Ask students to make these sentences superlatives.

- **Note 4:** Read the example sentence aloud. Ask, *Is China the biggest country in the world? How do you know?* Explain that it is not because the text says *one of the* + plural noun. Then explain that *one of* is used when the item belongs to a larger group. To illustrate this, give two more examples: *Bill Gates is one of the richest people in the world.* (I don't know if he is #1.) *Katie is one of my best friends.* (I have other very good friends.)

6 page 224 — 10 min.

1. This is the least popular state park in California.
2. Canada is the largest country in North America.
3. Tokyo has the biggest population in Japan.
4. This is the least expensive apartment in the building.
5. Alan drives the fastest of my three brothers.
6. Jane is one of the most intelligent students in her class.
7. That was one of the least interesting classes I've ever taken.
8. Mel works the least efficiently of all the people in this office.
9. This is the cheapest computer in the store.
10. That's one of the prettiest streets in this city.

7 SPEAK, page 224 — 5 min.

Answers will vary.

- **Tip:** Before you begin exercise **7**, elicit ideas from students for possible topics to talk about.

PRACTICE

8 page 225 — 5 min.

1. the most modern
2. the rarest
3. one of the worst things
4. one of the best things
5. the most important thing
6. the most convenient place
7. the least expensive
8. the least helpful salespersons/salespeople

- **Expansion Tip:** Have students read the conversation aloud. Encourage them to use appropriate intonation and stress. Then ask if students agree with or have had similar experiences to the speakers in the conversation. Have students discuss this in groups of 2–3.

- **Tip:** Before students begin the reading, have them look at the picture of the camel. Ask what they already know about camels. Based on this slogan, what do they think the article will be about? Explain that *litter* is garbage that is left in the open, on the street, or in this case, in the desert.

The Arabian Desert in the Middle East is one of the ~~most hot~~ hottest environments on Earth, and it has the ~~less~~ least amount of rainfall. But to the camel, it is home. The camel is one of the ~~most strong~~ strongest animals in the world. Camels can go for many days with only a little food and water. When they do find water, they probably drink the most quickly of any land animal. Adult camels can drink about 25 to 30 gallons (95–114 liters) in ten minutes. Unfortunately, finding water is not the ~~seriousest~~ most serious problem camels face. ~~Most~~ The most dangerous threat to camels comes from humans. Tourists in the desert leave trash behind. Camels think the trash is food and eat it. This is very dangerous for the camels, because it can kill them.

One of the most polluted parts of the desert is outside the city of Abu Dhabi. Each year, many camels die there from eating trash. Cameron Oliver has been trying to change this. Since he was eight years old, Cameron has been telling people that trash is very dangerous for camels. Of all the young people in Abu Dhabi, Cameron has worked ~~most hard~~ the hardest to help the camels. When he was 12, Cameron became the ~~most young~~ youngest person to win an Abu Dhabi award for community service.

A 1. Mount Everest is the highest mountain on Earth.

2. The cheetah is the fastest animal in the world.

3. The Nile River is the longest river in the world.

4. The Pacific Ocean is the widest ocean on Earth.

5. Australia is the smallest continent.

6. The blue whale is the largest animal on Earth.

7. Antarctica is the coldest place on Earth.

8. Mercury is the closest planet to the sun.

B *Answers will vary.*

C *Answers will vary.*

D *Answers will vary.*

- **Alternative Apply:** Have students work in groups of 2–3 to create a quiz with superlative questions and answers about the school where they are studying, e.g., *Which classroom is the largest one in the school? (a) 206 (b) 301 (c) 208.* Have each group give the quiz to another group. Ask each group to read their most interesting question and answer aloud to the class.

1 READ & WRITE, page 227   15 min.

- **Tip:** Before beginning the activity, make sure that students understand what the chart represents (how environmentally conscious or *green* each country is). Explain that the headings for each sentence set tell us which column to look at. For example, first section is about transportation, so students should use the information in the transportation column to complete these sentences. Model the first two sentences with the class.

A 1. the greenest

2. the least green

3. greener

4. not as green as

5. not as concerned as/less concerned than

6. the most concerned

7. more concerned than

8. not as concerned as/less concerned than

9. as responsibly as

10. the most responsibly

11. less responsibly than

12. the least responsibly

B *Answers will vary.*

- **Expansion Tip:** Search for the *Greendex Calculator* online. The calculator has a list of questions that students can answer to calculate how green they are, compared to the rest of the world. This can be assigned for homework, or printouts can be made and students can answer the questions in class. Students can compare their answers in groups.

2 EDIT, page 228   10 min.

- According to a recent Greendex survey, people in India were the ~~most green~~ greenest consumers in the world. They scored lower in transportation than the Chinese ~~were~~ did, but they scored ~~the highest~~ higher than the Chinese in three other categories.

- Mexicans were more concerned about green transportation ~~as~~ than green food or goods. For them, the ~~low~~ lowest score of all was in the housing category.

- Germans scored as highly in the transportation category ~~than~~ as they did in the food category. However, they were ~~least~~ less concerned about housing than goods.

- The Japanese were one of the least concerned ~~nationality~~ nationalities overall. They had one of the ~~most bad~~ worst scores in the housing category.

- Americans had the lowest overall score of all the nationalities in the survey. Food was the only category in which Americans did not score lower ~~then~~ than the other nationalities.

3 LISTEN & SPEAK, page 229   25 min.

A 1. greener than

2. more carefully than

3. as hard as

4. more difficult

5. more popular

6. as quickly as

7. more comfortable

8. easier

B *Answers will vary.*

C *Answers will vary.*

4 WRITE & SPEAK, page 229   20 min.

Answers will vary.

- **Tip:** In exercise **C**, encourage higher-level students to explain why they have made these choices. Have their partners ask as many follow-up questions as possible, e.g., *Why do you think a computer is less important than a smartphone?*

1 READ & NOTICE THE GRAMMAR,
page 230   25 min.

A *Answers will vary.*

B   I needed to buy a new sleeping bag for a winter camping trip. So, I went to a camping store and compared three different brands of sleeping bags: Ultra Comfort, Snowy Down, and Northern Trek. I wanted to look at each sleeping bag very carefully. For winter camping, the Snowy Down had (the highest) rating. But in some ways, the other two sleeping bags were <u>better than</u> the Snowy Down. Of the three sleeping bags, the Snowy Down was (the warmest), but it was also the (most expensive). The Northern Trek cost <u>less than</u> the Snowy Down, but it was just <u>as expensive as</u> the Ultra Comfort. The Ultra Comfort was <u>warmer than</u> the Northern Trek. Finally, the Ultra Comfort was <u>lighter than</u> the other sleeping bags, so it was <u>easier</u> to carry.

     I decided not to get the Northern Trek for camping outside. It wasn't <u>as warm as</u> the other sleeping bags. But we were having a mild winter, and I didn't need (the warmest) kind of sleeping bag. So I looked more closely at (the lightest) sleeping bag, the Ultra Comfort. That's the one I chose.

C

Product Details	Ultra Comfort	Snowy Down	Northern Trek
Cost	as expensive as the Northern Trek	the most expensive	less than Snowy Down
Warmth	warmer	the warmest	warm
Weight	lightest	heavier than Ultra Comfort	heavier than Ultra Comfort

2 BEFORE YOU WRITE, page 231   10 min.

Answers will vary.

3 WRITE, page 231   15 min.

WRITING FOCUS, page 231

Choose a sequence of 2–3 sentences from one of the readings in this unit. Write these on the board and make them run-on sentences by omitting capitalization at the beginning of sentences and periods or conjunctions. Ask students how they could correct the sentences. Then direct them to the reading where the sentences occur. Have them find the writer's well-written sentences and compare them to students' corrections. Note that there can be more than one correct answer.

- **Alternative Writing:** Have students write online reviews of three places in their hometown that they think people would like to visit. If possible have students look at a travel websites such as TripAdvisor as models. Have students make charts similar to the one in exercise **2** and fill out information about the three places. Then have them write advice for others. (If students share a hometown, they can work in pairs.) Encourage students to use as many superlatives and comparatives as possible. Then have students read their sentences in groups of 4–5. Have the other students decide which of the three places they would like to visit.

Conjunctions and Adverb Clauses

Unit Opener

Photo: Have students look at the photo. Ask, *What do you see? What looks interesting or unusual about this plant?* Have students read the caption with you. Explain that Bouvardia is a group of evergreen herbs and shrubs that have flowers.

Location: This kind of plant is usually found in Mexico and Central America, but one type is found in the southern part of the United States. This Bouvardia is in Lincoln, the capital city of the state of Nebraska. Lincoln has a population of about 300,000.

Theme: This unit is about the natural world. It includes information about meat-eating plants, cacti, scientists who study volcanoes, and communication of whales and dolphins.

Page	Lesson	Grammar	Examples
234	1	Conjunctions	I like Texas, **so** I moved to Dallas. Linda likes to swim, **and** so does Luc. Mae doesn't eat fish, **and** Kim doesn't either.
242	2	Adverb Clauses: Cause and Contrast	We got lost **because it was dark.** **Since it was raining hard**, we stayed home **Even though I was sick**, I went to work.
250	3	Adverb Clauses: Future Conditional	**If you study hard**, you'll pass the test. **When they go hiking tomorrow**, they'll take a lot of pictures.
258	**Review the Grammar**		
260	**Connect the Grammar to Writing**		

Unit Grammar Terms

adverb clause: a kind of dependent clause. Like single adverbs, they can show time, reason, purpose, and condition.
> ➤ *When the party was over, everyone left.*

clause: a group of words with a subject and a verb.
> ➤ *We watched the game. (one clause)*
> ➤ *We watched the game after we ate dinner.*
> *(two clauses)*

conjunction: a word used to connect information or ideas. *And, but, or*, and *because* are conjunctions.
> ➤ *He put cheese **and** onions on his sandwich.*
> ➤ *I wanted to go, **but** I had too much homework.*
> ➤ *We were confused **because** we didn't listen.*

future conditional: expresses something that we believe will happen in the future based on certain conditions; the *if* clause + simple present gives the condition, and *will* or *be going to* + the base form of the verb gives the result.
> ➤ *If you don't go to practice, the coach will not let you play in the game.*

Student Learning Outcomes	• **Read** an article about meat-eating plants. • **Say** sentences with conjunctions. • **Complete** sentences using conjunctions. • **Find** and **edit** errors with conjunction usage and *too, so, either,* and *neither.* • **Write** and **share** sentences with conjunctions.
Lesson Vocabulary	(n.) edge (n.) insect (n.) seed (v.) shine (v.) trap (v.) escape (adj.) pleasant (n.) shelter (n.) soil (n.) tube

EXPLORE

1 READ, page 234   15 min.

• **Tip:** Use the photos to elicit or teach vocabulary such as *insect, catch,* and *trap*. Point out that the shape of the plants allows them to *catch* or *trap* an insect. Use your hands to demonstrate grabbing something. This will help students anticipate the content of the article.

• **Tip:** Have students use context clues to guess the meaning of *nutrients, pleasant, tasty,* and *shine*. Ask questions: *What do plants get from the soil? What are nutrients? What is a pleasant smell—is it good or bad? Do you think insects like tasty liquids? What verb is related to tasty?* If students are advanced, you may ask them to identify the parts of speech for each new word.

Be the Expert

• Carnivorous plants are found around the world, but they are not very common. They are usually in bogs, very wet land that has plenty of sunlight and water, but soil that is poor in nutrients. There are five ways that these plants capture food:

1. Pitfall traps such as pitcher plants use rolled up leaves filled with a liquid containing bacteria that digests the insects.

2. Flypaper traps are sticky. When insects land on the leaves, they can't escape.

3. Snap traps have leaves that move rapidly to catch the insect.

4. Bladder traps use a vacuum to suck the insect in.

5. Lobster-pot traps are easy to enter, but hard to exit because of hairs that point inward.

• Although their most common prey are insects, these plants also sometimes eat frogs or small mammals.

• **Expansion Tip:** Ask students: *How do animals catch their prey?* Elicit ideas and write them on the board. For example, ask about snakes, tigers, humans, alligators, and hippos. Have students write sentences individually to compare a plant's method of catching food to an animal's method, and then have them share their ideas in pairs.

2 CHECK, page 234   5 min.

  1. d   2. a   3. e   4. c   5. b

• **Tip:** Have students work in pairs to write answers to these questions: *Why do plants sometimes eat insects? How do they get their food? How are such plants different from other plants?*

• **Expansion Tip:** Have students go online to research an example of a carnivorous plant and answer these questions: *What is the name of the plant? Where does it live? Which method does it use to capture food? What kind of food does it eat?* Then have students present the information in small groups.

3 DISCOVER, page 235   5 min.

A 1. a   2. a   3. b

B *Answers will vary.*

• **Tip:** To help students understand the rules that apply to these sentences, refer to notes 2, 4, and 5 in chart 9.1 as you discuss the answers.

LEARN

Chart 9.1, page 236   10 min.

• **Note:** Students usually understand the meaning of most of these conjunctions. The one that can cause difficulty, however, is *so.* Make sure students understand that *so* comes before the result, or second thing that happens. To check students' understanding of the meanings of the conjunctions, write several example sentences from the notes on the board in random order.

Leave blanks where the conjunctions go. Have students choose the appropriate conjunction for each sentence and explain their choice.

- **Note 6:** Knowing when to use commas can be difficult for students. Point out that we use commas between items in a list when there are more than two. We use commas before a conjunction when it connects two independent clauses. Point out that an independent clause can stand alone as a sentence. Write pairs of sentences on the board that students can combine (e.g., *She likes to swim. She likes to play the drums. Tennis is fun. Tennis is difficult. Tonight I'll watch TV. Tonight I'll go to the gym. It was raining hard. I took the bus.*). Have students combine the sentences using conjunctions.

4 page 236   5 min.

| 1. and | 3. and | 5. but | 7. so |
| 2. or | 4. so | 6. or | 8. but |

- **Expansion Tip:** Challenge students to work in pairs to write a different ending to each sentence using the other conjunction option. Students will usually have to add more words for the sentence to make sense. Do the first sentence as an example. *Pitcher plants attract insects with bright colors, light, and tasty liquids, so they can capture them for food.* Have volunteers read their sentences aloud to the class. If students have difficulty, you may ask the class to identify the rule that applies to each new sentence.

5 page 236   10 min.

| 1. or | 3. and | 5. , but | 7. and |
| 2. , but | 4. , so | 6. or | 8. , so |

6 SPEAK, page 237   5 min.

| 1. c | 3. a | 5. g | 7. h |
| 2. e | 4. f | 6. d | 8. b |

- **Expansion Tip:** On the board, write: *English is difficult.* Then write conjunctions and phrases or clauses to complete the sentence in different ways (e.g., *but important; but I like it*). Ask students what different ideas are expressed (e.g., *English is difficult; English is important; I like English.*). Point out that when two clauses have the same subjects and verbs, we don't have to repeat them. Then review the content of note 1 on page 236. Have students work in pairs to complete each sentence using their own ideas and words, phrases, and clauses (e.g., *Last week, I went shopping and swimming. Last week, I went shopping and bought some shoes. Last week, I went shopping and there was a robbery at the store!*). Have students write examples on the board.

Chart 9.2, page 237   10 min.

- **Notes 1, 2 & 3:** Students may have difficulty understanding how the word order differs for *and + too* and *so*, and for *either* and *neither*. To clarify the differences for each rule, write the example sentences on the board using different colors for the subjects and verbs, including auxiliary verbs. For example, in the first sentence *Linda* and *Luc* might be in green, and *likes* and *does* in blue, while the other words are in purple. This highlights the word order issues in the different structures.

- **Tip:** Write sentences on the board with errors in word order and in the form of the auxiliary (e.g., *Linda likes to swim, and Luc likes too. Linda likes to swim and so Luc does.*). Have students correct the sentences.

7 page 238   10 min.

1. so do	5. so has
2. neither is	6. neither will
3. does not/doesn't either	7. is too
4. did too	8. neither has

- **Tip:** Working in pairs, have students take turns saying the sentences in another way. For example, the first sentence could be *Ellie likes to watch nature films, and her children do too.*

REAL ENGLISH, page 238

To demonstrate the use of *so* and *neither +* auxiliary verb, say sentences about yourself (e.g., *I've eaten sushi. I don't like classical music.*). Call on students and elicit agreement with both affirmative and negative statements (e.g., *I have too. So have I./I don't either. Neither do I.*). Have students write six statements, three affirmative and three negative, about themselves. Encourage them to use multiple verb forms/auxiliaries. Then have them walk around the room to talk to classmates one-on-one. Have them take turns in their pairs saying affirmative and negative statements as their partner responds in agreement in both ways. Remind students to use the appropriate auxiliary. Monitor the conversations and correct as needed. After a minute or two, have students find new partners.

8 page 238   5 min

| 1. a/b | 3. a/c | 5. a/b | 7. a |
| 2. c | 4. b | 6. b/c | 8. a/c |

PRACTICE

9 page 239   5 min.

1. or the day after
2. , but she doesn't like roses
3. , so I'm not hungry
4. and learn to play it
5. , but tickets are very expensive
6. and a sleeping bag
7. or go for a walk
8. , so she is free tonight

- **Expansion Tip:** Have students write five sentence starters using various tenses and so that different auxiliaries are required (e.g., *I ate pizza last night and . . . , Lisa's not going to Mexico this summer and . . .*). Divide the class into two groups. One group forms a circle facing out. The other group forms a circle outside the first circle facing in. At your direction, the students take turns saying their sentence starters to their partner and eliciting an appropriate completion. After 30 seconds, instruct the outside circle to move one position to their right. Have students practice with their new partners. Continue until students are more comfortable with the target structure.

10 page 239   15 min.

1. my brother has not/ hasn't either
2. Aunt Jill does too
3. neither are the red ones
4. so has Jane
5. I am/I'm not either
6. neither does his brother
7. their parents do too
8. so will Sally

- **Alternative Speaking & Writing:** Have students work in pairs to find these things in common: something they have done several times, something they did last week, something they will do tomorrow, something they haven't done, something they like, etc. Have the pairs write sentences describing the things they've done using at least five different auxiliaries and both negative and affirmative statements. They should write the sentences together, and then find new partners and tell what their previous partner liked and disliked (e.g., *I like pizza, and Ana does too.*).

11 EDIT, page 240   5 min.

- **Tip:** Have students look at the photo and read the caption before they complete the task. Ask, *What is this land like? What do you think the climate is like? What do you know about cacti?*

- Saguaros can reach a height of over 40 feet (12.2 meters), ~~so~~ but in their first ten years they only grow around one inch (2.54 cm).

- The fruit of the saguaro is red, ~~so~~ and it contains around 2000 seeds. It is very tasty, ~~but~~ and/so it is popular with local people.

- Saguaros grow arms, ~~but~~ so they have room for a lot of flowers and fruit. This gives them a better chance to reproduce.

- The largest known saguaro is in Maricopa County, Arizona, in the United States. It is 45.3 feet (13.8 m) tall and 10 feet (3.1 m) wide.

- Saguaros live in the desert. There are hardly any rivers there, and it doesn't rain much ~~neither either~~. When it rains, saguaros store the rainwater inside their stems.

- Old western movies show saguaros in Texas and New Mexico, but Texas does not have any saguaros, and New Mexico doesn't either.

- The saguaro used to provide both food ~~or~~ and shelter for Native Americans.

- Bats help spread saguaro seeds, and birds do ~~so~~ too.

12 LISTEN & WRITE, page 241   5 min.

- **Tip:** Before they do the exercise, have students look at the photo and read the caption. Ask what they know about redwoods, or they can guess about redwood trees from the picture.

A
1. a. California   b. Oregon
2. a. 379 feet   b. 26 feet
3. a. long   b. flat
4. a. shallow   b. strong
5. a. tallest   b. oldest

B *Answers will vary. Sample answer:*

The giant redwood is found in California, and so are other types of redwood trees. They are tall and wide. Their leaves are long and flat. Their roots are shallow but strong. The tallest trees are in deep valleys, and so are the oldest trees.

C *Answers will vary.*

13 APPLY, page 241   10 min.

Answers will vary.

- **Expansion Tip:** Have students write a paragraph using one of the sentences from exercise **A** as the beginning. If it's helpful, model the activity by telling a story using a sentence as a prompt (e.g., *Do you want to go to the movies, or would you rather stay home? Personally, I like going to the movies. My job is stressful, so I escape by watching movies. The characters on the screen have a problem, and so do I.*). Their paragraphs should use as many conjunctions as possible. Then have students pair up and share their paragraphs.

Student Learning Outcomes	• **Read** an article about a volcano that scientists are studying in Africa. • **Combine** sentences using adverb clauses of cause and contrast. • **Listen** to and **talk** about ideas presented in a lecture. • **Write** sentences with adverb clauses about a natural place. • **Ask** and **answer** questions about a natural place.
Lesson Vocabulary	(adj.) active (v.) collect (n.) eruption (n.) lava (n.) relationship (n.) climate (adj.) dangerous (adj.) huge (v.) predict (n.) view

EXPLORE

1 READ, page 242   15 min.

• Write these words on the board: *volcano, lava, eruption/erupt, crater.* Have students work in pairs to write sentences about the photos using the words. They may use dictionaries if needed. Ask volunteers to write sentences on the board.

• **Expansion Tip:** Dictate the sentences of the last paragraph in random order. Then have students renumber the sentences in an order that makes sense. Encourage students to use their understanding of connecting words, logic, and pronoun referents to put the sentences in order. Have students compare ideas in pairs.

Be the Expert

• Mount Nyiragongo is inside Virunga National Park. The main crater is 1.3 miles (2 kilometers) wide and usually is filled with a lake of liquid lava. It is one of the largest lava lakes in an active volcano. The volcano has erupted 34 times since 1882. The lava is more fluid than most lava, so instead of flowing slowly, it races down the volcano at up to 60 miles an hour. This is what makes it so dangerous.

• Ken Sims, a professor at the University of Wyoming, is a volcanologist (a scientist who studies volcanoes). Visiting Mt. Nyiragongo and descending into the lava lake is one of his favorite adventures, along with diving in a submersible and going to Antarctica.

• Ask students what other fields of science put researchers in physical danger (e.g., *studying storms, exploring the depths of the ocean, Antarctica,* or *space*). If students are at a high level, have them go online to research another dangerous field of science and share their findings

2 CHECK, page 243   5 min.

1. It's an active volcano.

2. They want to know when it will erupt again.

3. He's a scientist.

4. He climbed into a volcano.

5. It will help Sims predict the next eruption.

• **Tip:** Have students identify where they find the answers in the text. This will help them practice skimming and scanning.

3 DISCOVER, page 243   5 min.

A   1. Although   3. Even though

     2. since   4. because

B   1. although; even though   2. since; because

• **Tip:** This lesson focuses on the subordinating conjunctions that indicate cause and contrast. As students go through the lesson, and help them relate the content to the previous lesson. Ask, *Which words are similar in meaning to* but? *Which conjunction introduces a result? What is the relationship between that conjunction and* because *and* since? Point out that the chart on page 244 focuses on adverb clauses of reason that use *since* and *because.*

• **Expansion Tip:** To help students apply the knowledge they gained from Lesson 1, have them write four sentences about the content of the article on page 242 using *but* and *so.*

LEARN

Chart 9.3, page 244   10 min.

• **Note 1:** Write the question words *why, when, how,* and *under what condition* on the board. Explain that adverb clauses answer these questions. Students have already learned some adverb clauses of time. Have them look at the example sentences, and ask them to make up questions that could be answered by the examples: *Why did we go to the park? When is she going to call us? Under what conditions will we have a picnic?*

- **Notes 2, 3 & 4:** Subordinating conjunctions (e.g., *because, when, if*) define the relationship between the main clause and the dependent clause. Encourage students to check that they have two clauses (subject + verb) in every sentence they write that includes these conjunctions. Write sentences containing errors on the board (e.g., *Since I missed the bus. I was sick because I stayed home. When she broke her foot. Because she was late.*). Have students correct the sentences.

4 page 244   5 min.

1. Since Mount Nyiragongo is so close (C), the city of Goma is in danger (R).
2. Scientists study volcanoes (R) because they want to predict their eruptions (C).
3. The people of Goma are worried (R) since there was a lot of damage after the last eruption (C).
4. Because some volcanoes don't erupt often (C), people don't worry about them (R).
5. Since volcanoes are so interesting (C), I like to read about them (R).
6. The film about volcanoes was popular (R) because it had wonderful photography (C).
7. Since I'm afraid of volcanoes (C), I don't go near them (R).
8. Lava is dangerous (R) because it is extremely hot (C).

- **Tip:** Have students rewrite the sentences to change the order of the causes and results. Encourage them to use a different conjunction if the old conjunction is no longer appropriate. Remind students to use correct punctuation.

5 page 245   10 min.

1. Since there are around 1900 active volcanoes on Earth, it is important to study them.
2. Since my friend and I were in Sicily, we saw Mount Etna.
3. Mount Etna is interesting because it erupts frequently.
4. Because it was a hot day, we wore shorts and t-shirts.
5. Because the volcano was very high, we didn't climb to the top.
6. We had a wonderful view because it was a clear day.

7. Since we climbed for several hours, we were very tired.
8. My friend was excited because he found some lava.

- **Expansion Tip:** Write the following sentences on the board or dictate them to students: *The lava in the volcano is very fluid. It moves very quickly. It kills more people than most volcanoes. The government moved the city farther away. The lava lake is very large. Scientists have to be careful.* Have students work in pairs to write as many new sentences as they can by combining the original sentence with *because* or *since.* Set a time limit of three minutes. The pair with the most sentences that use the conjunctions correctly wins.

Chart 9.4, page 245   10 min.

- **Note 1:** Have students close their books. Write the clauses in the note on the board as separate sentences without the conjunctions. Ask students what the relationship is between the two ideas. Then ask which piece of information is a surprise. Have students open their books and read the note. Then have them use the information in the note to identify the main clause.

- **Note 2:** Speakers often put the more interesting or surprising information at the end of a sentence, so sentences that begin with *even though* or *although* are common. If your students are higher level, ask them to look for examples in articles or texts that use *even though* and *although*, and note which order of clauses is more common.

6 page 246   10 min.

- **Tip:** Read the two sentences in item 1 aloud. Elicit which contains the surprising information.

1. Even though the lava was hot, the scientist picked it up.
2. Even though Erica looked everywhere, she couldn't find her book.
3. Although I am tired, I'm going to go to the gym.
4. The book was useful even though it was very old.
5. Marsha likes her new apartment even though it's very small.
6. Although I went to bed early last night, I'm tired today.
7. Mark didn't pass his math test even though he studied hard.
8. Although the movie was exciting, a lot of people left early.

- **Expansion Tip:** Use three sets of ten note cards or slips of paper. Each set will contain the words for one of the sentences below. For sentence 1, write one word on each card of set 1. Do the same for the remaining sentences. *Luisa is a great basketball player although she's not tall. The flight took off on time even though it snowed. Although the work is dangerous, volcanologists often go inside volcanoes.* Use a different colored marker for each set. Shuffle the cards in each set. Divide students into groups of ten. Give each student a card and have the groups put themselves in order to make correct sentences. The first group to finish wins. Collect the sets and redistribute to play again.

PRACTICE

7 page 246   5 min.

| 1. g | 3. h | 5. f | 7. c |
| 2. a | 4. b | 6. e | 8. d |

- **Expansion Tip:** Follow the pattern in exercise **7** to write other sentences with two parts. Copy each part onto a separate piece of paper or cardstock. Use large letters, so all students can read the words. Shuffle the papers or cards and tape them to the board with the words facing in. Divide the class into two teams. Have teams take turns sending a member to the board to turn over two cards. If the sentence parts make sense together, the team keeps the cards. If not, turn them over and replace on the board. The team with the most matches wins.

8 page 247   5 min.

1. because	4. since	7. Because
2. Although	5. although	8. since
3. Since	6. Since	

9 page 247   10 min.

1. Marie wants to move to another city although/even though she likes her hometown.

2. Since/Because Dana likes her hometown, she wants to stay there for the rest of her life.

3. Miguel is good at basketball since/because he is tall and fast.

4. Although/Even though Alan is not very fast, he is good at basketball.

5. I studied math in college although/even though it wasn't my best subject in high school.

6. Since/Because my sister enjoyed history in high school, she decided to study it in college.

7. The children didn't eat much at the party since/because they didn't like the food.

8. Lin liked the food at the party although/even though she didn't eat very much.

10 WRITE & SPEAK, page 248   15 min.

Answers will vary.

- **Tip:** Call on volunteers to share their ideas by reading one or more sentences aloud to the class.

- **Expansion Tip:** Explain the activity. Students form groups of four or five and sit in a circle. The first student says a sentence with a single clause (e.g., *I like to go to the beach.*). The person to the right adds a clause of cause (e.g., *I like to go to the beach because it is relaxing.*). Then student 2 says a sentence and student 3 adds a clause of contrast. They continue around the circle alternating the types of clauses added. Monitor the groups as they go around the circle 2–3 times.

- **Alternative Writing & Speaking:** Write several topics on the board (e.g., *taking classes online, studying abroad, jobs that require travel, moving to a new city*). Have students choose a topic and write a list of positive and negative aspects of the topic. Then have students discuss the topic with a partner, using adverb clauses of reason and contrast (e.g., *Taking classes online is a popular trend because it is convenient. Although online classes are flexible, many students don't feel like they are part of a community.*).

11 LISTEN & SPEAK, page 249   15 min.

A 1. b   2. a   3. b   4. b   5. a

B *Answers will vary.*

12 APPLY, page 249   15 min.

Answers will vary.

- **Alternative Speaking:** Have students prepare a 1–2 minute speech on their favorite natural place and present it to a small group or the whole class. They should use as many adverb clauses of reason and contrast as they can.

Student Learning Outcomes	• **Read** an article about the effects of noise on dolphins and whales. • **Use** sentences with future conditional. • **Complete** conversations using future conditional sentences. • **Find** and **edit** errors in future conditional sentences. • **Write** and **talk** about plans using future conditional sentences.
Lesson Vocabulary	(adj.) distant (adj.) industrial (v.) lend (v.) search (n.) storm (v.) disturb (v.) interfere (v.) locate (n.) shore (n.) wildlife

EXPLORE

1 READ, page 250   15 min.

• Use the photo to teach the meanings of *dolphin* and *underwater*. Ask, *What do you feel when you look at the dolphins swimming? What do you know about them? How would you describe the place where they live?*

• **Expansion Tip:** Have students use the information in paragraphs 2 and 3 to make a cause/effect diagram (see below). In the boxes on the left, have students write the three things that cause dolphins and whales to stop communicating, and in the boxes on the right, the three things that result from their not communicating.

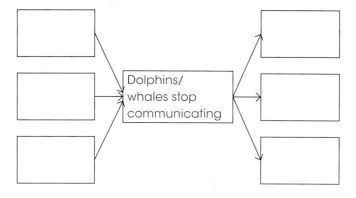

Be the Expert

• Most whales use clicks as a form of vocal communication and as a form of echolocation, which also helps them navigate. Humpback whales also "sing" to communicate with other whales over enormous distances. Whales in different communities vocalize differently. Whale sounds have gotten louder in recent years because of the other noises in the ocean.

• Dolphins whistle to communicate, but they can also yelp and click. Each dolphin has a unique whistle, so they can recognize each other. They also use echolocation by listening to how their clicks sound bouncing off objects. This helps them get a mental picture of their world.

• The three largest sources of noise pollution in the ocean are ship noise, oil and gas exploration, and military sonar. Ask, *How do animals communicate?* If necessary, ask about specific animals such as dogs, birds, apes, or chimpanzees. Elicit ways in which other animal species communicate. Ask students to rank the ways animals communicate in terms of complexity.

2 CHECK, page 251   5 min.

    1. T   2. T   3. F   4. F   5. F

• **Expansion Tip:** Have students write sentences about the content of the article. Sentences should use *and, but, so, or, because, since, although,* or *even though* to describe causes and contrasts. Model the activity by writing a sentence on the board (e.g., *Even though people don't live in the ocean, they make noise that whales can hear.*). Then ask volunteers to write sentences on the board. Have the class edit as necessary. Remind students to check for the appropriate use of commas.

3 DISCOVER, page 251 · 5 min.

A 1. gets; will stop

2. stop; will be

3. do; will

B b

LEARN

Chart 9.5, page 252 · 10 min.

- **Note 1:** Explain that if something is conditional, it may happen or it may not. The result will only happen if the condition is met.

- **Note 2:** Students often have difficulty using the simple present in the *If*-clause when talking about the future. Write sentences on the board that use *will* or *be going to* incorrectly in the *If*-clause. Have students correct the errors.

- **Note 3:** *If*-clauses are like other adverb clauses—when they are before the main clause, they are set off by a comma.

- **Tip:** After reviewing the notes, have students close their books. Write the example sentences on the board leaving blanks for the verbs. Elicit the correct verb forms from students.

4 page 252 · 5 min.

1. finds

2. make

3. will continue

4. don't

5. watch; will learn

6. will be; don't leave

7. will get; keeps

8. will help; has

- **Tip:** Confirm that students recognize the future forms in the sentences by having students highlight them.

5 page 252 · 5 min.

1. go; will/'ll bring

2. have; will/'ll help

3. snows; will not/won't have

4. does not/doesn't call; will/'ll be

5. goes; will stay

6. will miss; do not/don't hurry

7. are; will not/won't go

8. want; will/'ll drive

6 SPEAK, page 253 · 5 min.

Answers will vary.

- **Tip:** Follow up exercise **6** by calling on students to tell the class about their partner using conditional clauses (e.g., *If Sara passes this class, she will take English 101 next semester.*).

Chart 9.6, page 253 · 5 min.

- **Notes 1 & 2:** Before you go over the notes in the book, write the two example sentences on the board. Elicit which sentence sounds more certain.

- **Note 2:** Remind students that they studied future time clauses, including those with *when* in Unit 7. Here the focus is on contrasting *When*-clauses with *If*-clauses. Point out that the verb forms are the same in both types of sentences: future in the main clause, present in the adverb clause.

7 page 253 · 10 min.

1. If the dolphin swims too close to the shore,

2. If the whale comes near the boat,

3. When I see Ray,

4. if Noor leaves her job

5. when they go to Paris

6. When the lecture ends,

7. If it rains tomorrow,

8. When my brother graduates,

- **Expansion Tip:** Write sentences on the board that express possibility (e.g., *I may get a new job.*) and certainty (e.g., *She's going to get married in June.*). Have students use those sentences as adverb clauses and their own ideas for the main clause of new sentences they compose (e.g., *If I get a new job, I'm going to move.*).

PRACTICE

8 page 254 · 10 min.

1. If I do not/don't work

2. If the weather is

3. If it is not/it's not/ it isn't

4. When you get

5. if we do

6. If you see

7. if you make

8. if we go

- **Tip:** Working in pairs, have students practice manipulating verb forms for different subjects. Have them take turns retelling the information in the conversation from a different point of view (e.g., *Ivan and his wife are going to see the new Matt Damon movie. Meg's sister is coming for a visit.*).

9 WRITE & SPEAK, page 255 15 min.

A 1. If there is a storm tonight,

2. If I miss two weeks of class,

3. When my friend arrives tonight,

4. if I get a new job

5. when I see you at the party tomorrow

6. if I miss the train

7. If my foot still hurts tomorrow

8. When the store opens in five minutes,

9. When I get home later,

10. If it snows this afternoon,

B *Answers will vary.*

- **Alternative Writing:** Have students identify the expressions in the sentences in exercise **9** that indicate something is not certain (e.g., *Maybe; It's possible that . . . , ___ will probably . . .*). Ask, *How do you know something is certain?* Have students write three sentences that refer to future events that are not certain and three that refer to events that are certain. Then have students exchange papers with a partner and use their partner's sentences as *If-* or *When-* clauses, adding their own ideas to form main clauses.

10 EDIT, page 256 5 min.

- **Tip:** To help students anticipate the content, have them look at the photo and read the caption. Ask, *What problems might the people nearby face? How do you think people cause problems for wildlife?*

Jean: Today, I'm talking to Dr. Ruth Lowe, an expert on the Sundarbans region of Bangladesh and India. Dr. Lowe, if you ~~will be~~ are ready, we'll start the interview now. Can you explain why the Sundarbans are so important?

Dr. Lowe: Of course, Jean. First, the mangrove forests of the Sundarbans are home to wildlife such as the Bengal tiger. These forests also protect the region from serious storms that hit the coast every year. If the forests ~~will~~ disappear, millions of people will be in danger. Unfortunately, people are harming the Sundarbans. If they do not stop, they ~~is~~ will be in serious danger.

Jean: What exactly will happen if the mangroves ~~will~~ continue to disappear?

Dr. Lowe: Well, ~~when~~ if people don't stop destroying the mangroves, the Sundarbans won't be able to protect towns and cities on the coast from storms. If the storms ~~will~~ hit these places, there will be a lot of damage, and people's lives will be at risk.

Jean: That sounds like a real problem.

Dr. Lowe: Well, yes, it really is . . .

11 APPLY, page 257 20 min.

Answers will vary.

- **Alternative Writing:** Model the activity. Tell a story about the future activities of a famous person, either real (e.g., Princess Kate) or fictional (e.g., Iron Man, Harry Potter). The story can be realistic or ridiculous, but it should use clauses with *if* and *when.* Then tell students to choose a famous person to write a paragraph about and describe the person's future plans using *if* and *when.* When students have finished, call on volunteers to read their paragraphs aloud. Have the other students listen and take notes on any errors they hear. When all the readers have finished, elicit the errors their classmates noted.

1 page 258 5 min.

1. and   3. but   5. If   7. when
2. and   4. so   6. or   8. when

2 page 258 5 min.

1. John was upset because his flight was delayed./
   Because John's flight was delayed, he was upset.

2. My parents are going on vacation, and so am I.

3. Lin didn't pass the exam, and Brian did not/
   didn't either.

4. Anne didn't go out even though it was her
   birthday./Even though it was her birthday, Anne
   didn't go out.

5. Patricia enjoyed the trip, and her sister did too.

6. I'm going to visit my uncle since I have a few
   days off./Since I have a few days off, I'm going
   to visit my uncle.

7. Although Boris was sick, he still went to work./
   Boris still went to work although he was sick.

8. Jane didn't go to the party, and neither did
   Danny.

3 EDIT, page 259 5 min.

- **Tip:** Have students look at the photo to activate
  background knowledge and predict content. Ask,
  *What do you know about lightning? When are
  people in the most danger from a lightning strike?
  When is lightning most common here? How do you
  protect yourself from lightning?* After students finish
  the exercise, have them write tips or facts to add to
  the list. Have volunteers write them on the board
  as the class checks for errors.

1. We do not see most lightning ~~even though~~
   because/since it happens inside clouds.

2. Lightning usually strikes near the center of a
   storm, ~~because~~ and/but it can also strike far
   from the center.

3. Rubber shoes do not protect people from
   lightning, and ~~so~~ neither do small buildings.

4. Lightning can travel through wires, ~~although~~
   so it's dangerous to use electrical equipment
   during a storm.

5. Lightning doesn't just happen in thunderstorms.
   People have seen lightning during forest fires,
   snowstorms, ~~but~~ and volcanic eruptions.

6. Many people believe that lightning never strikes
   in the same place twice, ~~so~~ but that is not true.
   Keep away from places that attract lightning.

4 LISTEN, WRITE & SPEAK, page 259 20 min.

A 1. They live in Africa. Both

2. They have tails. Neither

3. They are intelligent. Both

4. They eat meat. Chimpanzees

5. They are strong. Both

6. They can be aggressive. Both

7. They behave in a funny way. Chimpanzees

B *Answers will vary.*

- **Expansion Tip:** Have students use the chart in
  exercise **A** to write paragraphs to compare and
  contrast gorillas and chimpanzees. Remind them
  to use expressions such as *and, both, neither, and
  so does . . . , and neither does . . .* to talk about their
  similarities. To talk about differences, remind
  students to use expressions of contrast such as
  but, although, and *even though.* After students
  finish, have them work with a partner to exchange
  paragraphs and edit as needed.

1 READ & NOTICE THE GRAMMAR, page 260   20 min.

A *Answers will vary.*

- **Tip:** Have students read the title and look at the photo. Ask volunteers to predict the content of the article, and have them explain what they based their predictions on.

B   <u>Since we can't see, smell, or touch noise pollution</u>, many of us don't notice it. People that do notice it think it's annoying, but they don't worry too much about it. However, noise pollution is all around us,(and) it sometimes causes some very serious problems.

Many things that we see every day cause noise pollution. Trucks, motorcycles, airplanes, loud machines,(and) power tools all make a lot of noise. Even music is noise pollution when people play it very loudly.

Noise pollution can cause a number of health problems. For example, it can lead to hearing loss. It can also lead to sleep problems. Near airports, people often wake up at night <u>because the planes are so loud</u>. They don't sleep enough,(so) they get sick more easily. Noise pollution also makes people feel stressed. Stress makes it difficult for them to concentrate,(so) they can't do their work very well. For example, if a child goes to a noisy school, he or she will probably get lower grades than a child in a quiet school.

These are just some of the ways that noise pollution affects our daily lives.

C

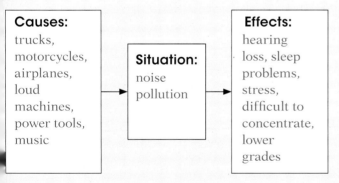

Causes:		Effects:
trucks, motorcycles, airplanes, loud machines, power tools, music	**Situation:** noise pollution	hearing loss, sleep problems, stress, difficult to concentrate, lower grades

2 BEFORE YOU WRITE, page 261   15 min.

Answers will vary.

- **Tip:** Begin the brainstorming process with the class as a whole, so they broaden their choices. Ask, *What things in the environment have a direct effect (either positive or negative) on you?* Encourage students to think about both good things and bad. If available, have them look out the window to get ideas (e.g., *noise, weather, crowdedness, availability of resources, trash, crime, etc.*).

3 WRITE, page 261   15 min.

> ### WRITING FOCUS, page 261
>
> Write examples of comma splices on the board and have students correct them. After students write their paragraphs, have them exchange papers with a partner, so the partner can check for comma splices.

- **Alternative Writing:** Brainstorm other topics in the unit that involve or describe causes and effects (e.g., noise pollution and problems with whale communication, scientists studying volcanos because they are dangerous, etc.). Have students choose a topic, and then create a diagram as in exercise **2B**. Then have students write two paragraphs on the topic.

Gerunds and Infinitives

Unit Opener

Photo: Have students look at the photo and read the caption. Discuss what students see in the picture. Ask, *What is this person doing? Have you ever been to a water park? If so, did you enjoy it? If not, would you like to go?*

Location: There are over 2000 water parks around the world. Water parks have slides where visitors of all ages can slide into a pool at the finish. Water parks rely on physics for the safety of visitors. Accidents have been drastically reduced in the last 30 years.

Theme: This unit is about work and play. Ask, *What do you enjoy doing in your free time?* Have students look at the photos in this unit. Ask, *Which of these activities would you like to try?*

Page	Lesson	Grammar	Examples
264	**1**	Gerunds	**Swimming** is fun. I enjoy **running**. He has a good reason for **missing** class.
271	**2**	Infinitives; Infinitives and Gerunds	They wanted **to live** in Mexico. She allowed the children **to leave** early. I started **driving** last year. I started **to drive** last year.
279	**3**	More Uses of Infinitives	I went to the store **to buy** some food. It's not too far for us **to walk**. He spoke loudly enough for us **to hear**.
287	**Review the Grammar**		
290	**Connect the Grammar to Writing**		

Unit Grammar Terms

gerund: an *-ing* verb form that is used as a noun. It can be the subject of a sentence, or the object of a verb or preposition.
> ➤ **Surfing** *is a popular sport.*
> ➤ *We enjoy* **swimming**.
> ➤ *The boy is interested in* **running**.

gerund phrase: an *-ing* verb form + an object or a prepositional phrase. It can be the subject of a sentence, or the object of a verb or preposition.
> ➤ **Swimming in the ocean** *is fun.*
> ➤ *I love* **eating chocolate**.
> ➤ *We are thinking about* **watching TV**.

infinitive: *to* + the base form of a verb.
> ➤ *He wants* **to see** *the new movie.*

infinitive of purpose: *to* + the base form of the verb used to express purpose or answer the question *why*.
> ➤ *Scientists studied the water in order* **to learn** *about the disease.*
> ➤ *We went to the store* **to buy** *milk.*

Student Learning Outcomes	• **Read** about Jason deCaires Taylor, a sculptor who creates underwater sculptures. • **Complete** stories using gerund forms. • **Read** a chart and **discuss** surprising information. • **Listen** to different people talking about their free time. • **Ask** and **answer** questions about your own life.
Lesson Vocabulary	(n.) choice (ph. v.) consist of (v.) damage (n.) free time (n.) statue (v.) combine (v.) create (ph. v.) feel like (n.) passion (adj.) typical

EXPLORE

1 READ, page 264   10 min.

• Use the photo and ask, *Are these real people? Where are they? Do you like the sculptures? Explain.*

• Explain *diving* through hand gestures. Then explain that *coral reefs* are underwater structures created by tiny animals; coral looks like rock, but is actually alive. If possible, show the class images of coral reefs.

Be the Expert

• Jason deCaires Taylor was born in 1974 and grew up in England and Asia. He spent his childhood exploring the coral reefs of Malaysia, and went to art school in England. In 2006, he created the world's first underwater park, which has been named one of the top 25 Wonders of the World by *National Geographic*.

• *The Silent Evolution* is one of Taylor's many projects, with 400 figures in an area of approximately 420 square meters. The figures represent different kinds of people. They are made out of environmentally friendly materials that encourage coral to grow. Taylor works with marine biologists to design areas that will attract certain sea life, and creates these parks in shallow water so that it is possible to view them when diving, snorkeling, or using a glass bottom boat.

• Search *Jason deCaires Taylor sculptures* for more images of his work.

2 CHECK, page 265   5 min.

   1. T   2. F   3. F   4. T   5. F

• **Tip:** Ask higher-level students to correct the false statements.

3 DISCOVER, page 265   5 min.

A   1. Combining   3. diving   5. growing
     2. Saving   4. seeing

B   a, b, c

• **Expansion Tip:** Have students read the article again and find four more examples of gerunds (. . . *Taylor has succeeded in doing exactly that; Taylor often went diving for fun . . . ; He also enjoyed swimming with the fish . . . ; Placing them on the sea floor . . .*). Ask, *Do these follow the pattern for a, b, or c in exercise B?* Notice that *were growing* in the last paragraph is not a gerund.

LEARN

Chart 10.1, page 266   5 min.

• **Notes 1, 2 & 4:** Gerunds can be confusing for students because they look like verbs in the progressive tense. For this reason, students are usually comfortable using gerunds as the object of a sentence, but avoid using them as a subject. To build students' comfort level with gerunds as subjects, write gerunds on the board and have volunteers complete the sentences for the class.

Eating _____. Not eating _____.

Finishing English assignments on time _____.

Not finishing English assignments on time _____.

• **Note 5:** Explain that *go + gerund* is usually used to talk about activities (e.g., *I went shopping today* sounds more natural than *I shopped today.*).

4 page 266   10 min.

   1. diving   4. seeing   7. going
    2. Swimming   5. touching   8. waiting
    3. visiting   6. Taking

5 WRITE & SPEAK, page 266   5 min.

Answers will vary.

- **Expansion Tip:** Have students write their answers on slips of paper. Emphasize that each answer should include a gerund. They should not write their names on the papers or show their answers to classmates. Collect the papers, and then distribute them to the people in the class. Have students ask questions to find who wrote the answer on their paper, e.g., *Is skiing your favorite sport? Do you enjoy cooking?*

- **Expansion Tip:** If students finish early, have them look at note 3 in chart 10.1 and create sentences with the verbs, e.g., *I avoid driving in the rain.* Have students share their answers with the class.

Chart 10.2, page 267   5 min.

- **Note 3:** Students may have difficulty with this point because their native languages use different prepositions to convey the same meaning (e.g., English combines *worry + about*, while other languages may combine *worry + on.*). Explain to students that they will need to memorize these combinations. Have students find the list on page A5 in the Appendix and quiz each other.

6 page 267   10 min.

1. on seeing
2. in taking
3. by studying
4. about going
5. between fixing; buying
6. at solving
7. for leaving
8. of studying
9. by practicing
10. of swimming

7 SPEAK, page 268   10 min.

Answers will vary.

- **Tip:** If students feel uncomfortable providing personal information, bring in magazine photos, and have them pretend to be the people in the photos and answer the questions from their point of view (e.g., *a supermodel: I feel like eating a big meal. I'm afraid of gaining weight.*). If no magazines are available, have students choose a celebrity and answer the questions as that person.

PRACTICE

8 page 268   10 min.

1. between taking
2. becoming
3. skiing
4. doing
10. posting
11. at taking
12. about working
13. getting

5. being
6. helping
7. at teaching
8. sitting
9. Finding
14. going
15. seeing
16. leaving
17. Traveling
18. going

- **Expansion Tip:** Have students read the conversations aloud in groups of three. Have them pretend to be each of the three people and ask and answer follow-up questions, based on the information in the stories, e.g., *Nick what sporting event do you enjoy photographing most?*

9 READ, WRITE & SPEAK, page 269   25 min.

- **Tip:** Students may not have much experience analyzing charts. To help them, ask a student to read the description of the chart aloud. Ask, *Where are these students from? How do you know?* Ask students to think about which activities they do in their free time. Look at the example sentence as a class. Ask, *How do you know this is true?* Explain that some sentences have a percentage in parentheses, which can help students find the answer.

A 1. Listening to music
2. Surfing the Internet
3. Going shopping
4. Going to a friend's house
5. texting friends; talking on the phone
6. Listening to music; watching TV/DVDs/ Watching TV/DVDs/listening to music
7. surfing the Internet; reading books or magazines
8. Playing computer games

B *Answers will vary.*

- **Expansion Tip:** Have students write 2–3 additional questions about the chart. Have them ask the class. Encourage the other students to answer using a gerund.

10 LISTEN & SPEAK, page 270   15 min.

A *Answers will vary.*

B 1. going for a hike on weekends
2. watching another action movie
3. visiting the museum
4. not going to the/missing the
5. not going to all the attractions/missing some attractions
6. going to the beach
7. Dealing with any problems
8. to keep waiting

C *Answers will vary.*

- **Tip:** Have students write first-person sentences for the speakers in exercise **B**, and then read their sentences to a group of three or four. The other students should guess who they are pretending to be (e.g., student A: *I love being outside in nature.* student B: *You're Elizabeth!*).

11 APPLY, page 270   25 min.

A 1. missed doing   5. terrible at doing

    2. stopped doing   6. thinking about doing

    3. interested in learning   7. enjoy doing

    4. good at doing   8. reason for taking

B *Answers will vary.*

C *Answers will vary.*

- **Tip:** Explain that if you *miss doing* something, you are sad that you don't do something now that you liked doing before. *Thinking about doing* something means that you might do it in the future.

- **Alternative Apply:** Have students imagine that they are interviewing each other for the school newspaper. Tell them that this is the end of the year, and they are being asked about their experience in English class, and their plans for the future. Have students adapt the questions in exercise **A** (e.g., *What have you missed doing this year?* can be changed to: *What will you miss doing in class?*). After students have interviewed each other, have them write the interview as if it were in a newsletter.

Student Learning Outcomes	• **Read** an article about Felix Baumgartner and the world's highest skydive. • **Complete** a blog about mountain climbing using the gerund or infinitive form. • **Practice** pronunciation of the infinitive *to*. • **Listen** to a woman talking about a recent trip and **complete** sentences. • **Write** about your hobbies and interests. • **Ask** and **answer** questions about hobbies and interests.
Lesson Vocabulary	(v.) aim　　　(n.) goal　　　(v.) lift　　　(v.) retire　　　(n.) space (n.) canyon　　(n.) landing　　(n.) record　　(n.) skill　　　(n.) victory

EXPLORE

1 READ, page 271　　10 min.

• Have students look at the photo. Ask, *What is happening in this photo? Would you like to skydive? Why, or why not?*

Be the Expert

• Felix Baumgartner was born in 1969. He had already broken many skydiving records before his famous jump from space. He spent five years preparing for this jump, broke the sound barrier, and set the world record for the highest skydive. In 2012, when he stepped out of the capsule to make his historic jump, he said, "I'm going home now." He fell for over four minutes before opening his parachute.

• Search *Felix Baumgartner* or *supersonic freefall* for footage of his skydive from space.

2 CHECK, page 272　　5 min.

1. a　　2. b　　3. b　　4. a

3 DISCOVER, page 272　　5 min.

A 1. to become

2. to make; to skydive

3. to fly

B infinitive

• **Tip:** Have students read the article again and circle the infinitives and underline the gerunds.

LEARN

Chart 10.3, page 273　　5 min.

• **Note 3:** Students' native languages may use a different structure from English to negate an infinitive. Explain that the infinitive, *to* + base form, should not be separated in English: *not* should come before *to*. To practice this, have students make each sentence in the chart negative.

4 page 273　　10 min.

1. The skydiver decided to jump from space.

2. My brother wants to go skydiving.

3. Bruce is planning to take a skydiving class.

4. Shelly seems to love dangerous sports.

5. Fred pretended not to be nervous about skydiving.

6. He never forgets to check his equipment.

7. I refused to go skydiving with my friends.

8. Kyle agreed to stay and help us.

REAL ENGLISH, page 273

Ask students to create a list of fun activities. Then ask them to invite their partner to join them, using *would you like* + infinitive.

Chart 10.4, page 274　　5 min.

• **Note 2:** Have students substitute different verbs on the list for the first two sentences in the chart: *We ＿＿＿ to be there. We ＿＿＿ her to be there.* Have them discuss how the meaning changes. Note that all of the verbs are logical except for *help*.

5 page 274   10 min.

1. to do/their children to do

2. us not to go

3. him to come

4. to stay/my sister to stay

5. us to finish

6. to paint/me to paint

7. everyone to leave

8. me to take

9. to be/you to be

10. your friends to borrow

11. children to play

12. to wait/you to wait

- **Expansion Tip:** If students finish early, ask them to use the sentence openers in exercise **5** to write original sentences for sentences 4, 5, 7, 8, 9, 10 (e.g., *The professor reminded us to finish our research before we start writing.*).

Chart 10.5, page 275   5 min.

- **Note:** Higher-level students may be interested to learn that there are a few verbs that change meaning when an infinitive or a gerund follows the verb, e.g., *remembered* + gerund = you had a memory of the past. *I remembered walking to school every day.* Remembered + infinitive = you needed to do something and you didn't forget to do this action. *I remembered to lock the door.* When you *stop doing something,* you no longer do this action, e.g., *I stopped eating sugar. = I don't eat sugar anymore.* When *you stop to do something,* you interrupt your action to do something else. *I stopped to tie my shoe. = I paused to tie my shoe.* Other verbs whose meanings change with infinitives and gerunds include *forget* and *try.*

6 page 275   10 min.

1. playing   5. to exercise

2. waiting   6. to swim

3. being   7. to play

4. giving; cooking   8. to live

7 SPEAK, page 275   5 min.

Answers will vary.

PRACTICE

8 page 276   10 min.

1. to climb/climbing   6. to take

2. to visit   7. to reach

3. to go   8. reaching

4. to have   9. not to continue

5. to get   10. reading/to read

- **Expansion Tip:** After students have finished reading, ask, *What do you think about the blog? Do you think Lili and her older brother should have turned back? What would you have done? Why?* Encourage students to use gerunds and infinitives in their answers.

9 PRONUNCIATION, page 277   10 min.

B *Answers will vary.*

- **Expansion Tip:** After students have shared their sentences with a partner, have them find new partners and share what they have learned about their first partner. Be sure to explain this additional activity at the start of exercise **9** (e.g., Malik: *I hope to be an engineer.* Nadia: *Malik hopes to be an engineer.*). Use the hand gesture in the tip above to correct the pronunciation of *to* when necessary.

10 LISTEN, page 277   10 min.

1. invited her to climb

2. refused to go

3. loves climbing/loves to climb

4. wanted to spend time; agreed to go on/agreed to make

5. needed to borrow

6. can't stand getting wet

7. didn't mind going

8. prefers climbing mountains/prefers to climb mountains

11 WRITE & SPEAK, page 278   25 min.

Answers will vary.

- **Tip:** Students may notice that this activity is similar to exercise **9B**. Encourage students to expand on their ideas. Explain that further practice can help with fluency. Have students work with different partners from exercise **9B**.

12 APPLY, page 278   25 min.

Answers will vary.

- **Alternative Apply:** Have students research a hobby or activity. Tell students to write five to six sentences about this hobby with at least 4–5 gerunds and infinitives.

Student Learning Outcomes	• **Read** about Kakani Katija, a scientist who studies the movement of water in the oceans. • **Ask** and **answer** questions using infinitives of purpose. • **Complete** a conversation with *enough* and *too (much/many)*. • **Listen** and **choose** sentences with similar meanings. • **Find** and **edit** errors in an article about langur monkeys in India. • **Write** about the positive and negative aspects of a job.
Lesson Vocabulary	(n.) assignment (n.) criminal (v.) mix (adv.) overnight (n.) staff (v.) board (v.) gather (n.) movement (adj.) realistic (n.) tide

EXPLORE

1 READ, page 279   10 min.

• Have students look at the photos. Explain that *ocean currents* refers to the movement of water in oceans. *Tides* and *wind* influence these currents. Ask, *Can sea creatures influence the climate?* Tell students to read to see what one scientist says.

Be the Expert

• This reading is about a bioengineer, Kakani Katija, who has an interesting background. She was a competitive ice dancer with her brother, and then studied aeronautics, before she decided to focus on oceans.

• Katija has said that her work ethic in ice dancing has helped her as a scientist. Skating taught her that when she fell, she should make adjustments. The same is true in scientific research.

• Katija's research highlights the need for ocean conservation. Ocean currents affect climate systems, which affect all of us, whether we live near the ocean or not.

• Katija also says that there is a lot more to discover about our oceans. In fact, there are scientists who discover new species every time they dive.

2 CHECK, page 280   5 min.

1. b   2. a   3. a   4. b

3 DISCOVER, page 280   5 min.

A b

B b

• **Tip:** On the board, write the following sentences:

I am taking English classes to _____.

I'm too young to _____.

I have enough money to _____.

Have students answer these questions in pairs. Ask volunteers to share their answers with the class.

LEARN

Chart 10.6, page 281   5 min.

• **Note 3:** Infinitives of purpose can also be stated as *in order to* + base form. Have students read each example sentence with *in order to* before each infinitive of purpose. Explain that this answers the question *why?*

4 page 281   10 min.

1. to start a discussion about jobs

2. to show his interest in the ocean

3. to understand climate systems

4. to do some research and finish her project

5. To get a good grade

6. to find some answers to her questions

7. to get good grades

8. to ask the professor questions

5 SPEAK, page 281   5 min.

Answers will vary.

- **Expansion Tip:** Have students write a list of five things they need to do this week, and then read the list to a partner. Have partners ask and answer *why* they need to do each item (e.g., A: *I need to go shopping.* B: *Why?* A: *To buy a present for my friend's birthday.*). Encourage students to use as many infinitives of purpose as possible.

Chart 10.7, page 282   5 min.

- **Note 1:** Students might try to use *too* as a synonym for *very/a lot of*. On the board, write: *I have a lot of friends. I have too many friends.* Ask, *What is the difference between these two sentences?* Elicit the response that in sentence 2, you are not happy about your friends. Explain that *too* means that there is a problem.

6 page 282   5 min.

1. too late to speak
2. too long to read
3. too many patients to take
4. too much work to finish
5. too slowly to reach
6. too experienced to make
7. too many e-mails to answer
8. too many books to carry

7 page 282   10 min.

1. too quickly for me to understand
2. too much homework for the teacher to correct in one night
3. too much work for one person to do
4. too dangerous for an inexperienced person to do
5. too many calls for the employees to answer
6. too much money for John to spend
7. too many assignments for us to do
8. too old for me to take

- **Expansion Tip:** Have students work in pairs and repeat the sentences in exercise **7**. Have the partner give advice to resolve the problem (e.g., A: *The teacher spoke too quickly for me to understand.* B: *Ask her to speak more slowly*).

LEARN

Chart 10.8, page 283   5 min.

- **Note 1:** Word order is a common difficulty with *enough*. If possible, write sentences a, b, and c on paper, and cut them up into individual words. Have students close their books, and work in pairs to form the words into sentences. Compare answers with the class.

- **Note:** Explain that *enough* means sufficient. The negative, *not + verb + enough*, means *too little* or *too few*. Read the sentences in exercise **6** again. Ask students to work together to write the sentences with *not + verb + adverb/adjective + enough* rather than *too*. Complete the first sentence as a class: *The businessman arrived too late to speak at the meeting.* OR, *The businessman didn't arrive early enough to speak at the meeting.*

8 page 283   10 min.

1. enough salespeople to help
2. well enough to get
3. enough staff to fill
4. good enough to win
5. enough money to take
6. easy enough to follow
7. enough sugar to make
8. comfortable enough to sleep

9 page 284   10 min.

1. loudly enough for everyone to hear
2. enough time for me to finish
3. small enough for everyone to know
4. light enough for him to carry
5. enough room for all of us to stay
6. warm enough for me to wear
7. quickly enough for the flight to leave
8. enough books for every student to have

PRACTICE

10 page 284 — 10 min.

1. too many mistakes to work
2. too much new vocabulary for me to remember
3. too fast for me to follow
4. slowly enough for us to understand
5. too fast for us to understand
6. enough time to get
7. enough students to keep
8. interesting enough to attract

- **Expansion Tip:** Have students who finish early use the phrases from exercise **10** to talk about their English language learning. Have them adapt the sentences (e.g., *I speak English well. I don't make too many mistakes to work in England.*).

11 LISTEN & SPEAK, page 285 — 15 min.

A 1. a   3. b   5. a   7. a
    2. b   4. a   6. a   8. a

B *Answers will vary.*

12 EDIT, page 286 — 10 min.

- **Tip:** To create interest, have students look at the photo and the title before reading the article. Ask, *What do you know about monkeys? What do you think the monkey's job could be?*

In the Great Indian Desert, it's too hot and dry for langur monkeys to live comfortably all year round. That's why over 2000 of them come into the city of Jodhpur ~~for~~ to find something to eat. Local people like the langurs, so they bring food to ~~sharing~~ share with the monkeys. It's ~~enough easy~~ easy enough for langurs to survive in the city, but it's not all fun and free food! Many of them have to work for a living . . . controlling other monkeys!

Langurs are welcome in Indian cities, but other kinds of monkeys aren't. There are too ~~much~~ many of these monkeys to control, and they sometimes attack people to get food. Langurs scare other types of monkeys, so cities use them to keep these monkeys away. In Delhi, for example, during a big sports event in 2010, 38 langurs patrolled the streets, and the other monkeys were too ~~much~~ scared to stay in the area. The plan was successful enough for most people ~~enjoying~~ to enjoy the event in peace.

13 APPLY, page 286 — 20 min.

Answers will vary.

- **Alternative Apply:** Have students work together to make a list of positive and negative aspects of a celebrity job, such as a movie star, football player, or skydiver. Have students present their lists in groups of six, and then discuss whether the positive aspects outweigh the negatives.

1 page 287   10 min.

1. to get	6. working
2. to take	7. getting
3. defending	8. to hurt
4. me to do	9. strong enough
5. to do	10. to get

• **Tip:** Have students look at the photo. Ask, *What sport is this? What skills do you need to be good at hockey?* Explain that *shooting the puck* means hitting the puck toward the goal.

2 page 287   10 min.

1. studying	8. working
2. helping/to help	9. teaching
3. becoming	10. teaching/to teach
4. to study	11. working
5. to work	12. to finish
6. to do	13. knowing
7. becoming	

3 page 288   10 min.

1. reading magazines	5. being late for work
2. Exploring new places	6. working/to work
3. me to wait	7. short to be useful
4. in skiing	8. me to swim

4 EDIT, page 288   15 min.

    In 2007, Barrington Irving became famous ~~on~~ for being the youngest person to fly solo around the world. Irving was born in Jamaica and lived there until his parents decided to move to Miami. Although life was not always easy, Irving has always been good at ~~overcome~~ overcoming difficulties. When he was 15, Irving met a professional pilot who invited him to take a look at his plane. That was when Irving became interested in learning to fly. He didn't have ~~money enough~~ enough money to go to flight school, so he earned money by washing planes. He practiced ~~to fly~~ flying in video games. When he was 23, Irving built his own plane and succeeded in flying around the world in 97 days.

    After this success, Irving created exciting programs ~~for~~ to encourage children to learn about science, math, and technology. He believes in showing children that studying hard brings success. If they do their best, no goal is too difficult to achieve.

5 WRITE & SPEAK, page 289   15 min.

Answers will vary.

• **Expansion Tip:** Have students write interview questions using the prompts in the box, and then interview each other. Have students write one to two paragraphs about their partner. Then have the partner read and edit the paragraph for grammar and content.

Connect the Grammar to Writing

1 READ & NOTICE THE GRAMMAR,
page 290   20 min.

A *Answers will vary.*

B   When Carlos was five years old, he moved
in with his *abuela*, or grandmother. She loved
(to cook), and Carlos spent a lot of time with her in
the kitchen. Being in the warm kitchen with his
grandmother was fun. She liked telling stories
about her childhood, and Carlos enjoyed listening
to her. He also enjoyed learning (to cook) by
watching and helping her. In the beginning, most
dishes were too difficult for him (to make). First,
he chopped vegetables and stirred beans. Then,
he learned how (to make) soups and other simple
dishes when he was seven. By the time he turned
13, Carlos was cooking full meals for his family
and friends. He enjoyed making people happy with
his food.

Eventually, Carlos realized that he had
enough talent (to become) a chef. At the age of 18,
he began working at a local restaurant. Then, 12
years later, after a lot of hard work, Carlos opened
his own restaurant. He invited his family and
friends (to come) to the grand opening. (To honor)
his grandmother, Carlos named his restaurant
Abuela's Kitchen.

C Age 5: Moved in with Grandma

Age 7: Learned to make soup and simple dishes

Age 13: Was cooking full meals

Age 18: Began working at a restaurant

Age 30: Opened his own restaurant

- **Expansion Tip:** Have students close their books
  and retell the story in their own words. Have them
  use as many infinitives and gerunds as possible.

2 BEFORE YOU WRITE, page 291   15 min.

Answers will vary.

3 WRITE, page 291   20 min.

> ## WRITING FOCUS, page 291
>
> Have students write three sentences about what
> they did this morning, or what they did when they
> returned home last night. Have them begin with
> *first* and use *then* where appropriate. Have them
> compare stories with a partner and make sure that
> they have used commas correctly.

- **Alternative Writing:** Have students imagine
  that it is twenty years in the future and they are
  writing their autobiography using the chart in
  exercise **2**. Encourage students to be creative and
  positive about their future, and to use gerunds and
  infinitives.

- **Alternative Writing:** Have students work
  individually or in pairs to research one of the
  people featured in this chapter: Jason deCairnes
  Taylor, Felix Baumgartner, Kakani Katija, or
  Barrington Irving. Have students prepare one-
  to three-minute presentations about the person
  of their choice and present the material to the
  class or to small groups of five or six. Encourage
  students to use at least five examples of infinitives,
  gerunds, or *too/enough*. As the students give their
  presentations, have the listeners take notes on
  at least one new piece of information that they
  learned from each presentation.

People and Places

Relative Clauses

Unit Opener

Photo: Have students look at the photo and read the caption. Ask, *How do people usually row boats? Why do you think the man is rowing in this way?* Men use this technique to row because the lake is covered by tall reeds and rowers can't see when they sit down.

Location: Inle Lake is in the middle of the country of Myanmar. About 70,000 people live in cities and towns on the edge of the lake and on the lake itself. Most people live in simple bamboo houses on stilts. Have students find Myanmar on the map.

Theme: This unit is about interesting people and places. Have students look through the photos in the unit. Ask, *Which people or places look the most interesting to you?*

Page	Lesson	Grammar	Examples
294	1	Subject Relative Clauses	We met the woman **who owns the shop.** I have a friend **who likes traveling.**
301	2	Object Relative Clauses	The house **that she bought** is blue. They are the people **I met** on the tour.
308	3	Relative Clauses with Prepositions and with *Whose*	Did you find the book **that you were looking for?** The author **whose book won the award** writes beautifully.
314	**Review the Grammar**		
316	**Connect the Grammar to Writing**		

Unit Grammar Terms

preposition: a word that describes the relationships between nouns. Prepositions show space, time, direction, cause, and effect. Often they occur together with certain verbs or adjectives.
➢ I live **on** Center Street.
➢ We left **at** noon.
➢ I'm worried **about** the test.

relative clause: a clause that describes a noun or indefinite pronoun in a sentence. It comes after the noun or pronoun it describes. It is also called an *adjective clause*.
➢ The student **that I am sitting next to** is from Peru.
➢ I know everyone **who lives in my building**.

relative pronoun: a pronoun that introduces a relative clause. Common relative pronouns are *who, whom, whose, that,* and *which.*
➢ We met the woman **who** owns the shop.
➢ Here's the book **that** you were looking for.

Student Learning Outcomes	• **Read** a conversation about a town in Jordan. • **Listen** to the full and reduced pronunciation of *that* in relative clauses. • **Write** original sentences using relative clauses. • **Listen** to and **complete** a conversation about the World Cup in South Africa. • **Write** definitions of objects and jobs. • **Say** sentences that have relative clauses.
Lesson Vocabulary	(adv.) certainly (n.) event (adj.) impressed (v.) settle (n.) tribe (n.) crop (adj.) flat (n.) report (n.) souvenir (n.) village

EXPLORE

1 READ, page 294   15 min.

- **Tip:** Use the photo and caption to elicit guesses about what the location is like. Have students explain their reasoning. Ask, *What do you think the conversation will be about?*

- Use the conversation to teach the meaning of *carved.* Have students use context cues to guess the meaning of *tribe, settle,* and *crop.*

Be the Expert

- Petra, Jordan, is famous for its buildings that are cut into the rocks and for its water system. The stone that the buildings are carved into is rose-colored, so Petra is also known as the Rose City. Although Petra is in the desert, it occasionally has flash floods. Ancient residents developed a system of dams, cisterns, and conduits to save and control this water.

- More than 2000 years old, Petra is a UNESCO World Heritage site. More tourists visit Petra than any other place in Jordan.

- The Bedul Bedouin only number around 1000. They raise goats and grow wheat and barley when there is rain. They also produce yogurt and have a dried form of it. For most of the 20th century, they lived in tents woven of goat hair, rock shelters, and also tombs in the area. Now many live in a village.

2 CHECK, page 294   5 min.

   1. F   2. F   3. T   4. F   5. T

- **Tip:** Have students do this exercise as a prediction exercise before they read and listen. After they read, have them rewrite the false statements to make them true.

- **Expansion Tip:** Have students write three more statements based on the information in the conversation. At least one of their statements should be false. Have students exchange sentences with a partner to identify and correct the false statements.

3 DISCOVER, page 295   5 min.

A 1. that was on TV last night

    2. which make up the oldest part of the city

    3. that has lived in the area for over 200 years

    4. who visit Petra

    5. who prefer to keep goats and grow crops

B that, which, who

LEARN

Chart 11.1, page 296   10 min.

- **Notes 1 & 2:** Write two sentences on the board: *We live next to a woman. She is from Lebanon.* Underline *a woman* and *She.* Point out that both refer to the same thing. Have students follow the model in the note to write a sentence that combines the two. (*We live next to a woman who is from Lebanon.*) Have a student write the new sentence on the board. Then draw a line from the relative clause to the noun it modifies.

- **Note 3:** When a relative clause is used to identify which person, place, or thing is being discussed in a sentence, *that* is used much more frequently than *which* to introduce the clause (e.g., *The car that got scratched belonged to my uncle.*). These identifying (or restrictive) clauses do not have to be set off by commas. When referring to people, it is more common to use *who* than *that.* Suggest that students note examples of relative clauses that refer to objects or people when they find them in text or hear them on TV or in movies.

- **Note 4:** Have students write the example sentences as two separate sentences (e.g., *I like the guide. The guide showed us the sites.*). This will help them see more clearly that the relative pronoun is the subject.

4 page 296   5 min.

1. The Bedul are people who live near Petra, Jordan.

2. Tourists that visit Petra buy souvenirs from the Bedul.

3. The Bedul used to be farmers who lived simply.

4. The building that is most popular with tourists is the Treasury.

5. The guides that show tourists around Petra are often Bedul.

6. The name *Petra* comes from the Greek word that means "stone."

7. The buildings that make up the old part of Petra are carved into the hills.

8. Anyone who wants to know more about Petra can find information on the Internet.

- **Tip:** Students may have difficulty seeing the relationship between the ideas in the two clauses. To clarify this relationship, have students break each sentence into two sentences without relative clauses. This can also help them understand the next chart.

Chart 11.2, page 297   10 min.

- **Notes 1, 2 & 3:** Write several sentences with errors on the board—either the subject is repeated in the relative clause (e.g., *That's the boy who he was late to class.*), or the verb in the main clause does not agree with the subject of the main clause (e.g., *The book that has lots of pictures are very interesting.*). Have the class correct your errors.

5 page 297   10 min.

1. is   4. takes
2. sells   5. does not/doesn't talk
3. understands   6. are

- **Tip:** Have students underline the main clauses and circle the relative clauses to help them notice which verb needs to agree with which subject. The underlined verb needs to agree with the underlined subject. Similarly, the circled verb needs to agree with the circled subject.

- **Expansion Tip:** Have students work in pairs to extend two or three conversations from exercise **5** by adding more interactions between the speakers. Model the activity by extending the first conversation (e.g., A: *Yes, thanks. It lists places that we should see.* B: *Are they places that are close to our hotel?* A: *I don't know yet, but now I can look it up in the book.*). Suggest they add three more exchanges. Encourage students to use at least two new relative clauses in each conversation.

6 page 297   5 min.

1. was   5. doesn't arrive
2. have   6. has been
3. cost   7. travel
4. have lost   8. goes

PRACTICE

7 page 298   5 min.

- **Tip:** If students are more advanced, you can explain that certain clauses in English are called restrictive, or identifying, relative clauses. These are clauses that identify who or what the speaker is talking about (e.g., *I saw the car that won the race yesterday.* The clause *that won the race* identifies which car I saw.). Restrictive clauses are usually (but not always) introduced by *who* or *that*. *Which* is much more likely to be used in a non-restrictive clause—one that adds information but is not necessary for identification (e.g., *I am from Rhode Island, which is the smallest state in the United States.*). When a clause is used to add information but not to identify a person or object, it is set off by commas.

1. that/which explains   5. that/which offer
2. that/who lives   6. that/which allows
3. that/which attract   7. that/who tell
4. that/who visit   8. that/which has

8 PRONUNCIATION, page 298   5 min.

- **Tip:** Remind students that *that* is a demonstrative pronoun or determiner when it is pronounced fully. It is reduced when it is a relative pronoun. Write sentences on the board: *I didn't know that. That shirt looks great on you. That's interesting news about Monica. She's the student that came late yesterday.* Say the sentences and ask students which *that* is reduced. Then, working in pairs, have students practice saying the sentences.

1. I like visiting places that are warm, sunny, and relaxing.

2. I have friends that don't like to fly.

3. I don't like guides that talk all the time.

4. My friend likes trips that allow plenty of time to shop.

5. I don't buy souvenirs that break easily.

6. My classmate likes places that aren't very crowded.

7. I like to stay in hotels that have exercise rooms.

8. My mother likes to eat at restaurants that have fixed menus.

B *Answers will vary.*

• **Tip:** Model the activity by writing the first three sentences on the board using your own experiences.

C *Answers will vary.*

> **REAL ENGLISH, page 299**
>
> Have students bring in examples of relative clauses they find in articles, websites, or hear on TV or the radio. Ask them to tally how many of each type of relative pronoun they find to confirm that *that* is generally the most commonly used relative pronoun.

9 LISTEN, page 299   5 min.

1. that took place
2. who watched
3. that made
4. who were using
5. that have happened
6. which brought
7. who thought
8. who came
9. that spoke

• **Tip:** Working in pairs, have students practice the conversation. Remind them to use reduced pronunciation for *that* in relative clauses. After students have practiced, have volunteers role-play the conversations in front of the class. Correct pronunciation as necessary to focus on the reduced *that*.

A   1. b   3. d   5. c
      2. e   4. f   6. a

B   1. A vuvuzela is an instrument that/which is similar to a horn.

2. Archaeologists are scientists that/who study historic places and objects.

3. A magnifying glass is a tool that/which makes small objects look bigger.

4. Statisticians are scientists that/who calculate and analyze numbers.

5. A carving is a piece of art that/which is cut from stone, wood, or another material.

6. A spreadsheet is a computer program that/which allows you to organize numbers or data.

C *Answers will vary.*

D *Answers will vary.*

• **Alternative Speaking:** Write the names of famous people or places on slips of paper. Tape one slip to each student's back so that the student can't read what is on his or her back. Students walk around the room to ask and answer questions with relative clauses in order to guess the person or place (e.g., *Is this a place that most people have been to? Is this a person that is on TV or in movies?*). Students only have to answer questions truthfully if the question uses a relative clause correctly.

Student Learning Outcomes	• **Read** an article about a person who helps elephants.

- **Read** an article about a person who helps elephants.
- **Complete** sentences with object relative pronouns.
- **Listen** to people talk about photos of interesting places.
- **Discuss** a photo with a partner.
- **Edit** paragraphs from a travel brochure.
- **Write** statements about yourself using relative clauses.

Lesson Vocabulary

(adv.) badly	(adj.) extraordinary	(adj.) historic	(adj.) narrow	(ph. v.) take care of
(adj.) concerned	(n.) forest	(v.) interview	(v.) provide	(n.) technique

EXPLORE

1 READ, page 301   15 min.

- Have students look at the photos and read the captions. Ask, *What do you know about elephants and their relationships with people?*

- **Tip:** After students read and listen, have them work in pairs to ask and answer questions about the article using relative clauses (e.g., *Who is Lek Chaifert? She is someone who works with elephants.*).

Be the Expert

- The Elephant Nature Park in Chiang Mai provides a natural environment for elephants, dogs, cats, buffaloes, and many other animals. Volunteers can come and work at the park for up to four weeks, taking care of the elephants and other animals. Ask, *Do you want to work with elephants? Why, or why not? What animals (if any) would you like to work with? Why?*

- Many of the elephants at the park are blind because their trainers punished them by stabbing them in the eye. Elicit opinions about why the elephants may have been punished this specific way (e.g., *Their skin is too tough. The eye is a vulnerable spot.*).

- Sangduen "Lek" Chailert was born in 1962. Her grandfather was a traditional healer. When she was young, Lek grew close to an elephant her family took care of.

2 CHECK, page 302   5 min.

1. b	2. c	3. b	4. a	5. c

- **Expansion Tip:** Have students use the Internet to find another rescue park or preserve that specializes in helping injured animals. Then have them write one or two paragraphs describing the park and comparing it to the Elephant Nature Park. Encourage students to use relative clauses in at least two sentences. If Internet access is not available in the classroom, the activity could be assigned as homework.

3 DISCOVER, page 302   5 min.

A b, c

B The word that comes after *that* in the clauses in the sentences from exercise **A** is a noun. In a subject relative clause, the word that comes after the relative pronoun is a verb.

- **Tip:** Review the definition of a direct object: It is a noun or pronoun that recieves the action of the verb. On the board, write: *I saw a doctor last week.* Then ask, *Who or what was seen?* Write a sentence on the board that uses the content of the first sentence in a relative clause (e.g., *The doctor that I saw last week was on TV.*). Ask students what they think an object relative clause might be (e.g., *a relative clause in which the relative pronoun is the object of the verb*). This will lead into note 1.

LEARN

Chart 11.3, page 303   10 min.

- **Note 1:** Write the two simple sentences on the board. Ask which person, place, or thing is in both sentences. Ask whether he is the subject or object in each sentence (subject in first, object in second). Then read aloud the third sentence. It contains a relative clause. Point out that the relative clause is an object relative clause because the relative pronoun *that* is the object in the clause.

- **Note 2:** *Whom* is used to introduce object relative clauses in formal settings or in writing.
- **Notes 3 & 4:** Write two more pairs of sentences on the board that students can combine using object relative clauses (e.g., 1. *The teacher was great. I had her last semester.* 2. *The movie was boring. We saw it last night.*). Ask volunteers to write the new sentences on the board.

4 page 303   10 min.

1. that/which; use
2. that/who/whom; meets
3. that/which; helps
4. that/which; visit
5. that/which; find
6. that/who/whom; hires
7. that/which; receives
8. that/who/whom; admire

Chart 11.4, page 304   10 min.

- **Notes 1 & 2:** Direct students back to exercise **4**. Read the first two sentences without the relative pronoun. Have students rewrite the other sentences without the relative pronouns. Make sure students know the symbol Ø means that something is not needed.

5 page 304   5 min.

1. Jan Peng is an elephant ~~that~~ people treated badly.
2. Jan Peng worked in a camp ~~that~~ loggers built.
3. The trees ~~which~~ Jan Peng moved were large and very heavy.
4. As Jan Peng got older, the work ~~that~~ she was doing became too hard for her.
5. The people ~~whom~~ Lek interviewed about Jan Peng promised not to make her work again.
6. Jan Peng seemed afraid when she had to go with people ~~that~~ she did not know.
7. The team members ~~that~~ Lek brought to the logging camp took good care of Jan Peng.
8. Jan Peng liked the new home ~~that~~ Lek and her team provided for her.

6 page 304   10 min.

1. that/which/Ø
2. that/which/Ø
3. that/who/whom/Ø
4. that/which/Ø
5. that/who/whom/Ø
6. that/who/whom/Ø
7. that/who/whom/Ø
8. that/which/Ø

- **Tip:** Have students read the different forms of the sentences aloud. Ask students which form sounds the most natural for each sentence.
- **Expansion Tip:** Write a sentence on the board using the subject + verb + object pattern, e.g., *I ate sushi.* Then demonstrate how the sentence can be turned into an object relative clause, e.g., *The sushi that I ate was delicious. I didn't like the sushi I ate.* Have students write four sentences that follow the subject + verb + object pattern and exchange their sentences with a partner. Then have students create new sentences using their partners' sentences as object relative clauses.

PRACTICE

7 page 305   5 min.

1. The notebook ~~that~~ I lost had important information in it.
2. The person ~~that~~ I talked to on the phone was rude to me.
3. The car ~~that~~ my sister bought is easy to drive.
4. Most of the people ~~who~~ I met on vacation speak German.
5. The doctor ~~whom~~ I called is not taking new patients.
6. The song ~~which~~ Alan was singing was beautiful.
7. The report ~~that~~ I'm writing is really difficult.
8. Do you have a map of the city ~~that~~ I can use?
9. Have you seen the books ~~that~~ I left on the table?
10. Meryl Streep is an actress ~~whom~~ I would like to meet.

- **Alternative Writing:** Have students rewrite the ending of the main clause and/or replace the object relative clause for the first five sentences in exercise **7**. For example, the first sentence might be rewritten as, *The notebook I lost was red.* OR, *The notebook Lily found had important information in it.*

8 LISTEN & SPEAK, page 305   20 min.

A *Answers will vary.*

B *Answers will vary.*

C 1. b   3. a   5. b   7. b

    2. a   4. a   6. a   8. a

D *Answers will vary.*

- **Alternative Speaking:** Bring in other interesting photos, or have students choose another photo in a previous unit to describe to a partner, using object relative clauses.

9 EDIT, page 306   5 min.

Kyoto

Kyoto, was the capital of Japan for over a thousand years. It is a city which visitors find ~~it~~ fascinating. In the eastern part of the city, there are many temples and gardens ~~who~~ that/which/Ø you can see on a short walk. The Golden Pavilion is a beautiful building you can visit ~~it~~ in the northwestern hills. Another wonderful building in the center of town is Nijō-jō. This is a famous palace ~~whom~~ that/which/Ø every visitor wants to see.

Kuala Lumpur

The Malaysian capital, Kuala Lumpur (or "KL"), has changed a lot in the last 50 years. The historic buildings ~~whom~~ that/which/Ø you can visit in Kuala Lumpur are now mixed with modern skyscrapers such as the Petronas Towers. KL is a busy but friendly place, and the different cultures that you can experience ~~them~~ will make your visit fun.

- **Alternative Writing:** Have students write a paragraph about a city they know well. Their paragraphs should have at least five relative clauses. Then, working in pairs, have students exchange paragraphs to check for errors and edit as necessary.

10 APPLY, page 307   15 min.

Answers will vary.

- **Tip:** Model the activity by completing the first two sentences with details about yourself.

- **Expansion Tip:** After students have shared their sentences, have them find new partners and describe their first partners' preferences and experiences (e.g., *The last city Tomas visited was Muscat.*).

Student Learning Outcomes	• **Read** an article about cycling on the Isle of Man. • **Use** relative clauses as objects of prepositions. • **Write** sentences using *whose* in relative clauses. • **Edit** articles about Vikings and Tanzania. • **Ask** and **answer** questions using relative clauses.
Lesson Vocabulary	(n.) cycling (n.) geography (n.) signature (adj.) successful (adj.) tough (v.) develop (n.) race (n.) strength (n.) trader (n.) violence

EXPLORE

1 READ, page 308   15 min.

- Have students look at the photo and read the caption. Ask, *What does the photo tell you about the place where these people are cycling? Would you like to take a bike tour through an area like that? Why might people from this place be good cyclists?*

- **Expansion Tip:** Have students work in pairs or small groups to discuss how the characteristics of a place can affect the particular abilities that people develop. For example, why are so many good climbers from Nepal?

Be the Expert

- The Isle of Man is only about 130 kilometers from Dublin, and roughly the same distance from England, Scotland, and Wales. The island is about 52 kilometers long, but only 22 kilometers wide. It was part of Norway until the 13th century. After that, it became part of Scotland, and then part of the British kingdom in 1765. It has cool summers and mild winters. A central valley cuts through the middle of the island.

- Originally from the Isle of Man, Mark Cavendish became a professional cyclist in 2005. He has won 25 Tour de France stages (a stage is a one-day segment of the race), which is the third most of all Tour de France racers. He has also competed in the Olympics and is known as a very fast sprinter.

- Cycling is popular in many countries, including China, India, Norway, and the Netherlands. European countries such as France and Italy have produced some of the best cyclists in the world.

2 CHECK, page 309   5 min.

1. F (between Great Britain and Ireland)
2. T
3. F (hills and valleys)

4. F (in 2011)
5. F (under 90,000)

- **Tip:** Have students write three more statements that are true or false about the information in the article. Then have students exchange statements with a partner and identify each others' statements as true or false.

3 DISCOVER, page 309   5 min.

A 1. for   2. about

B b

- **Tip:** Ask students to identify the relative pronouns and relative clauses, if any, used in exercise **A**. Note that both sentences have null relative pronouns. The relative clauses are (Ø) *they are looking for*, and (Ø) *everyone is talking about*.

LEARN

Chart 11.5, page 310   10 min.

- **Tip:** After you go over the notes, have students rewrite the example sentences in another way to practice both formal and informal relative clauses. For example, *The people I met with were customers* could be rewritten as, *The people with whom I met were customers*.

4 page 310   5 min.

1. that she rode in
2. that Roberto is/was most interested in
3. [for] whom you are looking/were looking/have been looking [for]
4. you are/were friends with
5. Valerie was talking to
6. your brother works/is working for
7. [on] which Sue decided/had decided [on]
8. I haven't spoken/haven't been speaking/didn't speak to

9. you worked/were working with

10. that we talked/were talking/had talked about

- **Tip:** Suggest that students rewrite the first five sentences using relative clauses of their own creation. Then have students share their new sentences with a partner.

- **Expansion Tip:** Ask, *What sport are you most interested in?* Elicit answers that use relative clauses (e.g., *The sport (that/which) I am most interested in is football.* OR, *Football is the sport that I am most interested in.*). Write these phrases on the board: *listen to, pay attention to, study with, talk to, travel with, go to.* Explain that each phrase has a verb and a preposition. Then have students write questions that use each phrase, and that can be answered in sentences with object relative clauses (e.g., *What kind of radio programs do you listen to? The programs that I listen to play classical music.*). Then, working in pairs, have students take turns asking and answering questions with object relative clauses.

Chart 11.6, page 311   10 min.

- **Notes 1 & 2:** Write the pairs of sentences without relative clauses on the board. Have students identify the person, place, or thing that appears in both (e.g., *the author/her*). If necessary, write the sentences to repeat the noun (e.g., *The author writes beautifully. The author's book won the prize.*). Explain that *whose* replaces *the author's/her.* Repeat with the sentences in note 2.

5 page 311   10 min.

1. His	4. the team's	7. her
2. Their	5. the bike shop's	8. Its
3. His	6. Her	

PRACTICE

6 page 312   5 min.

1. whose signature you need

2. whose movies have made millions of dollars

3. that/which/Ø my son goes to

4. whose name is Freddy

5. that/who/Ø Marianne spoke to/[to] whom Marianne spoke [to]

6. whose mother is a doctor

7. that/which/Ø we went to last night

8. that/who/Ø Lucy works with/[with] whom Lucy works [with]

- **Tip:** Have students work in pairs. Partner A reads the original pairs of sentences. Partner B reads the new combined sentence with a relative clause. Have them identify which is emphasized more: *whose* or the word(s) it replaces.

7 WRITE & SPEAK, page 312   10 min.

A 1. that/which/Ø Tim is interested in

2. that/which/Ø you talked/were talking about

3. that/which/Ø you applied for

4. that/which/Ø we traveled to

5. that/who/we spoke to/we've spoken to/[to] whom we spoke/we've spoken [to]

B *Answers will vary.*

- **Alternative Speaking:** Write these phrases on the board: *a person's job, an animal's home, a city's sights, someone's car, a teacher's class.* Have students work in pairs to make sentences about the prompts using relative clauses with *whose* (e.g., *I have a friend whose job allows her to travel all over the world. Mammals whose homes are in the desert are often tan.*). Have each pair join another pair to share their sentences.

8 EDIT, page 313   5 min.

- **Tip:** Have students look at the painting and describe the boat. Ask students to name and describe other countries/peoples that are known for their love of the sea (e.g., *Ancient Egyptians, Phoenicians, Polynesians*). Ask more advanced students to use relative clauses in their descriptions (e.g., *Phoenicians, who lived in the Middle East thousands of years ago, were traders.*).

The people that we think of ~~them~~ as Vikings were not in fact one group of people. They were different groups of people whose native countries ~~they~~ were in southern Scandinavia. The areas that they lived in ~~them~~ are now called Norway, Sweden, and Denmark.

In addition to the violence that they are famous for ~~it~~, the Vikings were explorers whose love of the sea everyone ~~know~~ knew about. The Vikings were great travelers and traders. They sailed their small wooden ships as far as Russia to the east and to North Africa to the south. They were also the first Europeans to reach America. The Vikings even settled for a short time in an area ~~who~~ whose Norse name was *Vinland.* Its modern name is Newfoundland, Canada.

9 APPLY, page 313   15 min.

A *Answers will vary.*

B *Answers will vary.*

- **Expansion Tip:** Have students prepare a one- to two-minute speech on one of the topics from exercise **A**. Have students give their speeches to a small group or to the class. Have the other students take notes on the relative clauses each presenter uses.

1 page 314　　5 min.

1. that/which/Ø my son took on our vacation

2. that/which/Ø I visited yesterday

3. that/which/Ø Stefan applied for was in Mexico City

4. whose wallet I found

5. that/who travels all over the world

6. that/which/Ø we took on Saturday was wonderful

7. that/which/Ø our guide told us about yesterday

8. that/which/Ø I bought for my family weren't very expensive

2 EDIT & SPEAK, page 314　　10 min.

A　　I come from the Tanga region of Tanzania, Africa. It is a place that/which is full of history and beauty. Tanga has many tourist destinations such as Mount Kilimanjaro that ~~is~~ are famous around the world. People ~~whom~~ who/that go to see this mountain will never forget it. There are guides ~~which~~ who/that take people up the mountain. These trips can be dangerous, so only people that ~~they~~ are physically fit should try to climb to the top of the mountain. Another place is Zanzibar. This is a group of islands that/which became famous for its spices. These days, Zanzibar's economy depends more on tourism than spices. The Serengeti National Park also attracts a lot of tourists. Here you can go on safari and see the many amazing animals that live there.

B *Answers will vary.*

- **Expansion Tip:** Have students work in pairs to write a travel ad for a place they know well. Their ads should use several relative clauses appropriately. Post the ads around the room. Have students walk around the room to read the ads, and then vote for the three places that sound the most interesting.

3 LISTEN & SPEAK, page 315　　15 min.

A 1. you just took

2. who went

3. that I'll never forget

4. that you chose

5. who flew

6. whose mother was

7. who loves

8. I took

B *Answers will vary.*

- **Tip:** Have students look at the photo and read the caption. Ask why balloon tours are a good way to see this place or any place. Then ask volunteers to describe to the class what they might see if they took a balloon trip over a well-known location nearby. Encourage volunteers to use relative clauses in their descriptions.

1 READ & NOTICE THE GRAMMAR, page 316 — 20 min.

A *Answers will vary.*

B

treatments I learned about

neighbor who is from Italy

tea that has sage and bay leaves in it

tea that my friend Deedee drinks

classmate whose grandparents are from Turkey

cereal she calls jook

soup that my friend Jason's grandfather from Hungary makes

person whose remedy was most unusual

tree that grows there

people I know

place that hurts them

remedy that many people use.

C

Topic: Cold Treatments Around the World

Group 1: drinks	Group 2: foods	Group 3: activities
tea with sage and bay leaves; tea with herbs and honey	*jook* (hot rice cereal); chicken soup; bark of a tree	(sit in a) room full of steam; (take a) hot shower; (put a) hot stone (on the place that hurts); (sit in) the sun

- **Tip:** Explain that a classification essay talks about things that can be classified or grouped. Ask students what are some ways they could classify the places they have lived or visited. Then elicit other things that can be easily classified (e.g., *climates, animals, things students do during the summer, music, jobs*). Write their ideas on the board. This will help them with exercise **2**.

2 BEFORE YOU WRITE, page 317 — 15 min.

Answers will vary.

- **Tip:** Students will be writing several paragraphs. Help them identify topics that are not too broad or too narrow. Refer to the ideas students have generated in previous activities, and discuss whether these ideas would make good essays and why or why not. To illustrate how to narrow the focus of a topic, choose an idea that is very broad (e.g., *jobs*). Point out that there are too many jobs to write about in just a few paragraphs. Elicit ways that the topic can be narrowed (e.g., by workplace: *jobs in a hospital, jobs outside, jobs in stores*). Have students use this technique to focus on an idea to identify a topic and subtopics that can be reasonably covered in four or five paragraphs.

3 WRITE, page 317 — 15 min.

WRITING FOCUS   page 317

Brainstorm other ways students can organize their essays using a logical progression. For example, if they are writing about climate, they might move from the equator to the poles. If they are writing about movies, they might move from the most recent movies to the earliest movies. Have students write topic sentences for each of their paragraphs using these ideas and share them with partners to get feedback.

- **Expansion Tip:** Have students exchange charts from exercise **2B** with a partner. Then have students write a topic sentence for each group in their partner's chart. Have students compare their own topic sentences with the ones their partners have written.

- **Alternative Writing:** Assign students to write a classification essay on a topic suggested by the unit theme: people and places. Students should classify people or places according to their own classification system. For example, they might classify the people in their cities according to background, work, or language. Or they might classify areas of their country geographically. Or they could choose to classify friends or vacation spots.

Unit Opener

Photo: Have students look at the photo and read the caption. Explain what *graffiti* is, and ask whether students think it is an art form. Ask students for their ideas about the photo. Ask, *Are art and music important in your life? Your culture? Why, or why not?*

Location: São Paulo, Brazil, is the largest city in both South and North America. Have a student locate São Paulo on a map.

Theme: This unit is about art and music. Have students look at the photos throughout the unit. Ask, *Which photo interests you most? Why? What artistic talents do you have?*

Page	Lesson	Grammar	Examples
320	1	Ability: Past, Present, and Future	I **can paint** with watercolors. She **couldn't speak** before the age of three. I'm **able to see** the stage clearly.
330	2	Possibility and Logical Conclusions	That song **may become** a big hit. He **couldn't be** at lunch. He's in a meeting. She **must practice** a lot. Barbara **must not eat** meat. She never buys it.
336	3	Permission and Requests	**May we sit** in these seats? **Could I have** your autograph?
344	**Review the Grammar**		
346	**Connect the Grammar to Writing**		

Unit Grammar Terms

modal: an auxiliary verb that adds a degree of certainty, possibility, or time to a verb. *May, might, can, could, will, would,* and *should* are common modals.
  ➢ *You **should** eat more vegetables.*
  ➢ *Julie **can** speak three languages.*

Student Learning Outcomes	• **Read** an article about using trash as art. • **Pronounce** *can* and *can't* appropriately. • **Find** and **edit** errors with modals of ability. • **Listen** to conversations about creative activities. • **Interview** classmates about their artistic abilities. • **Write** sentences about abilities.
Lesson Vocabulary	(adv.) absolutely (n.) attention (ph. v.) have trouble with (v.) organize (n.) trash (n.) aging (n.) awareness (v.) look forward to (n.) sculpture (adj.) wasteful

EXPLORE

1 READ, page 320   10 min.

• Have students look at the photo. Ask, *What are these sculptures made of? What do you think they represent?*

Be the Expert

• Born in Germany in 1939, HA Schult studied at the Academy of Art in Düsseldorf. He has created many other interesting art installations, including the Corona Beach Garbage Hotel, which is made of garbage found on European beaches and represents what could happen if we are not more environmentally conscious. Search these names for images to show students.

• There are 500 people in the Trash People exhibit. The exhibit has been traveling around the world for the past 18 years. As well as the places mentioned in the article, the statues have appeared in places including the Arctic, Rome, Cairo, and Washington, DC.

• **Expansion Activity:** If students have read about the underwater sculptures in Unit 10, page 264, ask them to compare the two types of sculptures. Ask, *How are the sculptures of Jason DeCairnes Taylor and those of HA Schult similar? How are they different? Which sculptures would you most like to see? Why?*

2 CHECK, page 321   5 min.

1. change people's behavior
2. thousand
3. less wasteful
4. still

3 DISCOVER, page 321   10 min.

A 1. is able to change
2. were able to view
3. could see
4. couldn't understand
5. aren't able to see; can learn

B

	Present or Future	Past
Affirmative	is able to change; can learn	were able to view; could see
Negative	aren't able to see	couldn't understand

• **Tip:** Write the sentences on the board and have students complete them with their own ideas.

LEARN

Chart 12.1, page 322   5 min.

• **Note:** Students are usually quick to understand the concept of *can* and *could* but may make errors with the form. Write the following sentences on the board for students to correct: *The boy cans run a mile. They don't can speak English. She could sang beautifully. We can to call you later.*

• **Note 3:** Have students ask and answer questions with *can* and *could*. Make sure that students use *can/can't* or *could/couldn't* in short answers, not *do/did*.

4 page 322   10 min.

1. can create
2. Can we see
3. could not/couldn't hear; could create
4. could not/couldn't discuss; can talk
5. cannot/can't understand
6. Could van Gogh write; could paint
7. could da Vinci do; could do
8. can I

Read the box or ask a student to read it. Explain that *can't* is the most informal of the three ways to write *can + not*.

5 PRONUNCIATION, page 323 — 10 min.

A 1. can   2. can't   3. can't   4. can   5. can

B *Answers will vary.*

Chart 12.2, page 324 — 5 min.

- **Note 3:** Explain that, in situations where *can* and *be able to* are both possible for the future, *be able to* is more formal than *can*. Have students think of situations where they would be more likely to use *be able to* (e.g., *in a job interview*).

6 page 324 — 10 min.

1. are/'re able to
2. is able to/will be able to
3. are; able to; are/'re able to
4. was not/wasn't able to; was able to
5. will be able to
6. is not/isn't able to/will not/won't be able to
7. was able to
8. are able to, weren't able to
9. will be able to
10. is/'s able to

Chart 12.3, page 325 — 5 min.

- **Note 1:** *Be able to* can convey the idea that something took effort, e.g., *He can play the piano well. He is able to play the piano well. Can't* and *not able to* have similar meanings, but *not able to* is often used to express frustration, e.g., *I can't understand her. I'm not able to understand her.* The second sentence conveys that the speaker has tried and failed to understand.

7 page 325 — 10 min.

1. was able to/could
2. wasn't able to/couldn't
3. was able to; wasn't able to/couldn't
4. Were you able to/Could you; wasn't/couldn't
5. was able to
6. were able to/could
7. was able to
8. were able to/could

9. was able to
10. wasn't able to/couldn't

- **Expansion Tip:** Have students talk about their own past abilities. Have them choose a year and write a list of 3–5 sentences about themselves at that age (e.g., *When I was five, I wasn't able to pronounce the letter "s." I could swim, but I couldn't ride a bike.*). Have students compare their lists with a partner, and then have them share some of the information that they learned with the class.

PRACTICE

8 page 326 — 10 min.

1. can play; Chris is able to play the piano fairly well.
2. could not/couldn't go; My parents were not/weren't able to go to the concert yesterday.
3. cannot/can't dance; Tanya hasn't been practicing, so she will not/won't be able to dance next week.
4. Could you understand; I could not/couldn't; A: Were you able to understand the actors last night? B: No, I was not/wasn't.
5. could not/couldn't find; I wasn't able to find the artist's biography on the website.
6. can finish; The children will be able to finish their paintings tomorrow.
7. cannot/can't teach; The professor will not/won't be able to teach the art class tomorrow.
8. could not/couldn't hear; I was not/wasn't able to hear the movie because people were talking.

9 LISTEN & SPEAK, page 326 — 20 min.

- **Tip:** Have students look at the photo of the sculpture and read the caption on page 327 before they listen to the audio. Explain to students that the conversation is between the director of an art museum or gallery and an assistant.

A 1. is not/isn't able to help
2. Are; able to come
3. will not/won't be able to get
4. were able to do
5. is/'s able to create
6. was not/wasn't able to see
7. will; be able to meet
8. will be able to relax

C ANALYZE THE GRAMMAR, page 327

1. cannot/can't   5. can
2. Can   6. could not/couldn't
3. cannot/can't   7. can
4. (were able to)   8. can

REAL ENGLISH, page 327

Have students work in pairs to write two short conversations about their plans for next Monday: (1) talking to their boss, the head of their school, or another person with whom they need to speak formally and (2) making plans with a friend. Have students act out the two conversations for the class. Remind students to pay attention to the pronunciation of can and can't.

10 EDIT, page 328   10 min.

• **Tip:** Before beginning the activity, explain that a podcast is an audio file that people can download. Call students' attention to the photo. Explain that this is a museum in New York City, and the interviewer has asked the visitors to the museum a question in order to hear different opinions.

Host: Welcome to the Guggenheim Museum in New York. This is Ava Paterson, and I'm talking to visitors here about this week's question: Can art ~~keeps~~ **keep** us young? What do you think, sir? Are people able **to** fight the effects of aging with creative activities?

Man: Yes, I think so. My grandfather was able to organize his thoughts easily, and he thought art helped him. He was a painter. A lot of older people have trouble with their memories. People with Alzheimer's disease sometimes can't remember their own families, for example. My grandfather was 93 when he died, and he ~~can~~ **could** remember absolutely everything! The last time I saw him, I ~~could~~ **was able to** ask him many questions about his life.

Host: And what do you think, miss? Can art have positive effects on people as they age?

Woman: Well, research shows that people ~~are~~ **will be** able to live longer in the future, but is art the reason? I'm not sure. I like to believe that it can help. I love to see and create art, so I hope when I'm older, I will **be** able to think clearly.

• **Expansion Tip:** Have students imagine that they were at the Guggenheim Museum, and the interviewer asked them the same questions. What would they say? Have students write 3–4 sentences and share their answers in small groups.

11 LISTEN, page 329   10 min.

1. F   3. T   5. F   7. T
2. T   4. T   6. T   8. F

12 APPLY, page 329   15 min.
Answers will vary.

• **Alternative Apply:** Have students work in groups of 3–4 to create a list of 10 interview questions for their classmates. Have them write five questions with *can/could* and five questions with *are/were/will be able to*. Make sure that each member of the group has a copy of the questions. Then pair each student with a partner from a different group. Have students interview each other and take notes on their responses. Finally, have students write about their partner and share their answers in small groups or with the class.

Student Learning Outcomes	• **Read** a radio interview about music in Latin America. • **Speak** with a classmate and make plans for after class. • **Write** sentences that show possibility. • **Complete** sentences to make logical conclusions. • **Write** and **speak** about logical conclusions.				
Lesson Vocabulary	(n.) audience (n.) beat	(n.) capital (adj. + p.) familiar with	(n.) hit (n.) instrument	(n.) melody (n.) performer	(n.) popularity (v.) spread

EXPLORE

1 READ, page 330   5 min.

• Explain that *folk music* is music that is traditional from a certain area.

Be the Expert

• This reading is about *nu-cumbia*, which began in the 1990s. As well as Colombia, Panama, and Argentina, bands in Peru, Mexico, and the United States are experimenting with this new sound and making it their own. In 1994, Selena's single, *Techno Cumbia* was one of the first attempts at *nu-cumbia*. Since then, other bands include Dengue, Dengue, Dengue; Bomba Estereo; DJ Javier Estrada; and Royal Highness.

• Search *La Yegros* (a singer-songwriter from Argentina) or some of the above names to find clips of music to play in class. Note: You may want to make sure that the videos are suitable before showing these in class.

• Ask students about folk music in their native countries. Can they hear the influence of older music in more modern songs? Have them explain their answers.

2 CHECK, page 331   5 min.

  1. a   2. b   3. a   4. b

3 DISCOVER, page 331   5 min.

A 1. may   3. must   5. could

    2. might not   4. may

B 1. may, might, could   2. must

• **Tip:** Write the following sentences on the board: *It must be raining. It might be raining.* Then say, *Sue comes to class and her hair is wet.* Ask, *It might be raining or it must be raining?* The answer is *might*. Then say, *She is shaking her umbrella and Bob walks into class wearing a raincoat.* Ask, *It might be raining or it must be raining?* The answer is *must*.

LEARN

Chart 12.4, page 332   5 min.

• **Note 1:** Remind students to use the base form of the verb following the modal.

• **Note 1:** To practice the differences between the modals, draw a stick figure on the board with a sad face. Ask students to brainstorm ideas about why the stick figure is sad. On the board, write full sentences with examples of each modal (e.g., *He might be lonely. He might not have any friends.*). Then draw a second stick figure of a person holding a box and facing the first person (e.g., *It could be a present. It couldn't be a new car because the box isn't big enough.*). Have students brainstorm more sentences about the situation and write these on the board as well.

• **Note:** Students may ask how to form sentences about possibility in the past. Explain that they will learn more about this in the future, but that past can be formed with the perfect tense (e.g., *He might have eaten too much.*).

4 page 332   10 min.

  1. Alisha could become a great DJ.

  2. Eric Clapton might play the guitar better than anyone else.

  3. *The Nutcracker* may be the best ballet I have ever seen.

  4. That website might provide free music.

  5. The art gallery could become more successful next year.

  6. His new movie could win a lot of prizes.

  7. La Yegros might soon have a lot more fans.

  8. Her latest album may surprise her followers.

5 ANALYZE THE GRAMMAR, page 333   10 min.

1. FP	3. PA	5. PA	7. FP
2. PA	4. PP	6. FP	8. PP

6 SPEAK, page 333   10 min.

Answers will vary.

Chart 12.5, page 334   5 min.

- **Notes 1 & 2:** Students may be hesitant to use *must/must not* in this context because they have already learned *must/must not* for obligation. Write the following sentences on the board and have students decide if they are obligation or logical conclusion: *Visitors must pay $5 admission. Your brother is an art historian, so he must know a lot about art. You must not touch the paintings. You must be hungry. You didn't eat anything.*

7 page 334   5 min.

- **Tip:** Before beginning this activity, make sure that students are aware of the cultural references. Bob Marley is a reggae musician. *Cats* is a musical.

1. must	5. must
2. must not	6. must
3. must	7. must
4. must not	8. must not

- **Expansion Tip:** In pairs, have students write their own sentences with logical conclusions. Have them include a blank for *must/must not*. Have them give their sentences to another pair to answer. Ask each group to share one interesting sentence with the class.

PRACTICE

8 page 334   10 min.

- **Tip:** Before beginning this activity, explain that *world music* refers to music from all over the world and *folk music* refers to music from a particular tradition.

1. must not	5. could
2. may	6. could be
3. might	7. Maybe
4. must	8. may not

9 WRITE & SPEAK, page 335   15 min.
Answers will vary.

10 APPLY, page 335   20 min.

A
1. United Kingdom	4. Jamaica
2. Japan	5. India
3. Portugal	

B *Answers will vary.*

- **Alternative Apply:** Have students look at photos of famous works of art. These can be from books or images online. Have students work in pairs and write sentences using *may (not), might (not), could (not),* or *must (not)* to make conclusions about the painting or the artist. Make sure that each pair keeps their painting hidden from the other students. Then display the pictures on the wall or on a desk. Have students choose two sentences that they have written and write these on the board, without revealing which picture they apply to. Have students read the sentences and try to match them to the correct painting.

Student Learning Outcomes	• **Read** three conversations that take place outside a theater. • **Ask** for and **give** permission using *may, can,* and *could.* • **Rewrite** informal questions using more formal modals. • **Practice** the pronunciation of *would you* and *could you.* • **Complete** a conversation using modals. • **Find** and **edit** errors in a conversation between a student and a professor. • **Role-play** situations that require asking for permissions and requests.
Lesson Vocabulary	(n.) autograph (n.) front (n.) microphone (n.) program (n.) speaker (v.) borrow (n.) fan (n.) play (v.) sign (n.) stage

EXPLORE

1 READ, page 336   5 min.

Be the Expert

- The term *autograph* comes from the Greek words *auto* (self) and *graph* (write). This is used to describe a person's handwritten signature, and usually refers to the signatures of famous people.

- One of the first known autographs was of El Cid, a Spanish nobleman and hero of the 11th century.

- Most people think of an autograph as a way to connect with someone famous. There are magazines and books written about autograph collecting, and stores that sell autographed items. People will pay a lot of money for autographs, and autograph dealers ask celebrities for autographs in order to make money. Because of this, some celebrities no longer sign autographs for their fans, or only sign a limited number.

- The 2013 pop song *Royals* by musical artist Lorde was inspired by a 1976 *National Geographic* photo of baseball player George Brett from the Kansas City Royals signing autographs for fans.

- **Expansion Activity:** Have students discuss autographs. Ask questions such as: *Have you ever asked a celebrity for an autograph. If so, what happened? If not, would you wait in line for an autograph? Would you pay a lot of money for an autograph? Why, or why not? If you were a celebrity, would you sign autographs? Why, or why not?*

2 CHECK, page 337   5 min.

  1. T   2. T   3. F   4. F   5. F

- **Tip:** Ask higher-level students to correct the false statements.

3 DISCOVER, page 337   10 min.

A 1. May   3. Can   5. Would

     2. would   4. will

B 1. 1, 3   2. 2, 4, 5

- **Tip:** Have students ask their classmates to borrow items. Then have them ask the same question with *lend*, e.g., *Can I borrow a piece of paper? Could you lend me a piece of paper?*

LEARN

Chart 12.6, page 338   5 min.

- **Note 2:** Students whose native languages have more specific ways to show formal and informal speech might miss some of the nuance that English has with polite speech. Point out that it is common to use *could* with a close friend or relative. The purpose is to convey that you understand you are asking something of this person. Explain that a person might say the following to the same friend: *Can I have a cookie? Could I borrow some money?* Ask students why these might be the right choices. Note that asking for money is usually a bigger favor than asking for a cookie.

- **Note 3:** Explain that when a sentence is about something that has already been decided, use *can* or *be allowed to* rather than *may.* For example: *You may begin the test* (right now). But, *We can/are able to use our dictionaries in class* (this is a rule that was established and that we all understood).

4 page 338   10 min.

A 1. may/can/could

2. may/can/could; may not/can't

3. may/can; may/can

4. may/can

5. may/can/could, may/can

6. may/can

B ANALYZE THE GRAMMAR, page 339

Answers will vary.

5 SPEAK, page 339   10 min.

Answers will vary.

- **Tip:** Explain that *No, you may not* or *No, you cannot* followed by an explanation for *why* something is not possible is a polite way to give the explanation.

- **Expansion Tip:** Have students who finish early ask and answer permission questions, e.g., *Can I borrow a piece of paper? Could we study together after class?*

Chart 12.7 page 339   5 min.

- **Note 3:** Explain to students that it is best to avoid using *won't* in a short answer. *Will you give me a ride home? No, I won't* means *I can, but I don't want to. I can't* or *I'm sorry/I'm afraid. . .* conveys to the listener that there is a reason why you are saying no. Explain to students that when they use the phrase *I'm afraid,* they need to continue with the next part of the sentence immediately. Model this by emphasizing: *I'm afraid I can't* rather than *I'm afraid (long pause) I can't.* Explain that the latter sounds as if you are scared, rather than using a term to describe that something isn't possible.

6 page 339   10 min.

A 1. Could you download the concert tickets?

2. Would you help me practice my lines for the play?

3. Could you listen to me play the new song I just learned?

4. Would you rent the new Wes Anderson movie?

5. Could you take our picture?

B SPEAK, page 340

Questions:

1. Could you download the concert tickets, please?

2. Would you help me practice my lines for the play, please?

3. Could you listen to me play the new song I just learned, please?

4. Would you rent the new Wes Anderson movie, please?

5. Could you take our picture, please?

Answers to the questions will vary.

> **REAL ENGLISH,** page 340
>
> Ask students to make a list of requests that they might make at a public place (e.g., at a restaurant: *Could I have some water, please? Could we have the check, please?*). Have students work in pairs and have them guess what place their partner is talking about? If time allows, practice responding to the requests as well.

7 PRONUNCIATION, page 340   10 min.

A 1. Could you tell me your full name?

2. Would you lend me five dollars?

3. Could you repeat the last question?

4. Would you speak more slowly?

5. Could you tell me the time?

6. Would you raise your hands in the air?

B *Answers will vary.*

PRACTICE

8 page 341   10 min.

A 1. Could/Can/May I take

2. problem

3. would you let

4. course

5. Could/Can/Would you try

6. Could/Can/Would you stand

7. Could/Can/Would you move

8. could/can/would you smile

9. could/can/may I see

10. can/may

11. Could/Can/Would you send

12. No

9 EDIT, page 342 — 10 min.

Kira: Excuse me, Professor Howard, may I ~~to~~ speak with you?

Professor: Yes, of course you may, Kira. What's the problem?

Kira: Well, it's about my report on John Coltrane. I spent a lot of time researching his life. I'm surprised at the low grade I received. ~~Would~~ **May/Could/Can** I ask you what I did wrong?

Professor: Yes, of course. If I remember correctly, you wrote too much about his life and not enough about his music and its influence on jazz. Could you come to my office to discuss it?

Kira: Yes, I ~~could~~ **can**. May I come in tomorrow or Friday?

Professor: Sure. ~~May~~ **Could/Can** you come and see me on Friday around 1:00 p.m.?

Kira: Um, I'm already seeing Dr. Stein then. ~~Would~~ **Could/Can** we talk at 1:30?

Professor: Yes, that's perfect, and would you please bring your report with you?

Kira: Yes, I ~~would~~ **will**. Thank you so much, Professor Howard. See you Friday.

- **Tip:** Explain that in U.S. universities, it is acceptable to ask a professor for more feedback on a paper or test, as long as it is done in a polite manner. This may differ from practices in other countries and students may be surprised by this cultural difference. Explain that although *can* and *could* are both correct for some of the corrections, *could* is more formal and thus more appropriate.

- **Expansion Tip:** Have students work in pairs to create a similar conversation between a student and an English language teacher. Have students act out their conversation for the class, and encourage them to pay attention to their pronunciation of the modals.

10 page 343 — 10 min.

A **Megan:** Hey, I'm looking forward to hearing you sing. <u>Can I help you set up your equipment?</u>

Angel: Thanks, that'll be great. <u>Will you put the microphone stand on the stage for me?</u>

Megan: Sure . . . Is this all right?

Angel: Yes, uh, <u>could you move it forward just a little?</u> It has to be in front of the speakers.

Megan: No problem.

B **SPEAK**, page 343
Answers will vary.

11 APPLY, page 343 — 25 min.
Answers will vary.

- **Expansion Tip:** Have students repeat one of the role-plays a number of times with different partners. Explain that they should speak for one minute, and then change partners when you say *switch*. Explain that by practicing the same scenario with different partners, they will become more comfortable with the language. When they have spoken to 3–4 partners, ask whether they were more confident by the end of the activity.

- **Alternative Apply:** Have students work in pairs. Have them think of some scenarios that could occur in a restaurant. Have them write conversations that could take place between a cook and a waiter, a waiter and a customer, and two customers who are conducting business over their lunch. Each conversation should include a request or permission and be more formal or less formal depending on who is talking.

1 page 344   10 min.

1. can't
2. Will you
3. was able to
4. I'm not able to
5. must
6. must not
7. you can
8. Will
9. Maybe
10. you'll be able to

2 LISTEN, page 344   10 min.

1. couldn't see; a
2. must not like; b
3. might buy; b
4. would you teach; b
5. may become; a
6. will be able to; a
7. could hear; b
8. can I use; b

3 EDIT, page 345   10 min.

• **Tip:** Before beginning this activity, explain what *ballet* is. If possible, search *Swan Lake ballet* or *Hee Seo*, and show students images or a short video clip.

Christine: What is your favorite art form, Joan?

Joan: Oh, ballet, without a doubt. I must ~~spending~~ spend half my money on ballet tickets!

Christine: Really? Could you explain why?

Joan: I appreciate the skill of the dancers. They must ~~not~~ work very hard to make it look so easy.

Christine: So, who is the best dancer you've seen?

Joan: Last summer, I ~~could~~ was able to get tickets to see South Korean ballerina Hee Seo dance in New York. She is amazing! She is able to communicate many emotions just with her movements. I think she could become one of the best ballet dancers of all time. This summer she is going to appear in *Swan Lake*, which I love. Unfortunately, I ~~maybe~~ may be out of the country then. If I'm here, I'm going to get tickets for the first night.

Christine: Would you ~~to~~ let me know when they go on sale? From what you say, I'm sure Hee Seo ~~might~~ must/will/would be amazing to watch.

4 SPEAK, page 345   15 min.
Answers will vary.

• **Tip:** Have students compare their charts in pairs and note what is similar and what is different. Explain that *art* can refer to any type of art form, from painting to dancing ballet.

• **Expansion Tip:** After their discussion, have students expand on their answers by writing 1–2 paragraphs. Encourage students to use modals where appropriate.

Connect the Grammar to Writing

1 READ & NOTICE THE GRAMMAR, page 346 *25 min.*

A *Answers will vary.*

B

Past	Present or Future
. . . I couldn't look at the world . . . I was able to see my place in the world . . .	. . . movie could change the way you see . . . . . . it might turn your view . . . They aren't able to get back . . . . . . and they will probably not . . . . . . viewers can experience floating . . . You may feel . . . . . . you too might leave . . .

C *Answers may vary. Sample answer:*

Title/Name: Gravity

Main characters: two astronauts

Basic idea: Disaster strikes while they are on a mission.

Setting (place): in space while on a space walk

Artistic quality: 3-D movie; can experience floating in space

Possible effects on viewer: could change your view of the world; may feel off balance; might turn your view of the universe upside down; might end up with a new sense of your place in the universe

2 BEFORE YOU WRITE, page 347 *15 min.*
Answers will vary.

3 WRITE, page 347 *25 min.*

WRITING FOCUS, page 347

Have students make a two-column chart with *Italics* and *Quotation Marks* as headings. Ask them to work in pairs to find at least one example of each type of title mentioned in this writing focus. Have students look through the units of the textbook that they have completed and make a list of the titles that they find. Have them compare their charts with another group and discuss the items on their list.

- **Tip:** Students may have a difficult time thinking of ideas for this writing activity. Model the thinking process for the students by giving an example of a book, movie, or song that is meaningful to you, explaining your choice.

- **Alternative Writing:** Remind students that reviewers don't always like what they see, read, or hear. Have them choose something that they strongly disliked. Ask, *Why didn't you like it? What would you have done to improve it?* Model an example. Have students write a negative review and encourage them to use modals where possible. Then have them share these reviews in groups of 3–4 and find out whether their classmates agree with them or not.

Modals: Part 2

Unit Opener

Photo: Have students look at the photo and read the caption. Ask, *What do you think* capoeira *is? What skills do you think you need to do this? Do people do this in your city?*

Location: New York City has more than 1700 parks throughout the five boroughs, and they include everything from wetlands and woodlands to swimming pools and skate parks. Central Park is the most well-known park, but Pelham Bay Park Bronx is the largest at more than three times the size of Central Park.

Theme: This unit is about sports. Some of the topics discussed are judo, folk racing, racing between men and horses, and tennis.

Page	Lesson	Grammar	Examples
350	1	Necessity and Prohibition	You **must arrive** on time. **Do** you **have to leave**? You **can't drive** without a license. I **don't have to take** the test.
359	2	Advisability and Expectation	You **ought to exercise** regularly to stay fit. He **shouldn't play** in the game. She's **supposed to call** in a few minutes.
366	**Review the Grammar**		
368	**Connect the Grammar to Writing**		

Unit Grammar Terms

base form: the form of the verb without *to* or any endings such as *-ing, -s,* or *-ed.*
➢ *eat, sleep, go, walk*

modal: an auxiliary verb that adds a degree of certainty, possibility, or time to a verb. *May, might, can, could, will, would,* and *should* are common modals.
➢ *You **should** eat more vegetables.*
➢ *Julie **can** speak three languages.*

LESSON 1 · Necessity and Prohibition

Student Learning Outcomes	• **Read** a conversation on an online forum about judo. • **Listen** to the reduced pronunciation of *have to, has to,* and *have got to.* • **Write** original sentences about your school expressing necessity or prohibition. • **Listen** to a radio feature about folk racing. • **Edit** and **correct** errors in modal usage in an article. • **Speak** with a partner about a to-do list using modals and modal-like expressions. • **Say** sentences that express necessity or prohibition about personal activities.
Lesson Vocabulary	(v.) apologize (adj.) disciplined (n.) license (n.) opponent (n.) safety (n.) coach (adv.) fairly (n.) martial arts (adv.) respectfully (n.) silence

EXPLORE

1 READ, page 350   15 min.

• **Tip:** Elicit or provide an explanation of what an *online forum* is (e.g., *a place on the Internet where people can communicate about a topic*). Have students look at the photos and read the captions. Ask, *What is judo? Where is it popular? Why do you think people like it?*

• Have students use context cues to guess the meaning of *opponent, martial arts, disciplined,* and *respectfully.*

Be the Expert

• Judo has its origins in *jujitsu,* a martial art that dates back to 16th-century Japan. In judo, participants use only their bodies to defend themselves. Competitors learn how to throw and grapple. Judo became an Olympic sport in 1964. The International Judo Federation includes more than 180 countries. Judo is good exercise—it burns 340 calories per session.

• Karate is also a martial art, but it is more focused on striking one's opponent than on throwing or grappling. Judo is primarily defensive, whereas karate can be more about offense. Suggest that students research the two sports and use a t-chart to compare and contrast them.

2 CHECK, page 351   5 min.

   1. F   2. F   3. T   4. F   5. F

• **Tip:** Have students identify where they found the answers in the text.

• **Expansion Tip:** Have students write three comprehension questions about the information, and then take turns asking and answering their questions with a partner.

3 DISCOVER, page 351   5 min.

A 1. don't have to   3. cannot   5. must not

     2. have to   4. may not   6. must

B 1. 2, 6   2. 1   3. 3, 4, 5

• **Tip:** Point out that when something is necessary or required, we use modals and modal-like expressions of necessity (e.g., *You have to be careful. They must behave respectfully.*).

LEARN

Chart 13.1, page 352   10 min.

• **Note 1:** Point out that *must* will not change form with different subjects, but *have to* will. Their meanings are the same, but their forms are different.

• **Notes 2, 3 & 4:** Point out that the expressions are listed in the general order of formality with the most formal first. Elicit or provide other examples of each expression used appropriately (e.g., *You must show identification when you fly. I have to get gas. He's got to apply soon.*).

• **Note 5:** To practice the past tense, have students rewrite all of the sample sentences in notes 1–4 in the simple past.

• **Note 6:** To practice questions and focus on using the correct auxiliary, have students write *Yes/No* questions for the sample sentences in notes 1–4. Then have students practice asking and answering the questions in pairs.

4 page 352 5 min.

1. must/have to	6. had to
2. have to	7. have to
3. must/have to	8. had to
4. have to	9. 've got to
5. had to	10. had

- **Expansion Tip:** Ask, *Where are the conversations happening? How do you know?* Have students work in small groups to write conversations for another setting (e.g., *a store, a classroom, a rental car agency, an airport*). Tell them to use at least one example of each expression in the notes. Then have students perform their conversations for the class.

5 page 353 5 min.

1. Students must arrive

2. Do we have to take off; You must remove

3. we have to wear; It has to be

4. you have to remove

5. you must/have to bring; I have/'ve got to hurry

- **Expansion Tip:** Have students look at the photos. Working in pairs, have them write three sentences about kung fu in China, using modals of necessity (e.g., *The children must stand in rows when they practice. They have to move at the same time. They must wear black uniforms.*).

Chart 13.2, page 354 10 min.

- **Notes 1 & 3:** Students sometimes have difficulty with the different meanings of *must not* and *don't/ doesn't have to.* Provide more examples and ask them which expression is appropriate (e.g., *It is OK to wear anything you want to school. You ___ wear a uniform. It is very dangerous to walk on the subway tracks. You ___ walk there.*).

- **Note 3:** Review the other uses of *can* and *can't* (for possibility and ability). Have students write sentences using the modal in different ways, and then put students in pairs to identify the meaning of the sentences (e.g., *I can't swim—I never learned.* ability; *He can't be in Japan—I just talked to him. They can't use a dictionary during the test.* prohibition.).

- **Note 4:** Call on students to put the example sentences in the past tense using *didn't have to* or *couldn't.* Then have students work in pairs to take turns, with one partner saying a sentence of prohibition or lack of necessity in the present as their partner responds with the sentence in the past.

- **Tip:** To help students practice using the guidelines in notes 1–5, write sentences containing errors on the board and have students correct them.

6 page 354 10 min.

1. must not	6. must not
2. must not	7. don't have to
3. doesn't have to	8. couldn't
4. can't	9. have to
5. didn't have to	10. may not

7 **WRITE & SPEAK,** page 354 5 min.
Answers will vary.

- **Expansion Tip:** Have students work in pairs to write guidelines for new students attending their school. They should include what is required, prohibited, and not necessary. Have each pair join another pair to compare ideas. If your students come from different countries, have them write guidelines for schools in their countries and compare ideas with someone from another country.

PRACTICE

8 **PRONUNCIATION,** page 355 5 min.

A 15 min.

1. have to	3. have got to	5. has to
2. has got to	4. have to	6. have to

B *Answers will vary.*

- **Alternative Speaking & Writing:** Call on students to say sentences with reduced forms of *have to* and *have got to* aloud as their classmates write the sentences with full forms.

9 page 355 5 min.

A
1. do we have to	5. can't
2. don't have to	6. can't
3. 've got	7. does he have
4. had to	8. 've got to

- **Tip:** Have students practice the conversation in pairs. Remind them to use reduced pronunciation for *have to, has to,* and *have got to.* After practicing, have volunteers say the conversations in front of the class. Correct pronunciation as necessary to focus on the reduced forms.

10 page 356 5 min.
Answers may vary. Sample answers:

1. Rosa couldn't eat sweets all weekend.

2. She didn't have to meet her study group.

3. She had to work from 8–noon on Saturday.

4. She doesn't have to go to work.

5. She can't/must not forget tennis practice.

6. She has to/must write a draft of her essay.

11 SPEAK, page 356　　　　　　　　　10 min.
Answers will vary.

- **Alternative Speaking:** Have students find new partners and report on their first partner's activities using modals and modal-like expressions.

12 LISTEN, page 357　　　　　　　　　10 min.

- **Tip:** Share some background information about folk racing to create interest. Folk racing is popular in Sweden and other Scandinavian countries. It is unusual in that it uses old cars, and the cars cannot be expensive. Other unusual car races around the world include: soapbox derbies in the U.S., in which the cars used to be made out of actual soap boxes; another U.S. race in which ambulances race while towing cars; the Gumball Run, which takes racers across countries if not continents; China's Macau GP, which runs on city streets; and perhaps the most dangerous, the Dakar Rally that begins in Paris and ends in Senegal, Africa.

A 1. b　　2. c　　3. b　　4. b　　5. a　　6. a

B 1. have to　　　　　　4. can't

2. doesn't have to　　　5. must not/can't

3. couldn't　　　　　　6. must not/can't

13 EDIT, page 358　　　　　　　　　5 min.

You ~~may not~~ **don't have to** be an expert rock climber to enjoy Yosemite National Park, but it doesn't hurt. According to climbers, if you want the best views, you must ~~to~~ climb some of the park's famous mountains. If you are a climber, you have to visit Camp 4, the base camp where many famous climbs have started.

Lynn Hill arrived at Camp 4 for the first time as a 15-year-old in the 1970s. She was a gymnast, so she ~~hadn't~~ **didn't have** to learn to control her movements. She soon showed great ability.

In her thirties, she came back to Camp 4 with a goal. To reach her goal, she had ~~got~~ to 'free climb' the challenging route—the Nose, within 24 hours. Free climbing means it's just you and the rock. You have to put your hands and feet into cracks in the rock, and you ~~don't have to~~ **must not/cannot/can't** use ropes or other equipment. At times during her climb, Hill ~~must~~ **had to** hang by just her fingers. She completed her famous climb in 23 hours.

14 APPLY, page 358　　　　　　　　　20 min.
Answers will vary.

- **Alternative Speaking:** Have students research other races or competitions online and prepare a 2–3 minute presentation. Tell them to include tips and requirements for participants in their talks. Encourage them to use modals as often as possible in their presentations. Write these questions on the board as prompts: *Where does the competition take place? Who are the participants? What do participants have to do? What are they allowed to do? What is prohibited/not allowed? What are things they can do, but they don't have to do to compete?*

Student Learning Outcomes	• **Read** a conversation about a race where participants compete against horses. • **Give** advice using *should* and *shouldn't*. • **Write** and **speak** about what people are supposed to do. • **Identify** the correct modals required to express advisability and expectation in sentences. • **Edit** a survey to **correct** errors in modals. • **Discuss** answers to a survey.
Lesson Vocabulary	(v.) advise (n.) beat (n.) confidence (adj.) light (v.) register (n.) ankle (v.) compete (n.) entertainment (adj.) maximum (v.) risk

EXPLORE

1 READ, page 359   15 min.

• Have students look at the photo and read the caption. Ask, *Have you heard of this race? Is it something you'd like to do? Why, or why not? Why do you think runners compete in this race?*

• **Tip:** Have students find the words *beat, surface,* and *confidence* in the reading and use context to guess their meanings.

Be the Expert

• *The Guardian*, a British newspaper, calls the *Man versus Horse* race perhaps the most eccentric race in the world. It is a yearly competition in Wales that began in 1980. The course was changed in 1982 to make the competition between humans and horses a bit more fair. Huw Lobb was the first man to beat a horse in the race in 2004 with a time of 2 hours and 5 minutes. He won 25,000 pounds in prize money. In 2014, competitors began using electronic timers to improve accuracy.

• Llanwrtyd Wells, Wales, began as a spa town that developed around a local spring. The town has fewer than a thousand residents and is one of the smallest chartered towns in Great Britain.

• The horses have to stop periodically during the race to be checked by a vet, who makes sure they are healthy. Such vet checks take a few minutes, and the human runners are able to continue on. In 2009, the time spent at vet check was deducted from the overall race times. Ask, *Do you think the vet check times should be deducted from overall race times? Why, or why not?*

2 CHECK, page 360   5 min.

    1. F   2. T   3. T   4. F   5. T   6. F

• **Tip:** Ask higher-level students to correct the false statements.

3 DISCOVER, page 360   5 min.

A   1. I'm supposed to (run) in the "Man versus Horse" race in Wales in a few months.

    2. Well, you shouldn't (run) on hills all the time.

    3. Hills are important, but you ought to (run) on flat surfaces as well.

    4. And you should (do) at least one run that's longer than the race.

    5. So, you are supposed to (keep) away from the horses, right?

B   1. 2, 3, 4   2. 1, 5

• **Tip:** To ensure that students understand the terms *advice* and *expectation*, ask, *What is one piece of advice you might give the runners in this race? What is one expectation you might have if you ran in the race? For example, do you expect it to be difficult?*

LEARN

Chart 13.3, page 361   10 min.

• **Note 1:** *Should* is a modal, and like all modals, it does not change form with the subject. It is followed by the base form of the verb in the present tense. *Ought to* is an expression that has a similar meaning to *should*. It also doesn't change form with the subject and is always followed by the base form. *Ought to* is used mostly in affirmative statements.

• **Tip:** Have students work in pairs to come up with as many sentences as they can with *should* and *ought to* to give advice for staying healthy. Set a time limit of two minutes. Ask volunteers to write their ideas on the board.

4 page 361   10 min.

1. Should; should/ ought to
2. shouldn't
3. should/ought to
4. shouldn't; should/ ought to
5. shouldn't
6. should/ought to
7. shouldn't
8. should

- **Expansion Tip:** Have students work in pairs to create a similar advice sheet for an activity they know well (e.g., *swimming at the beach, hiking in the mountains, skiing*), following the model. Then have pairs exchange their advice sheets with another pair to write sentences using *should, shouldn't,* and *ought to*. When students finish, have them check their sentences with the other pair.

5 SPEAK, page 362   10 min.

A 1. c   2. d   3. a   4. b

B *Answers will vary.*

- **Expansion Tip:** Divide the class into two teams. Tell each student to make up three sentences that express a need for advice as in exercise **A**. Have one team form a circle facing out. Have the other team form a circle outside the inner circle and face in. Each student should be facing a partner. Direct students to take turns saying their sentences as their partners give advice in response. After 30–60 seconds, direct the outside circle to move one position to the right and repeat the activity. Continue a few more times. Encourage students to use different advice with each new partner if possible.

> **REAL ENGLISH, page 362**
>
> Have students bring in examples of *should* and *ought to* that they read or heard. Encourage them to note the entire sentence surrounding the expressions. With the class, tally the results of their findings to confirm that *should* is more common than *ought to*.

Chart 13.4, page 362   10 min.

- **Notes 1 & 2:** Point out that in these expressions the verb *be* does change form to coincide with the subject and to reflect tense. The rest of the expression *supposed to* + base form remains unchanged.

- **Note 2:** In the present and future, *be supposed to* indicates an expectation. In the past, it indicates an unmet expectation. To reinforce this idea, have students work individually to list three things they did not do last week that were expected of them. Call on volunteers to share their sentences and give an explanation (e.g., *I was supposed to finish the*

research paper, but I couldn't find enough sources. We were supposed to visit Kate, but she got sick.).

6 page 362   5 min.

1. are supposed to be
2. are not/aren't supposed to kick
3. Is, supposed to win
4. is supposed to call
5. was not/wasn't supposed to arrive
6. is supposed to go
7. Is, supposed to train
8. was supposed to drive
9. were supposed to arrive
10. are not/aren't supposed to wear

7 WRITE & SPEAK, page 363   10 min.
Answers will vary.

- **Expansion Tip:** Write these roles on the board: *parents, teachers, government officials, good students, responsible citizens.* Have students work in pairs or small groups to come up with expectations for each category. Then ask them to think of examples where each expectation was not met (e.g., *Government officials aren't supposed to take bribes. X wasn't supposed to take bribes, but he received $100,000 in gifts and cash.*).

PRACTICE

8 page 363   5 min.

1. shouldn't; should/ought to
2. was supposed to
3. ought to
4. isn't supposed to/shouldn't
5. 'm supposed to
6. should
7. ought to/should
8. wasn't supposed to

9 page 364   20 min.

- **Tip:** To help students anticipate content, after they look at the photo and read the caption, ask them to predict things participants should and shouldn't do.

1. was supposed to be
2. should call
3. shouldn't worry
4. Should I call
5. ought to learn
6. It's supposed to be
7. ought to provide
8. are supposed to use
9. Should I try

- **Alternative Speaking:** Have students work in pairs to create conversations about a different topic using all of the phrases in the box. Ask volunteers to perform the conversations for the class, and have the class vote on the most creative one.

10 EDIT, page 365   5 min.

This month's online survey was about the state of modern sports. Here are some of the replies we received to our questions.

1. Should top athletes ~~to~~ earn millions of dollars a year?

Tim in Texas: No, I think it's gotten crazy. There ought to be a maximum salary in every sport.

Gene in Georgia: Yes, I think so. Athletes should earn a fair amount. Sports stars are supposed **to** provide entertainment for millions of people. That is worth a lot of money. Also, college athletes don't earn any money, but they risk a lot. They should ~~to~~ get paid, too.

2. Should there be so much advertising in sports?

Tim in Texas: I understand the need for advertising—sports are a very expensive business. However, there ought to be more control.

Gene in Georgia: Sports **are** supposed to be attractive to fans, and advertising adds a lot of color to events. There shouldn't be more control.

3. Should children compete or ~~ought~~ should they just have fun?

Tim in Texas: Small children are suppose**d** to enjoy sports. They ought to concentrate on learning skills, not winning games.

Gene in Georgia: All sports **are** supposed to produce stars for world championships. If we want that to happen, then competition should start as early as possible.

- **Alternative Writing & Speaking:** Have students work in groups of four. Tell each student to think of a question with *should* to ask about sports, competition, or games, and write the question at the top of a piece of paper. Direct them to write their answer to the question, and then pass the paper to the next student to answer the question. When all students have answered the questions, have them discuss their ideas in small groups, and then share with the class.

11 APPLY, page 365   15 min.

Answers will vary.

- **Expansion Tip:** Have students research the pros and cons of one of these topics: competitive sports for young children, athletic scholarships for students, government support for athletes, sport requirements in secondary school. Tell students to prepare a 2–3 minute presentation on their topic and present it in a small group or to the whole class.

1 page 366   5 min.

   1. may not/can't/must not

   2. can't

   3. must/have to

   4. didn't have to

   5. 'm supposed to

   6. ought to/has to/should

   7. had to

   8. may not/can't

2 **LISTEN,** page 366   10 min.

1. People expect me	6. must
2. necessary	7. ought to
3. must	8. necessary
4. should	9. can't
5. didn't go	10. prohibited

3 **WRITE,** page 366   15 min.

Answers will vary.

4 **EDIT,** page 367   10 min.

   Perhaps, like many tennis players, you love playing the game, but hate serving. Well, good news! You don't have **to** feel that way anymore! We asked our readers to share their advice on serving like a pro. Here are the results.

- You shouldn't practice during a competition. You ought **to** practice your serve only when you don't have to worry about winning or losing.

- You ~~got~~ have/have got/'ve got to relax. Serving ought to be easy, but it can be very difficult if you are nervous.

- You must **not** take your eye off the ball! You should watch it all the way from your hand until you hit it.

- You shouldn't throw the ball too high. You're not supposed **to** wait a long time for the ball to drop. If you do that, you are throwing it too high.

- You ~~don't have to~~ should not/shouldn't throw the ball straight up. Instead, you should ~~to~~ throw the ball slightly to your right, if you are right-handed. Left-handers should throw to the left.

- You must not be afraid of your serve. It's the only time in tennis that you have complete control of what happens. Serving **is** supposed to be fun!

5 **SPEAK,** page 367   15 min.

Answers will vary.

1 READ & NOTICE THE GRAMMAR,
page 368   20 min.

- **Tip:** Have students look at the photo. Ask them to make predictions about what the student wrote.

A *Answers will vary.*

B Necessity: You **must practice** to become advanced; First, you **have to learn** to control the board on small hills.
Advisability: In fact, you **should rent** a board at first.

C Topic: → **Opinion:**
Snowboarding   You should try it!

Reason 1: → **Support/Explanation:**
great exercise   It strengthens your muscles and heart.

Reason 2: → **Support/Explanation:**
easy to get   Instructors are easy
started   to find, and you don't have to buy a lot of equipment.

2 BEFORE YOU WRITE, page 369   15 min.
Answers will vary.

- **Tip:** Brainstorm a list of sports with the class and write their ideas on the board. This will help them identify a sport they want to write about.

WRITING FOCUS, page 369

Have students look at exercise **13** on page 358 and identify the sentences that relate to the reader and sentences that state an opinion clearly.

3 WRITE, page 369   15 min.

- **Alternative Writing:** Have students research the pros and cons of one of these topics (or use their research from the Expansion Tip for exercise **11** on on page 365): competitive sports for young children, athletic scholarships for students, government support for athletes, sport requirements in secondary school. Tell students to use a chart like the one in exercise **1C** to organize the ideas for their opinion paper before writing. Students can then write an opinion essay on the pros and cons of their topic of choice.

Verbs

Unit Opener

Photo: Have students look at the photo and read the caption. Ask, *When was this photo taken? At the time, what made these phones special? How are these phones different from phones today?* Have students point out as many differences as possible.

Location: In 1964, people were invited to test a new invention called *Mod 1*, the picturephone, at Disneyland and at the New York World's Fair. However, many people didn't like it. They thought the machinery was too big and the picture was too small. In 1993, *Model 70* allowed people to communicate via computer screen, and this was received better than the *Mod 1*.

Theme: The theme of this unit is innovations. Have students look through the photos in the unit. Ask, *Which photo do you want to know more about? Why?*

Page	Lesson	Grammar	Examples
372	1	Transitive and Intransitive Verbs	Jen and Joe **rented a car** on their vacation. They **arrived** in the evening. He **sent** an e-mail to **his parents**. She **bought** a gift for **her brother**.
382	2	Phrasal Verbs	I **found out** the meaning of the word. Jen and Joe **got on** the flight to Beijing. Nancy **showed up** ten minutes late. Jack **looked** the word **up**. He **looked** it **up**.
390	**Review the Grammar**		
392	**Connect the Grammar to Writing**		

Unit Grammar Terms

direct object: a noun or pronoun that receives the action of the verb.
  ➤ Aldo asked a **question**.
  ➤ Karen helped **me**.

indirect object: indirect object is an object that receives the direct object.
  ➤ I gave **my mother** the present.

inseparable phrasal verb: a phrasal verb that cannot have an object noun or pronoun between its two parts (verb + particle). The verb and the particle always stay together.
  ➤ I **ran into** a friend in the library.
  ➤ Do you and your coworkers **get along**?

intransitive verb: a verb that cannot be followed by a direct object.
  ➤ We didn't **agree**.
  ➤ The students **smiled** and **laughed**.

phrasal verb: a verb and a particle that function as a single verb.
  ➤ **Turn off** the light when you leave.
  ➤ She's **figured out** the answer.

separable phrasal verb: a phrasal verb that can have a noun or a pronoun (object) between its two parts (verb + particle).
  ➤ **Turn** the light **off**.
  ➤ **Turn off** the light.

transitive verb: a verb that is followed by a direct object.
  ➤ We **took** an umbrella.

Student Learning Outcomes	• **Read** an article about cars without drivers. • **Identify** appropriate prepositions in an article about French chef Nicolas Appert and in a conversation about package deliveries by drones. • **Listen** to information about innovations in history and **complete** a chart. • **Write** sentences using direct and indirect objects. • **Discuss** with a partner whether drone deliveries are a good idea. • **Find** and **edit** errors in a conversation about an eyewear innovation. • **Write** a paragraph about an unusual invention.
Lesson Vocabulary	(adj.) automated (v.) blame (adj.) helpless (adv.) instantly (v.) react (adv.) automatically (n.) delivery (adj.) innovative (v.) permit (v.) reduce

EXPLORE

1 READ, page 372   5 min.

• Have students look at the photos and read the title. Ask, *Do you think allowing cars without drivers is a good idea? Why, or why not?* Have students read the article, and then ask if their opinions have changed.

Be the Expert

• Google is one company pioneering self-driving cars. The cars are programmed with very well-defined maps, and then the computers in the cars adjust this information as necessary, based on the actual situation on the road. As of April 2014, the test cars had driven 700,000 miles. Originally, each car needed to have a human driver in the driving seat. However, in June 2014, Google began to test a new kind of self-driving car that does not have a steering wheel or pedals.

• Sebastian Thrum, one of the inventors of Google Street View, is currently engineering self-driving cars. When he was 18, his best friend was killed in a car accident. Since then, Thrum has dedicated his life to reducing car accidents. He explains that most accidents are due to human error. Robotic sensors could eliminate these errors. He also argues that driverless cars would cut back on traffic jams, allowing commuters more free time, and reducing fuel consumption.

• Videos of self-driving cars show the cars as they stop for pedestrians and avoid animals in the road. Search *self-driving car video* for an example of a car moving without a driver.

2 CHECK, page 373   5 min.

1. b   2. b   3. c   4. b

3 DISCOVER, page 373   10 min.

• **Tip:** Before beginning this exercise, it may be helpful to remind students that a direct object is a noun or pronoun that receives the action of the verb.

A 1. difficult moral questions

    2. their passengers

    3. X

    4. driverless cars

    5. X

    6. its computer program

    7. X

    8. an instant response

    9. direction

    10. the morally wrong choice

B No

• **Tip:** On the board, write the three verbs from exercise **A** that don't take a direct object and group them with nouns as follows: *sun/appear/ sky, we/react/news,* and *story/happen/my family.* Ask students to create sentences with these words. Explain that these verbs are *intransitive,* and are followed by a prepositional phrase or adverb, not a direct object. Have students circle the prepositions.

LEARN

Chart 14.1, page 374   5 min.

- **Note 2:** Because verbs in other languages may not follow the same rules as English verbs with the same meaning, some students may find this grammar point challenging. Have students work in groups to create a two-column chart listing verbs that are usually used transitively and intransitively. Students can begin by listing the verbs in exercise **3** and note 2 in their charts. They can then add their own verbs. When there are 10–15 verbs in each column, have students compare their lists with lists from another group and see if they agree with their categorization.

- **Note:** Have students decide which of the following sentences are incorrect: *The engineers arrived quickly. They traveled plane. The kids rode the car. They liked.* Ask them to make corrections based on what they have learned from the chart. Note that students will need to add prepositions or objects sentences 2–4 (*by; in; it*).

4 page 374   10 min.

1. T; Eve always tries (the latest things).

2. T; Last week, she tested (a driverless car).

3. I; She traveled to the beach in the car.

4. I; She slept for about 30 minutes.

5. I; Then, a dog ran in front of the car.

6. T; Luckily, the car didn't hit (the dog).

7. I; Eve went to the store.

8. I; She arrived safely.

9. T; However, she didn't like (the car).

10. T; Eve won't buy (a driverless car).

- **Expansion Tip:** Have students write *Wh-* questions for the sentences in exercise **4**, e.g., 1. *What does Eve always try?* 3. *Where did Eve travel?* (latest things; to the beach) Make sure that students pay attention to transitive and intransitive verbs as they create their questions. Have students ask and answer the questions in pairs.

5 page 374   10 min.

1. a. T; the meeting	5. a. T; the class
b. I	b. I
2. a. I	6. a. I
b. T; the windows	b. T; us
3. a. T; the new car	7. a. T; the car door
b. I	b. I
4. a. I	8. a. I
b. T; the class	b. T; your tires

Chart 14.2, page 375   5 min.

- **Note:** Students may be confused that verbs with similar meanings follow different grammatical rules. The most common example of this is *say* versus. *tell*. (Correct: *I told my mother my password.* Incorrect: *I said my mother my password.*)

- **Note 1:** Students also may be confused because *to* can be used either to introduce an indirect object or as part of an infinitive of purpose. Compare: *He sold his bike to buy a car. He sold his bike to a friend.* Point out that students should check to see whether a verb or a noun follows the direct object. In sentence 1, the verb *buy* follows *to*, so *to* is part of an infinitive. In sentence 2, the noun *a friend* follows *to*, so it introduces an indirect object.

- **Note 3:** Point out that the prepositions at the end of the example questions are necessary. Otherwise they don't make sense: *Who did he send it? Who did you buy it?* To illustrate this point, write the examples on the board, and circle the preposition in the question and in the long answer. Then write two other sentences and have students write *who* questions for each: *She painted a picture for her sister. Her sister showed the picture to her friend.*

6 READ, WRITE & SPEAK, page 376   5 min.

- **Tip:** To create interest before reading, have students look at the photos. Ask, *Do you eat food from cans or jars? Why do people preserve their food in this way?* Elicit the meaning of *go bad* in this context (become rotten).

A
1. for	3. for	5. for	7. to
2. to	4. to	6. to	8. to

B 1. provide healthy food (for)

2. offered a prize (to)

3. solve the problem (for)

4. showed his ideas (to)

5. keep food safe (for)

6. gave the prize (to)

7. send fresh food (to)

8. explain the reasons (to)

C *Answers will vary.*

- **Expansion Tip:** Have students work in pairs to write 3–4 quiz questions about the article. Encourage students to create questions with *to/ for* and indirect objects (e.g., *Who did Appert need to provide fresh food for?*). Have students ask and answer their questions with a new partner.

Chart 14.3, page 377   5 min.

- **Note:** This grammar point can be difficult for students because other languages, including French and Spanish, do not have the same strict rules for indirect object placement. To practice word order, write down sentences from the chart and cut up each word in the sentence. Create one set of cut-up words for each group of 3–4 students. Have groups order the sentences using the rules they have learned, and then open their books to check their answers.

- **Note 1:** It may be helpful to explain that the verbs that follow this pattern are usually short, not long verbs. Compare these sentences: *She showed me a website to use. She recommended a website for me to use.*

7 page 377   10 min.

1. my cousin my e-book reader.

2. her husband the latest smartphone.

3. his boss the new product design.

4. me the new Internet password?

5. her professor her homework assignment.

6. her friend the article about robots.

7. me a new tablet.

8. my coworker the files.

- **Expansion Tip:** Have students reflect on what they have done during the past week. First, elicit a list of verbs they may want to use to describe their experiences (e.g., *sent, lent, got, e-mailed, bought, made)*, and write them on the board. Have students use the verbs to write 3–4 true sentences about themselves with direct and indirect objects. Then have students read their sentences to a partner. The partner should ask one follow-up question.

Model the activity by writing a sentence on the board (e.g., *Yesterday I sent my niece a birthday card.*). Elicit follow-up questions such as: *How old is she?*

8 page 378   10 min.

1. me a car/a car for me

2. me his car/his car to me

3. it to my brother

4. my grandfather a photo of it/a photo of it to my grandfather

5. me a nice e-mail

6. my sister a card/a card for my sister

7. her a card/a card for her

8. her the card/the card to her

9. it to my sister

PRACTICE

9 page 378   10 min.

1. a/b   3. c   5. a/c   7. a/b/c

2. a/c   4. a/c   6. a/b/c   8. a/b

- **Tip:** Encourage students to use the charts from the lesson to review the rules. Model the first question. Read the sentence and ask, *What is the verb?* Explain that *cause* means make something happen. Ask, *Do you think* cause *is transitive or intransitive?* Explain that it is transitive because you need to know what it is that makes something happen. Have students compare answers in groups of three before reviewing with the full class. Encourage students to explain why they arrived at their answers.

10 **READ & SPEAK,** page 379   10 min.

A 1. for   3. to   5. to   7. for

2. Ø   4. Ø   6. Ø   8. to

B *Answers will vary.*

- **Expansion Tip:** Have students work in two groups as follows: Group A—employees who work for the drone company and believe that this is a good system. Group B—customers who are deciding whether to order from their company. Have the employees write at least three reasons why the drones are a good idea. Have the customers write at least three questions. Then pair each student from Group A with a student from Group B. Have them role-play a telephone call where a customer wants to find out more about the drones. Encourage students to pay attention to transitive and intransitive verbs as they act out the dialogs.

11 WRITE & SPEAK, page 379 — 20 min

A *Answers will vary.*

1. (DO); (IO)   3. (DO); (IO)   5. (DO); (IO)
2. (IO); (DO)   4. (IO); (DO)

B *Answers will vary.*

12 LISTEN, page 380 — 25 min.

A 1. 1825   2. 1886   3. 1813   4. 1450

B

	Subject	Verb	Object
1. Rail Travel	Stephenson	changed	the way we travel
	He	operated	the first train for human passengers
2. The Dishwasher	Cochran	made	dishwashers for her friends
	She	started	her own business
3. The Circular Saw	Babbitt	invented	a large circular saw
	Men	used	large straight saws
4. The Printing Press	Gutenberg	did not invent	books
	The printing press	changed	the world

C *Answers will vary. Sample answers:*

1. George Stephenson changed the way we travel. He operated the first train for human passengers.

2. Josephine Cochran made dishwashers for her friends. She started her own business.

3. Tabitha Babbitt invented a large circular saw. Men used large straight saws.

4. Johannes Gutenberg did not invent books. The printing press changed the world.

- **Expansion Tip:** Have students discuss the importance of these four inventions today. Have them choose one invention and write 2–3 sentences about why this is important now.

13 EDIT, page 381 — 15 min.

Markus: Hey, Dave, I told ~~to~~ you how much I like my new phone, right? It gives me all the information I need when I'm away from my computer. Well, I just watched a video about a new pair of glasses that does the same thing. They show ~~for~~ you the same information as your phone, but right in front of your eyes!

Dave: Oh yeah, Mira sent me a photo of hers a couple days ago. Her parents got **(her)** a pair ~~her~~ **(for her)**. I don't understand the attraction. Can you explain ~~me~~ it to me?

Markus: Well, I guess they make life easier for people.

Dave: Are you serious? . . . I'm pretty sure they'd give **me** a headache ~~to me~~, and I really don't mind checking my phone for information. Are you seriously going to get a pair? I'm sure they will cost **you** a lot of money ~~you~~.

Marcus: Maybe, but I can't wait to get some.

Dave: I guess I won't need to buy a pair—you can lend ~~to me~~ **(me)** yours **(to me)**!

- **Expansion Tip:** If possible, search *Google Glass* for images and videos about the glasses. Show the class, and ask them if they would like to own Google glasses or not. Encourage students to use transitive and intransitive verbs correctly in their discussions.

14 APPLY, page 381 — 10 min.

A   The inventor <u>made</u> the picture phone for people who <u>wanted</u> more meaningful communication. The invention <u>looks</u> unusual, but nowadays people can easily <u>talk</u> to and <u>see</u> their friends and family on their phones or computers.

B *Answers will vary.*

- **Alternative Apply:** Have students brainstorm important inventions in history and make a list on the board. Then have each student choose one to research. Have students prepare and deliver a two-minute presentation to the class. Have students take notes during the presentations, and then vote on what they believe to be the top three most important inventions.

Student Learning Outcomes	• **Read** a podcast transcript about machines that can read brain waves (EEGs). • **Choose** the correct meanings for phrasal verbs. • **Read** a letter about keeping rivers clean and **identify** the correct particle to complete phrasal verbs. • **Complete** sentences with separable and inseparable phrasal verbs. • **Listen** to an excerpt from a lecture about inventors. • **Write**, **ask**, and **answer** questions using phrasal verbs.
Lesson Vocabulary	(adv.) carelessly (adj.) fascinating (ph. v.) get ahead (adj.) injured (n.) pond (n.) device (ph. v.) figure out (ph. v.) grow up (n.) official (adj.) portable

EXPLORE

1 READ, page 382   5 min.

• Have students look at the photos and read the captions. Have them read the title and ask, *What do you think this article will be about? How could the headset help people?*

Be the Expert

• TED Talks are online lectures about Technology, Entertainment, and Design.

• In her TED talk, Tan Le demonstrates that a symbol can move on a computer screen simply by visualizing this happening. She has a volunteer wear the EEG, and the computer reads his brainwaves in a neutral setting. Then he is asked to visualize an action such as pull. He imagines pulling the symbol closer toward him. The computer uses this as a basis for future readings. When he repeats this action, the computer recognizes these brain waves, and the symbol is pulled closer on the screen.

• Tan Le has given two TED talks, one about the headsets and one about her life. At age four, she escaped from Vietnam on a small boat. It took her five days to reach safety. If time permits, show students both videos in class.

2 CHECK, page 383   5 min.

1. F   2. T   3. F   4. F   5. T

• **Tip:** Ask higher-level students to correct the false statements.

3 DISCOVER, page 383   10 min.

A

about	ahead	from	out	up
talk thinking	get	comes	find check figure	hook grew give

B *Answers will vary. Sample answers:*
about: talk, think
ahead: get, go
from: come
out: drop, eat, figure, fill, find, go, help, look, move, put, run, sort, take, throw, watch, work
up: add, blow, break, bring, cheer, clear, dress, get, give, go, grow, make, pick, set, sign, speak, stand, stay, straighten, turn, wake

• **Tip:** After students have completed exercise **3**, write the phrasal verbs on the board. Have students copy them down, and ask them to number each phrasal verb based on how well they know each. Write the number system on the board:
1 = I know exactly what it means and can define it.
2 = I can use it in a sentence, but can't explain it.
3 = I can understand it, but I couldn't use it myself.
4 = I think I might know what it means.
5 = I have no idea what it means.
Have students compare their numbering in groups of 2–3 and define the difficult words for the other members of the group.

LEARN

Chart 14.4, page 384 — 5 min.

- **Note:** By this level, students are usually aware of phrasal verbs. Introduce the chart with a simple dictation activity. Read three sentences out loud: *Please hand in your papers. The bride called off the wedding. He wants to give up smoking.* Repeat these sentences three times and have students write what they hear. Then tell students to compare what they have written with a partner. Repeat the sentences one more time, and then have volunteers dictate the sentences back to you and write them on the board. Direct students' attention to the phrasal verbs and circle the *particles* in each sentence (*in; off; up*). Note that the meaning of each sentence would be different without the particle.

- **Note:** Students often find phrasal verbs challenging because the meanings are not always clear. However, these can be more logical than students may think. For example: *pick up* can be both literal—*I pick up the pen. A newspaper picks up a story.* Even though the newspaper doesn't literally lift the story, the meaning is related because the newspaper uses the story.

4 page 384 — 10 min.

1. find out; b	5. go away; b
2. give up; a	6. go back to; b
3. look up; a	7. call off; a
4. thinking about; a	8. turned off; a

- **Expansion Tip:** Have students work in pairs and choose 3–4 of the phrasal verbs in exercise **4**. Have them write true sentences. Model one example, e.g., find out: *I just found out that I got a raise at work.* Or, *Juan wants to find out more about phrasal verbs.* Have each pair of students read one sentence to the class.

Chart 14.5, page 385 — 5 min.

- **Note:** Remind students of what they have learned about transitive and intransitive verbs in Lesson 1 of this unit. Then direct their attention to pages **A7–A9** in the appendix. Have each student choose one separable and inseparable phrasal verb from the appendix that is useful in their daily communication. Create a list on the board.

5 READ & WRITE, page 385 — 10 min.

A

1. down	3. up	5. up	7. out	9. away
2. away	4. over	6. up	8. up	10. by

B throw away their garbage
talk over the problem
clean up these areas
set up an organization
send out teams
pick up garbage
come by our next meeting

- **Expansion Tip:** Ask students if they think that Riverwatch is a good idea. Why, or why not? Ask, *What is a problem in the area where you live? What is a solution for that problem?* Have students work in groups of 3–4 to write a similar letter about a different problem. Have students use at least five phrasal verbs in their letter. Then have volunteers read their letters to the class.

Chart 14.6, page 386 — 5 min.

- **Note:** Explain that separable phrasal verbs can have the direct object in the middle of the phrasal verb while inseparable phrasal verbs have the direct object at the end of the verb. Create this chart on the board.

	Type of ph. v.	Noun in middle	Noun at end	Pronoun in middle	Pronoun at end
Pick (DO) up	Sep.	I picked my mother up.	I picked up my mother.	I picked her up.	X
Go over (DO)	Insep.	X	We went over our notes.	X	We went over them.

Have students choose other verbs and add them to the chart.

6 page 386 — 10 min.

1. go	4. figure
2. out	5. over/about; come
3. from	6. over/about

- **Expansion Tip:** Ask students to read the statements again and tell a partner whether or not they would be a good innovator. Have them explain why they came up with this answer and see if their partner feels the same. Encourage students to use phrasal verbs whenever possible.

7 page 387   5 min.

1. a	3. a	5. a	7. a
2. b	4. a	6. b	8. a

- **Expansion Tip:** Have students read the lists on pages **A7–A9** and work in pairs to create 3–4 sentences using separable or inseparable phrasal verbs. Have them write multiple-choice options similar to the ones in exercise **7**. Have students write about their daily life (e.g., *Janna picked the kids up from school. a. picked them up b. picked up them.*). Then have them give the exercise to another group to complete. Allow the groups to use the appendix to find the answers.

PRACTICE

8 page 387   5 min.

1. up
2. the flight status up/up the flight status
3. off
4. off my speech/my speech off
5. out
6. into
7. over to
8. it over
9. along

9 page 388   10 min.

1. hand in	4. talk over
2. think over	5. talk about
3. turn down	

> ### REAL ENGLISH, page 388
>
> Ask students to read the e-mails in exercise **8** again and write a formal version for each. Model the first sentence: *When I awoke on the day of my flight, there was a terrible storm.* Have students compare answers with a partner.

10 LISTEN, page 388   10 min.

A
1. dream up	6. come from
2. wakes up	7. figure out
3. run into	8. bring up
4. give up	9. talking about
5. keep on	10. came up with

B
1. a	3. c	5. b	7. c	9. a
2. b	4. a	6. a	8. b	10. a

- **Expansion Tip:** Have students record the phrasal verbs from exercise **A** and the correct definition from exercise **B** in their notebooks. Have students work in pairs to quiz each other orally on the definitions.

11 APPLY, page 389   20 min.

A
1. Have you run into any problems recently?
2. How do you think up new ideas?
3. What have you found out about inventors?
4. What words have you looked up in this lesson?
5. Who do you count on for advice?

B *Answers will vary.*

- **Alternative Apply:** Have students discuss innovations that have changed their lives or that they could not live without. After the discussion, have students write a paragraph about important innovations in their lives. Have students use at least five phrasal verbs in their paragraph.

1 page 390   10 min.

- **Tip:** Before doing this exercise, have students look at the photo and read the caption. Ask, *Does this look like a typical spacecraft? Why, or why not? How do you think it is different?*

  1. sent me

  2. working on an assignment

  3. takes in energy/takes energy in

  4. hits the sail

  5. move

  6. take off

  7. arrived in space

  8. carried out its task/carried its task out

  9. going back/going ahead

  10. look it over

2 EDIT, page 391   10 min.

- **Tip:** To create interest, ask students to look at the photo and read the caption. Ask, *Have any of you ever used a 3D printer? How could the printer be useful to you?*

  [posted @ 10:20 pm by techwizard33]

  A few days ago, a friend showed ~~to~~ me his 3D printer. I wanted to see it because I might buy ~~for my son one~~ one for my son/my son one. The printer was smaller than I expected. It cost my friend a lot of money, too, but apparently the price is coming down. He turned ~~on it~~ it on, so I was able to see how it worked. My friend uses his computer to design items for other companies. To test his ideas, he needs to try ~~out them~~ them out. Making an item to test used to be a long process, but now my friend can make one quickly with his 3D printer. It seems incredible! I think I will buy one!

  [posted @ 10:33 pm by kbb4210]

  I agree. These sound great. The other day I ran ~~a friend into~~ into a friend when I was downtown. She does research on historical objects. She does a lot of work ~~to~~ for the Smithsonian Institution in Washington, DC. In the past, she had to travel twice a month to examine the real objects at the Institution, but recently she also bought a 3D printer. Now the Institution sends ~~to~~ her the exact measurements of an object and she prints ~~out it~~ it out at home. It's great!

3 LISTEN & SPEAK, page 391   10 min.

A *Answers will vary. Sample answers:*

  1. a computer disk notebook

  2. to take notes/to reuse old disks

  3. her uncle/her friends and family

  4. by wanting to make something useful with old disks

  5. yes, she couldn't figure out how to keep the disks and paper together

  6. no

- **Expansion Tip:** Have students give their own opinions about the computer disk notebooks. Would they like one? Why, or why not?

1 READ & NOTICE THE GRAMMAR, page 392   35 min.

A *Answers will vary.*

- **Tip:** Have students look at the photo and read the title. Before they read, ask, *Would you want to try this pill? Why, or why not? What would you want to know before you tried it?* After students read the article, ask them if they have changed their mind about the pill.

B *Answers will vary.*

- **Tip:** Have students compare their lists with a partner. If possible, on the board, create a chart with as many verbs as possible.

C *Answers will vary. Sample answers:*

What is the problem/need?	people have too many passwords to remember
Who invented the product?	the Motorola company
How does it solve the problem?	You take the pill and it reacts with the acid in your stomach, which then sends an electronic signal, or "password," to your phone, laptop, or other digital device.
When is it useful?	every day; whenever you are online, using a digital device
Why is (or isn't) it a good idea?	The FDA has approved the pill for sale in the U.S., but many might not feel comfortable with the idea of sending information with their bodies.

2 BEFORE YOU WRITE, page 393   15 min.
Answers will vary.

- **Tip:** Make sure that students have enough time to decide on an innovation. If possible, assign this for homework so that students can research an innovation or have more time to come up with their own ideas.

3 WRITE, page 393   25 min.

WRITING FOCUS, page 393

Have students read the titles in the next two units of this textbook. Ask, *Which ones are you interested in reading? Why?* Have students write the titles in their notebooks, and compare their lists with a partner's.

- **Alternative Writing:** Working in groups of 2–3, have students choose one of the innovations in this unit to write about. Have groups write commercials for their products using verbs correctly. Encourage everyone in the group to have a speaking role in the commercial. Then have students act out their commercials for the class. Have the class vote on the funniest/most persuasive/most informative commercial.

15 Windows on the Past

Passive Voice and Participial Adjectives

Unit Opener

Photo: Have students look at the photo and read the caption. Ask, *Where is Easter Island? What is it famous for? Why are people interested in the statues?*

Location: The Polynesian island Easter Island is in the southeastern Pacific Ocean. It is famous for its statues, known as *moai*, created by Rapa Nui people more than 500 years ago. Easter Island is more than 1000 miles (more than 1700 km) from the nearest inhabited place, and about 2300 miles (3700 km) from the closest continent of South America.

Theme: This unit is about the past. It includes information about an archaeological find in Peru, a recovered shipwreck from the American Civil War, and a "newspaper" from ancient Rome.

Unit Grammar Terms

active voice: a sentence in which the subject performs the action of the verb.
➤ *Michael ate the hamburger.*

intransitive verb: a verb that cannot be followed by an object.
➤ *We didn't agree.*
➤ *The students smiled and laughed.*

participial adjective: an adjective that is formed like a present participle (*-ing*) or past participle (*-ed*) form of a verb.
➤ *Martin had tired eyes.*
➤ *The movie was exciting.*

passive voice: when the focus of a sentence is on the object of the verb instead of the subject. The active voice focuses on the subject.
➤ *My wallet was stolen.*

transitive verb: a verb that is followed by a direct object.
➤ *We took an umbrella.*

Student Learning Outcomes	• **Read** an article about a group of people who lived in Peru over a thousand years ago. • **Complete** sentences using passive voice. • **Write** and **talk** about things that were found on an archaeological expedition. • **Edit** an article about Angkor Wat. • **Write** a paragraph about an item from the past.
Lesson Vocabulary	(n.) assistant (n.) database (n.) label (adv.) recently (n.) tomb (adj.) bright (n.) detail (adj.) mysterious (adj.) standard (v.) uncover

EXPLORE

1 READ, page 396   15 min.

• **Tip:** Use the photo to teach the meaning of the word *uncover* and *tomb.* Ask, *What do you see in the ground? Why is the body there? What is a tomb? What did the experts have to do to find the body and the objects? What does* uncover *mean?*

• **Tip:** Have students use context cues to guess the meaning of *inhabit, archaeologist, artifact,* and *priestess.* Ask, *Where did the Moche live? What does* inhabit *mean? What does an archaeologist do? What is an example of an artifact?*

Be the Expert

• The tomb was found at a site known as San José de Moro, a small community on the Chamán River in the Jequetepeque Valley in Peru. It is a very important burial site for the Moche people.

• Archaeologists have discovered many artifacts at San José de Moro. These discoveries suggest that priestesses played an important governing and spiritual roles in Moche society. Priestesses were often buried with necklaces, ceramic vessels, and sometimes, weapons.

• Archaeologists believe the woman was buried around A.D. 750. The bodies of seven other women of apparently high status have been found since excavation began at the site in 1991.

• **Expansion Tip:** Working in pairs, have students talk about the things that could be buried with them to show what was important to them in their lives.

2 CHECK, page 397   5 min.

1. e   2. c   3. d   4. a   5. b

• **Expansion Tip:** Have students go online to research another pre-Columbian culture in South or Central America such as the Inca, the Maya, the Toltec, or the Aztec people. Have students prepare and present a short report on the kinds of artifacts that archaeologists have found and what they say about the society. If possible, encourage students to include photos of artifacts in their reports.

3 DISCOVER, page 397   5 min.

A 1. are known   3. were used
    2. was found   4. will be uncovered

B

Verb Form	Passive Voice: *Be* + Past Participle
Present	are known
Past	was found; were used
Future	will be uncovered

• **Tip:** To help students understand the rules that apply to these sentences, refer to note 2 in chart 15.1 as you discuss the answers. Point out that the present and past verb forms in exercise **B** match the examples in the note particularly closely.

LEARN

Chart 15.1, page 398   10 min.

• **Notes 1 & 2:** Demonstrate the difference between active and passive voice by performing actions in the classroom such as giving a student a book, turning off the lights, and writing words on the board and then erasing them. For each action, say what you are doing using both active and passive voice, e.g., *I gave Hugo a book. Hugo was given a book by me. I write words on the board. The words were written by me.* Then write the sentences on the board, so students can see how the passive sentences are formed.

- **Note 3:** Write several sentences in active voice on the board, some of which have objects and some of which use intransitive verbs. Have students identify which can be written in passive voice, and then have students rewrite them in passive voice.

- **Expansion Tip:** To help students see how the active and passive voices are related, have them rewrite the sentences in the notes in the active voice.

4 page 398   5 min.

1. P	3. A	5. A	7. P	9. P
2. P	4. P	6. P	8. A	10. P

- **Expansion Tip:** Have students work individually to write some active sentences in which the agent is important or interesting and some in which the agent is obvious or not important (e.g., *People eat a lot of blueberries in the summer. Writers write books on a lot of different topics every year.*). Have students exchange sentences with a partner and rewrite them in the passive voice if they think that works better. Suggest that they write sentences in the simple present. Ask volunteers to write sentences in the passive voice on the board.

> **REAL ENGLISH, page 398**
>
> Have students look at the passive sentences in exercise **4** and identify the agent of each action if possible. Ask, *Why do you think the sentence uses the passive voice?* Make sure students see that sometimes the agent isn't known, is obvious, or is repeated.

5 page 399   10 min.

1. ruled	6. found
2. was discovered	7. knew
3. weren't known	8. were taken
4. was found	9. was removed
5. believed	10. found

- **Expansion Tip:** Have students go online to find an article about an archaeological discovery. (They can use the information they found in the expansion tip for exercise **2.**) Tell them to highlight or note all the examples of the passive voice. Elicit examples and write them on the board. Then have students explain why the authors probably chose to use passive voice.

Chart 15.2, page 399   10 min.

- **Note 1:** Point out that the tense of the passive voice is reflected only in the form of *be.* Suggest that students manipulate that first when forming the passive voice.

- **Expansion Tip:** Review past participles with students. Say the base form of a verb and call on a student to say the past participle. Have that student call on a classmate and say a base form of a different verb of his or her choosing. Continue until everyone has had at least one chance to respond. To keep the activity fast-paced, have students toss a ball to the student they call on.

- **Expansion Tip:** Have students look at exercise **5** and write questions for the passive sentences (e.g., *When was King Tut's tomb discovered? Where was it found?*). Have volunteers write the questions on the board, and then have all students practice asking and answering their questions in pairs.

6 page 400   5 min.

1. were used	6. Are; displayed; are
2. was discovered	7. will not be announced
3. were removed	8. was; prepared
4. will be completed	9. are; kept
5. is not owned	10. is not taught

- **Expansion Tip:** To reinforce students' understanding of how questions are formed, have them write *yes/no* or information questions for each statement in exercise **6**. Then have them take turns asking and answering in pairs.

PRACTICE

7 page 400   20 min.

A When team members <u>find</u> an artifact, they <u>follow</u> a standard procedure.

- A student assistant <u>places</u> the artifact in a special container.
- The assistant <u>writes</u> the information about the artifact on the container label.
- The assistant <u>records</u> the artifact in the project's database.
- Experts <u>analyze</u> the artifact at the laboratory.

B

1. is found	4. is written
2. is followed	5. is recorded
3. is placed	6. is analyzed

C 1. wasn't followed   5. Were; recorded

    2. were not labeled   6. was done

    3. Were; placed   7. was found

    4. were damaged

D WRITE & SPEAK

Answers will vary.

- **Alternative Writing & Speaking:** Brainstorm a list of recent problems in the news caused by people making mistakes. Have students work in pairs to write sentences about the problem using passive voice. When they are finished, have each student find a new partner and share their sentences with him or her.

> ### REAL ENGLISH, page 401
>
> Point out that we also use the passive voice when we don't want to say we did something wrong (e.g., *The application wasn't sent in on time.*). Put students in pairs to write a conversation in which the passive voice is used so as not to blame the speaker or someone else. Encourage them to be creative and use humor if possible. Ask volunteers to perform their conversations for the class.

8 EDIT & SPEAK, page 402   15 min.

- **Tip:** To help students anticipate content and practice the target structure before they complete exercise **A**, have them look at the photo and write three passive voice questions they think will be answered in the text (e.g., *Where is it located? When was it built? Who was it built for? Why is it located there?*). When students finish reading and editing, elicit which questions were answered in the text.

A   The temple of Angkor Wat in Cambodia was ~~build~~ built in the 12th century by a Khmer king. It was the state temple and also the place where the king was buried. Many parts of the temple are damaged. Water and time have done much of the damage. But also, the temple was constructed in a way that has not lasted. Recently, restoration work on one important part of the temple was completed by a team of specialists. Restoration is when a damaged building is brought back to a good condition.

For this restoration, special techniques were required, and the Cambodian team was well trained for the job. Gradually, over a five-year period, important parts of the temple were cleaned and dangerous cracks were filled. The project was a big success, and the team plans to continue its work on other buildings at the site. Hopefully, all of Angkor Wat will be restored in an equally successful way.

B 1. was; built   3. was; damaged

    2. was buried   4. Will; be restored

C *Answers will vary.*

9 page 403   5 min.

A   I have chosen a woodworking drill. It <u>was owned</u> by my grandfather and <u>was used</u> in his work as a carpenter on ships. Sadly, my grandfather <u>was lost</u> at sea when my father was a child, so I never knew him. His tools <u>are kept</u> carefully by my family. I like to do woodwork myself, so his drill <u>is</u> still <u>used</u>, and it works very well. I'm going to give the drill to my son. It's nice to think that my grandfather <u>will be remembered</u> through his tools.

B

	Item: Woodworking drill
Who was it owned by?	Paul's grandfather
How was it used?	for woodworking/ in his work as a carpenter
Where was it used?	on ships
Other details	still used and will be kept in the family

C *Answers will vary.*

D *Answers will vary.*

- **Expansion Tip:** Bring in unusual objects or photos of unusual objects. They can be artifacts that archaeologists have discovered, unique kitchen utensils, or work tools for an unusual occupation. Display the objects and have students create descriptions of the objects' use (e.g., *It is used to shave the scales off fish. It is found in a chef's set of kitchen tools.*). Have students use passive voice in their descriptions.

Student Learning Outcomes	• **Read** an article about the discovery of the SS *Republic*, a sunken ship.
	• **Ask** and **answer** questions about a ship.
	• **Read** and **talk** about an anthropology project.
	• **Listen** to a discussion about a disaster.
	• **Edit** an except from a project about the *Mary Celeste*.
	• **Write** statements using passive modals.

Lesson Vocabulary	(n.) artifact	(n.) coin	(adj.) everyday	(v.) load	(adj.) virtual
	(n.) ash	(n.) crew	(n.) goods	(v.) recover	(n.) wreck

EXPLORE

1 READ, page 404　　　　　　　　　　15 min.

- Before students read the text, have them look at the painting on pages 404–405. Have them work in pairs to write sentences about the ship using passive voice. Ask volunteers to write sentences on the board.

- **Tip:** To help students practice scanning for specific information, have them work individually to write questions about the numbers in the text (e.g., *How much money in coins was loaded onto the ship?*). Then have students exchange questions with a partner to answer.

Be the Expert

- Savannah, Georgia—founded in 1733—is a beautiful city on the southeast coast of the United States. It was an important port during the Civil War. It is known for its historic squares. The SS *Republic* was found on the floor of the Atlantic Ocean at a depth of 1700 feet (500 meters).

- The SS *Republic* was the first steamship to provide regular service between the United States and South America, but failed to make a profit at that. Later, it brought passengers to California during the Gold Rush, and then served as a warship for the Union Army during the Civil War. After it was damaged, it was repaired and used for shipping cargo.

- **Expansion Tip:** If your students are high-level, have them go online to research other famous treasure ships or wrecks that people have discovered.

2 CHECK, page 405　　　　　　　　　　5 min.

1. F　　2. F　　3. T　　4. F　　5. T

3 DISCOVER, page 405　　　　　　　　　5 min.

A 1. were loaded　　　4. were recovered

2. could be used　　5. can now be viewed

3. was discovered

B **Passive without Modal:** were loaded; was discovered; were recovered

Passive with Modal: could be used; can now be viewed

- **Tip:** To lead into chart 15.3, write one of the sentences with a modal on the board. Then have students label the parts of the sentence.

LEARN

Chart 15.3, page 406　　　　　　　　　10 min.

- **Note:** Review the meaning and use of modals for ability, possibility, advisability, necessity, etc. Point out that they have the same meaning in passive voice. Explain that just as modals in the active voice are followed by the base form, in the passive, they are followed by the base form of *be* + past participle.

- **Expansion Tip:** Dictate sentences in the active voice that use modals and objects (e.g., *Students should take the test in the testing center. You can submit your application online. You may not use your phone in class.*). Have students rewrite the sentences using passive voice. Ask volunteers to write the sentences on the board.

4 page 406　　　　　　　　　　　　5 min.

1. may be found	5. must not be moved
2. might be recovered	6. could be required
3. must be taken	7. should be worn
4. may not be used	8. can be consulted

- **Expansion Tip:** Have students work in pairs or small groups to write an information sheet for another activity they know well (e.g., playing soccer, checking books out of the library, using a search engine, using a language or computer lab). Set a time limit of five minutes. The pair with the most sentences using passive modals win.

- **Note:** It is common to use the *by* phrase with numbers, a person's name, and someone or something specific.

- **Expansion Tip:** Have students reread the first two paragraphs on page 404 and discuss, in pairs, why the *by* phrase is or is not used in each instance of the passive voice. If the agent is understood from context, have students identify the agent.

5 page 407   10 min.

The wreck of the SS *Republic* was discovered in 2003 by a private company called Odyssey Marine Exploration. The ship was found ~~by the company~~ at the bottom of the ocean 100 miles southeast of Savannah, Georgia.

The remains of the SS *Republic* were around 1700 feet (518 meters) deep. New high-tech equipment was used ~~by Odyssey~~ to aid in the exploration and recovery effort. For example, items were removed from the wreck by a robotic craft called ZEUS.

Over 51,000 gold and silver coins were recovered ~~by the Odyssey team~~ from the wreck. Everyday items such as shoes, cups, and bottles were also found ~~by the team~~. Photos of these artifacts are displayed on the company's website. Facts and details are also given ~~by the company~~ on the site for anyone who wants more information.

- **Tip:** The SS *Republic* is estimated to be worth between $120 and $180 million. Other valuable shipwrecks include the *Whydah Galley* off the coast of Massachusetts, United States, the Spanish ship *Nuestra Señora de Atocha* off the coast of Florida, United States, the *Belitung* in the Java Sea, the *SS Gairsoppa* on its way from India to Britain, and the *Antikythera* near Greece. Have students research one of these ships and report on it in small groups.

6 WRITE & SPEAK, page 408   10 min.

A 1. Who was the SS *Republic* discovered by?

2. Who was the company started by?

3. Who was the new equipment bought by?

4. Who was the ocean searched by?

5. What were the research teams attracted by?

B *Answers will vary.*

- **Expansion Tip:** If students researched a ship in the cultural tip for exercise **5**, have them ask and answer these passive questions in their small groups: *Who was the ship discovered by? What artifacts were found? Where was the wreck located?*

PRACTICE

7 page 408   5 min.

1. can be seen

2. can't be bought by groups

3. may not be parked

4. must not be used by adults

5. may be taken by children on school visits

6. should be left

7. might be changed

8. can be purchased

8 READ, WRITE & SPEAK, page 409   20 min.

A Theme — What <u>can</u> we <u>learn</u> from disastrous or mysterious events?

What to do

- <u>Choose</u> a historical event from any period.

- You <u>can</u> <u>write</u> about any country or culture.

- You <u>can</u> <u>do</u> the work alone or with a partner.

What to study

- <u>Read</u> accounts of the event soon after it <u>happened</u>.

- <u>Study</u> artifacts from the site.

- <u>Research</u> the opinions of archaeologists and anthropologists.

Resources to use

- <u>Visit</u> the college library.

- <u>Use</u> the Internet.

- <u>Interview</u> members of the faculty (for interviews, by appointment).

<u>Choose</u> a topic — January 31: Professor Lopez <u>has to approve</u> all topics.

<u>Complete</u> outline — February 7: A faculty member <u>must sign</u> your outline before you <u>begin</u> your project.

<u>Present</u> project — February 26: Dr. Henderson <u>will arrange</u> exact times.

B 1. be chosen

2. be written

3. be done

4. be read

5. be studied; be researched

6. be used

7. be interviewed

8. be approved; Professor Lopez

9. be signed; a faculty member

10. be arranged; Dr. Henderson

C 1. Who must the outline be signed by?

2. Can the work be done with a partner?

3. Whose opinions should be researched?

4. Can the Internet be used?

5. Who must the topic be approved by?

6. Who will the presentations be arranged by?

D *Answers will vary.*

• **Alternative Writing:** If your students are high-level, have them complete the project assignment but don't ask them to study artifacts or conduct interviews. Have them follow the other bullet points as appropriate to write one page on the event they choose. Suggest they choose an event that they already know something about (e.g., a recent disaster or mysterious event).

9 WRITE & LISTEN, page 410   10 min.

A 1. by disaster

2. by Mount Vesuvius

3. by archaeologists

4. by millions of tourists

B 1. can be shared

2. can't; be believed

3. should be included

4. should be respected

5. might be shown

6. can be found

7. might be chosen

8. may not be approved

10 EDIT, page 412   15 min.

I have chosen to research the mystery of the ship *Mary Celeste*. This famous story should ~~include~~ **be included** on any list of historical mysteries. In early November 1872, the ship left New York carrying goods to Italy. One month later, the ship was discovered in the Atlantic Ocean by another ship. There was no one on board, but the goods that the *Mary Celeste* was carrying were still on the ship.

There was no sign of trouble, but the sailors, the captain, and his family could not **be** found. The ship's lifeboat was missing, and a long rope was attached to the back of the ship. Some versions of the story say that a fully prepared meal could ~~see~~ **be seen** on the table, so maybe everyone left in a hurry. This, however, cannot be confirmed. Even now we don't understand exactly what happened, and the truth may never ~~know~~ **be known**.

In my opinion, the evidence should be examined again ~~by people~~. New information might ~~discover~~ **be discovered** using modern technology. Many people don't agree with me, though. They think some things just can't be explained.

• **Expansion Tip:** If students researched a disaster or mysterious event for the alternative writing assignment for exercise **8**, have them exchange and edit their papers. Walk around the room to provide help as needed.

11 APPLY, page 412   15 min.
Answers will vary.

• **Alternative Speaking:** Have students write passive questions about the places in exercise **A** (e.g., *Do textbooks have to be purchased before classes begin? Can the books at the library be checked out for two weeks? Are the museum's hours posted online?*). Have students find partners and take turns asking and answering their questions. Point out that they don't have to know the answers—they can just make them up. After one minute, have students switch partners.

Student Learning Outcomes	• **Read** an article about news in ancient Rome. • **Complete** an e-mail, an interview, and a blog using participial adjectives. • **Listen** to and **discuss** three conversations about an archaeology project. • **Edit** an article about garbology. • **Write** and **talk** about things that are thrown away.
Lesson Vocabulary	(n.) chess (n.) cosmetics (n.) emperor (n.) media (v.) review (n.) content (v.) date (n.) landfill (v.) publish (p.) throughout

EXPLORE

1 READ, page 413   15 min.

- Have students look at the photo and read the caption on page 414. Ask, *The Forum was an actual place in ancient Rome—what does the word* forum *mean now? What do you know about ancient Rome? How long ago was the Roman Empire? What is the title for a ruler of an empire?*

- **Expansion Tip:** Elicit the ways that people get news now and write them on the board: *newspapers, radio, TV, online news sources, social media sites, word of mouth.* Have students rank them according to how often they use them, and then according to how reliable they think the sources are. Then have students discuss their ideas in small groups.

Be the Expert

- During the Roman Empire, a main city center was called a *forum*. It was a public gathering spot surrounded by shops, offices, and arches. The most famous forum is the Forum Romanum in the center of Rome, which was used for gatherings and the Senate met there. The Forum was designed by the architect Vitruvius. Close by are several famous buildings such as the Arch of Septimius Severus, the arch of Titus, the Temple of Vesta and the Roman Forum Rostra.

- The first Acta Diurna dates back to 139 BCE. These "newspapers" included information on trials, military campaigns, births, marriages, and deaths.

2 CHECK, page 414   5 min.

   1. b   2. b   3. a   4. c   5. a

- **Expansion Tip:** To review information from the previous lessons, have students find examples of the passive voice in the text and identify the agent where possible.

3 DISCOVER, page 414   5 min.

A   1. disturbing   3. carved

      2. interested   4. fascinated; entertaining

B   1, 3, 5

LEARN

Chart 15.5, page 415   10 min.

- **Note:** Sometimes it can be difficult to identify if a past participle is an adjective or simply part of the passive verb when it follows *be*. For example, the active sentence *The TV program interested me* becomes *I was interested by the TV program* in the passive, which also follows the structure of subject + *be* + adjective.

- **Note 5:** Common phrases include: *annoyed by, frustrated with, confused about, concerned about, known for, frightened of, upset about, worried about.*

4 page 415   10 min.

A   1. qualified for   6. exhausted

      2. frightened of   7. excited about

      3. involved in   8. sold out

      4. surprised by   9. interested in

      5. satisfied with   10. disappointed with

B   1. for   4. of   6. about

      2. in   5. by/at   7. with/by

      3. with/by

- **Expansion Tip:** Have students write questions using five of the phrases (adjective + preposition) from exercise **A** (e.g., *What kind of job are you qualified for?*). Then have students take turns asking and answering their questions with a partner. Call on students to tell the class about their partners.

- **Note:** Although the chart focuses on feelings, present and past participial adjectives can describe other things. For example, we can talk about *the smiling woman, the sleeping baby*, and *the flying bird*. Point out that such present participial adjectives refer to an ongoing activity, not a feeling.

- **Note 4:** Some past participial adjectives refer to qualities: *determined, open-minded*.

- **Expansion Tip:** Dictate ten verbs that cause reactions. Have students work in pairs. Partner A should compose a sentence using one of the participial adjectives derived from the verb, e.g., *The storm was frightening.* Partner B then composes a different sentence using the other participial adjective, e.g., *The frightened boy hid in the closet.* Encourage students to vary the form they begin with.

5 page 416   5 min.

1. amazing
2. interesting
3. fascinating
4. disappointing
5. exciting
6. boring
7. exhausting
8. entertaining

PRACTICE

6 page 417   5 min.

- **Tip:** Before students do the exercise, have them look at the photo and describe the expressions on the Chessmen's faces. Encourage students to use participial adjectives in their descriptions.

1. buried
2. exciting
3. carved
4. known
5. made
6. interesting
7. disappointed
8. worried
9. amusing
10. boring

7 LISTEN, WRITE & SPEAK, page 418   20 min.

A *Answers will vary.*

B 1. disgusted
2. annoyed
3. interesting
4. boring
5. exciting
6. satisfied
7. excited
8. surprising

C 1. Why is Jesse disgusted?

2. Why is Tom annoyed?

3. Why does Sue think the work is interesting?

4. Why does Dave think studying garbage is boring?

5. Why would Dave like to do something more exciting?

6. Why isn't Rick satisfied with the amount of work they have done?

7. Why is Angela excited?

8. Why does Rick think their information is surprising?

D *Answers will vary.*

8 EDIT, page 419   5 min.

Most people think garbage is not very interesting, but archaeologists are ~~fascinating~~ **fascinated** by it. When archaeologists found 2000-year-old waste from Rome, they were excited about it. The waste taught them about the diet and daily life of people in ancient Rome. You can learn a lot about a culture by studying its trash.

Garbology can be described as the study of garbage to learn about a culture. Professor William Rathje and his students in Arizona invented the term when they were studying waste in modern America. Rathje and his students studied a number of landfill sites. Sorting through garbage can be a ~~tired~~ **tiring** and sometimes ~~disgusted~~ **disgusting** activity, but when the information from their research was collected, they were not ~~disappointing~~ **disappointed** with the results. The project led to some ~~interested~~ **interesting** discoveries. It was clear that some popular ideas about modern American garbage were mistaken. For example, the team discovered that almost half of the garbage in the landfills is paper—a fact that many people found ~~surprised~~ **surprising**.

9 APPLY, page 419   10 min.

Answers will vary.

- **Alternative Writing & Speaking:** Model the activity by listing what is in your trash at home. Then use participial adjectives to compose sentences about what can be inferred from a person's trash: *The people in this house eat fresh and packaged food. Their food scraps are not composted. There isn't any cardboard, so that is probably recycled.* Have students analyze trash from their own homes and write a description using at least five participial adjectives. When students have finished, have them share their ideas in pairs.

1 page 420   5 min.

1. should be supported
2. was made; was filmed
3. gave
4. must be completed
5. might finish
6. Is the mail delivered/Will the mail be delivered
7. must not be left
8. can obtain
9. can't be repaired
10. do you keep

2 EDIT, page 420   5 min.

The giant stone balls of Costa Rica are one of the most ~~fascinated~~ **fascinating** human artifacts. The balls **were** made in prehistoric times and are perfectly round. The stone comes from local mountains. It's likely that stone tools were use**d** to make the balls. The biggest ball is eight feet across and it ~~is weighed~~ **weighs** 16 tons.

Unfortunately, we may never ~~be discovered~~ **discover** the true purpose of the stones, since only a small number of stones can be studied in context. Many of the stones were removed from their original place.

Archaeologists are ~~annoying~~ **annoyed** about this situation. They say that when artifacts are found by members of the public, they must not be moved. Photos can ~~take~~ **be taken**, but the artifacts should not be pick**ed** up.

3 WRITE & LISTEN, page 421   5 min.

A 1. Where were the first public baths built?
   2. When was the first moon landing completed?
   3. Where were scissors invented?
   4. When was the first airplane flown?
   5. Who was popcorn invented by?
   6. When were the first CDs sold?

B 1. c   2. c   3. a   4. b   5. a   6. c

C *Answers will vary.*

4 WRITE & SPEAK, page 421   10 min.
Answers will vary.

Connect the Grammar to Writing

1 READ & NOTICE THE GRAMMAR, page 422   20 min.

- **Tip:** Have students read the title and look at the photo. Ask volunteers to predict the content of the article. Then have them explain what they based their predictions on.

A *Answers will vary.*

B

Passive Voice	Agent in text (necessary information)	Agent not in text (clear from context)
1. fountain pens were used		✓ (by people)
2. his name was engraved		✓ (by someone)
3. his mother was killed		✓ (by someone)
4. he was raised	✓ by his father	
5. his stories can . . . be enjoyed	✓ by people all over the world	

Other examples will vary, but the remaining examples of passive voice in the text are all examples of "agents not in text."

C *Answers will vary. Sample answer:*

	Event: Receiving gift from grandfather
What is the memory?	Receiving a special pen from my grandfather
What is this event important?	the pen was a gift for his 10th birthday; felt a connection with my grandfather
Details	grandfather is a writer; is rarely without his pen; the pen is very sentimental; I was stunned and incredibly happy

2 BEFORE YOU WRITE, page 423   10 min.

Answers will vary.

WRITING FOCUS, page 423

Have students look through the unit's *Explore* and *Edit* paragraphs and write down examples of strong concluding sentences. Then have students share the concluding sentences they have found with a partner. Call on volunteers to read aloud the best concluding sentences they have found, and ask them to explain why they think those sentences are particularly strong. Students who found particularly weak concluding sentences may also wish to share them with the class and explain why they are weak.

3 WRITE, page 423   20 min.

- **Alternative Writing:** Have students write about an object that is important to them. Model the activity by telling about an object that is important to you. Include answers to these questions: *Where did you get it? How does it make you feel? Why is it important to you? How often do you use it? What qualities make this object special?*

Noun Clauses and Reported Speech

Unit Opener

Photo: Have students look at the photo and read the caption. Ask, *What is happening in this photo? How do you feel when you see the man floating in space?*

Location: This image is of Bruce McCandless II. In 1984, he was the first person to fly in space untethered. McCandless traveled more than 300 feet from the ship, approximately 150 miles above Earth.

Theme: The theme of this unit is exploration. Have students look at the photos in the unit. Ask, *Which area would you most like to explore? Why?*

Page	Lesson	Grammar	Examples
426	1	Noun Clauses with *That*	Louis believed **that the professor was telling the truth.** The students were afraid **that the test was today.**
434	2	Noun Clauses with *Wh-* Words and *If/Whether*	I don't understand **how you knew that.** Do you know **where the museum is?** I'm not sure **if the workers are busy.** We don't know **whether they saw the e-mail.**
442	3	Quoted and Reported Speech	Rena **said, "I feel sorry for you."** Ben **said (that) Jeremy liked traveling.** Larry **told them (that) it's time for lunch.**
453		**Review the Grammar**	
456		**Connect the Grammar to Writing**	

Unit Grammar Terms

noun clause: a clause that can be used in place of a noun, a noun phrase, or a pronoun.
➢ *I didn't know **that she was here.***
➢ *I'm not sure **if the store is open yet.***

relative clause: a clause that describes a noun or indefinite pronoun in a sentence. It comes after the noun or pronoun it describes. It is also called an *adjective clause.*
➢ *The student **that I am sitting next to** is from Peru.*
➢ *I know everyone **who lives in my building.***

reported speech: a statement of what someone said that does not have quotation marks.
➢ *Adele said **that she was sick.***

quoted speech: a statement that includes the exact words someone said. Quotation marks ("/") are used around the exact words.
➢ *She said, **"I'm not feeling well."***

<table>
<tr><td>Student Learning Outcomes</td><td>
<ul>
<li>Read about the lost city of Thonis-Heracleion.</li>
<li>Identify subjects and verbs of noun clauses in statements.</li>
<li>Write and speak about Thonis-Heracleion using noun clauses.</li>
<li>Read a conversation about the Yonaguni monument and discuss your own ideas.</li>
<li>Listen to a podcast about Machu Picchu and answer questions.</li>
<li>Write true statements about your life using noun clauses.</li>
</ul>
</td></tr>
</table>

Lesson Vocabulary	(n.) century (v.) exist	(n.) expert (v.) found	(n.) monument (n.) pile	(v.) prove (n.) ruins	(adj.) separate (ph. v.) split up

EXPLORE

1 READ, page 426 5 min.

- Have students look at the photos and read the title and captions. Ask, *How do you think this city was lost? How do you think it was found?*

Be the Expert

- Franck Goddio worked with his team from the European Institute for Underwater Archaeology and the Egyptian Supreme Council of Antiquities. In 2000, they discovered the underwater city 4 miles (6.5 kilometers) off the coast of Egypt.
- The archaeologists discovered over 700 anchors and 60 shipwrecks, which led them to believe that this was an important port in ancient times.
- In the 5th century, Greek historian Herodotus wrote that Heracleion had a temple built to commemorate Herakles (also known as Hercules) landing in Egypt. Before the Trojan war, Helen and Paris were said to have visited Heracleion.
- Search *Franck Goddio Thonis-Heracleion images*. Note: Be sure to search for the underwater city, not Heraclion, Crete.

2 CHECK, page 427 5 min.

1. a   2. c   3. a   4. b

3 DISCOVER, page 427 10 min.

A

Subject	Verb	Clause with *That*
Stories	suggest	that some of these places are lost beneath the sea.
His work	has shown	that these lost places can be found.
Historians	thought	that Thonis and Heracleion were two separate cities.
Historians	think	that the city was founded in the 8th century B.C.
Experts	believe	that the city was hit by several natural disasters . . .

B 2

- **Tip:** Deciding on the answer for exercise **B** might be difficult for students, since the clauses include a noun and a verb. Explain that each noun clause could be replaced by the word *something*. Have students read the sentences in exercise **A** with this substitution. Then have students substitute a verb (*lose/find*), an adjective (*interesting*), or an adverb (*quickly*) instead. Students should note that only a noun can replace a noun clause.

LEARN

Chart 16.1, page 428 5 min.

- **Note 2:** One of the most common errors is to omit the subject in the noun clause, especially when the subject is the same as the subject of the sentence. On the board, write: *He realized that needed to work harder. I hope that will see you later.* Have students correct the errors.

- **Note 3:** Explain that noun clauses provide additional information in a smooth and fluent way. To demonstrate, on the board write: *Ana was smiling a lot today. I noticed this. She got a new job. She found out today.* Ask students to combine the sentences into two sentences. For example, *I noticed that Ana was smiling a lot today. She found out that she got a new job.*

4 page 428   10 min.

1. Explorers always hope that they will make discoveries.

2. Goddio decided that he wanted to look for Heracleion.

3. He thought that he and his team could find the city.

4. They discovered that the city was near the coast.

5. The team realized that the ruins were very old.

6. The divers noticed that the ruins contained statues and jewelry.

7. Archaeologists know that the site is very important.

8. They believe that it will help our understanding of ancient Egypt.

> **REAL ENGLISH, page 428**
>
> Ask students to circle the verbs in the box that were already used in exercise **4**. Then have them work in pairs and rewrite the sentences in exercise **4**, using the other verbs (e.g., *Explorers always dream that they will make discoveries.*).

5 page 428   10 min.

1. The students found out that the lecture on ancient Egypt was canceled.

2. Archaeologists learned that the city was important.

3. Scientists discovered that the statues were over 2000 years old.

4. I dreamed that I found a lost city.

5. Some explorers hope that their discoveries will be famous.

6. I believe that her book has information on ancient Greece.

> **REAL ENGLISH, page 429**
>
> Speakers often use reduced pronunciation. Encourage students to practice the reduced pronunciation by combining *that* + noun when they speak (e.g., *I hope that you can come to the party.*). Have students practice saying *that you* as one word. Then have them read the entire sentence. Have students circle *that* + noun for the sentences in exercise **5** and practice the reduced pronunciation.

6 WRITE & SPEAK, page 429   15 min.

A 1. it is under the sea.   3. it was a little boring.

2. they are the same.   4. it has improved a lot.

B *Answers will vary. Sample answers.*

1. I remember that Heracleion was hit by many natural disasters.

2. I learned that Thonis was the Egyptian name and Heracleion was the Greek name.

3. I thought that it was interesting.

4. I've realized that it takes time to learn a language.

- **Expansion Tip:** On the board, write the titles of 2–3 *Explore* articles in the textbook that students have read and discussed in class. Have students discuss the articles in pairs, using the same prompts found in exercise **6**: *I remember that . . . , I learned that . . . , etc.* After 2–5 minutes, have students share their observations with the class.

Chart 16.2, page 430   5 min.

- **Note 2:** These expressions are used more in formal, academic situations than in everyday conversation. People say, *It is a fact that the Earth revolves around the Sun.* We rarely say, *It is true that the café is open on Sundays,* unless they are refuting what someone else has said.

- **Note 3:** Students are often confused by the fact that the word *that* can be omitted. *That* is usually used more in formal situations such as academic writing than it is in speaking. *That* is also often used with less frequently used verbs (e.g., *I didn't know the test was today.* vs. *I didn't realize that the test was today.*).

7 page 430   10 min.

Ben: Is it true that <u>you're leading the search tomorrow</u>?

Lucia: Yes, it is. I'm surprised that <u>you know about it already</u>.

Ben: News travels fast! Anyway, I'm glad that <u>you've been chosen</u>. You'll be a great team leader. Dave doesn't have enough experience. I was afraid that <u>we were going to get lost today</u>.

Lucia: I know. I was worried that <u>someone might get lost</u> when he split us up into pairs. In my opinion, we should all stay together.

Ben: Yes, I agree. Professor Kim is disappointed that <u>we haven't found any sign of the city yet</u>. He's sure that <u>we're in the right place</u>, though.

Lucia: Well, it's true that <u>people have been looking for it for years</u> . . .

8 SPEAK, page 430   10 min.

Answers will vary.

- **Expansion Tip:** Have students write one false and three true statements before beginning the activity. Then have them work in groups of 3–4 and read the sentences. Have the group guess which sentence is false.

PRACTICE

9 READ, WRITE & SPEAK, page 431   15 min.

- **Tip:** Before starting the activity, explain that *man-made* means that humans created the object; it did not occur naturally.

A Professor: Great dive, everyone! So what do you think after seeing the Yonaguni monument for yourselves? Do you think <u>it's natural or man-made</u>? Is it a pile of rocks or the remains of an ancient civilization?

Kenji: Well, I can understand all the excitement. It's true <u>the rocks look like they have been carved</u>. The edges are so straight . . .

Pam: I agree. And I'm sure <u>I saw some steps</u>. They seemed to lead to the top of the monument.

Michaela: Hmmm. I'm not sure <u>I agree</u>. The rocks looked natural to me.

Kenji: What about the head-shaped rock? Did you see that, Michaela?

Michaela: No, I had to go back to the surface because I had a problem with my diving equipment. I was afraid <u>I didn't have enough air</u>.

Pam: I'm sorry <u>you didn't see it</u>.

Kenji: I know <u>there are some Japanese scientists who agree with us</u>, Pam.

Michaela: But the Japanese government doesn't agree. Don't forget <u>the monument is officially considered a natural site</u>.

B *Answers will vary. Sample answers:*

1. (that) Yonaguni was made by man

2. (that) it is natural, not man-made

3. (that) the head-shaped rock meas it is not natural

4. (that) the site is man-made

5. (that) his students thought about how the monument was formed

6. (that) the dive went well

7. *Answers will vary.*

8. *Answers will vary.*

C *Answers will vary.*

10 LISTEN & WRITE, page 432   15 min.

- **Tip:** To create interest, direct students' attention to the photo and ask what they already know about Machu Picchu. Ask, *What do you think the answers to exercise A will be?* Have students discuss the statements and decide. Then have them listen and see if they were correct.

A 1. F   2. T   3. T   4. F   5. F

B *Answers will vary. Sample answers:*

1. early morning/late afternoon

2. Sunday, fewest visitors

3. as early as possible; the number of tickets is limited

4. yes—there is only one road; it takes 2–4 days to walk the trail

5. bus (walking takes too long: 2–4 days)

C *Answers will vary.*

11 APPLY, page 433   15 min.

Answers will vary.

- **Alternative Apply:** Have students create stories together. Give students a blank sheet of paper and have them write the first line of a story, e.g., *One morning Bob woke up late* . . . Explain that they will continue the story using noun clauses. After each sentence, students should pass their paper to another student. On the board, write a list of verbs and phrases that students should use, e.g., 2. *sure,* 3. *disappointed,* 4. *surprised,* 5. *It is true,* 6. *think,* 7. *remember,* 8. *hope,* 9. *dream,* 10. *is afraid,* etc. Explain that sentence 2 should have the word *sure,* e.g., *He was sure that his alarm clock was broken.* Each story should have 5–10 sentences. Announce to the class when it is time to write a concluding sentence. Then have students read through the story that they have finished and correct any grammatical errors. Have students read the stories to the class or in groups of 3–4. Note: Lower-level students can write sentences in pairs.

Student Learning Outcomes	• **Read** about explorer Thor Heyerdahl and the voyage of the *Kon-Tiki*.
	• **Ask** and **answer** questions about Polynesia using noun clauses.
	• **Read** questions about exploring the city of Mumbai.
	• **Listen** to information about explorer Vasco da Gama and **write** sentences using noun clauses.
	• **Ask** and **answer** polite questions and questions using a map.

Lesson Vocabulary	(n.) cruelty	(n.) explorer	(n.) islander	(n.) material	(n.) theory
	(v.) demonstrate	(n.) harbor	(n.) kindness	(n.) spice	(n.) voyage

EXPLORE

1 READ, page 434   5 min.

• Have students look at the photo and read the title and caption. Ask, *Have you ever heard of the Kon-Tiki? What time period do you think the boat is from? What do you think the explorers were trying to do?* Then have students read the article to find the information.

Be the Expert

• This reading is about the explorer Thor Heyerdahl. He wrote a bestselling book about his journey. It was also the subject of an award-winning documentary and a 2012 feature film.

• Thor Heyerdahl and his five-man crew traveled 4300 miles (6900 kilometers) in the boat.

• *Kon-Tiki* was named after the Incan sun god Viracocha. Kon-Tiki is said to be an older name for this god.

• The original raft is on display at the *Kon-Tiki* museum in Oslo, Norway.

• Search *Thor Heyerdahl and crew images* to show the class photos from the journey.

2 CHECK, page 435   5 min.

  1. b   2. c   3. a   4. c   5. c

3 DISCOVER, page 435   5 min.

A 1. where   2. where   3. how

B 1. questions   2. statement

• **Tip:** On the board, write: 1. *Today we are going to discuss _____ we use noun clauses.* 2. *I'm not sure _____ noun clauses are.* Then write: *what/ how* in a separate column. Have students fill in the correct words in the sentences (1. *how;* 2. *What*). Ask, *How can you ask for this information as a direct question?* Write the direct questions under

the statements: 1. *How do we use noun clauses?* 2. *What are noun clauses?* Explain that these questions will be answered in the lesson.

LEARN

Chart 16.3, page 436   5 min.

• **Note:** Students often have difficulty with word order in noun clauses with *Wh-* words. Students know that direct questions are inverted and want to transfer this knowledge to any sentence with a *Wh-* word. To help with this, write the statements in the chart on slips of paper, with each word cut out, or write the words on the board in a scrambled order and have students order the words correctly in pairs. Have students check their answers in the book.

• **Note 4:** Remind students to pay attention to verb changes when they rewrite direct questions as noun clauses with *Wh-* words, e.g., *Where did you go? They wanted to know where we went.* Circle *go* and *went* and point out that both sentences are in the past tense, but without the auxiliary *did*, the main verb needs to be in the past tense form.

4 page 436   5 min.

  1. Polynesia is

  2. Thor Heyerdahl was

  3. the *Kon-Tiki* was built

  4. Heyerdahl sailed

  5. Heyerdahl was

  6. he was trying

  7. the *Kon-Tiki* sailed to

  8. the new research shows

• **Expansion Tip:** In pairs, have students read the statements and questions in exercise **4**, and answer based on the information in the article on page 434.

5 page 436　　　　　　　　　　　　　　10 min.

A 1. when people started

2. where the islands are

3. how many days the *Kon-Tiki* took

4. what the DNA results showed

5. who you believe

B *Answers will vary.*

- **Tip:** Ask students to work in pairs and write a list of 3–4 common questions (e.g., *What page are we on? What time is it?*) Have students rewrite these sentences using noun phrases to be as polite as possible. Have volunteers ask questions, and have the rest of the class vote on which version is the most polite.

> **REAL ENGLISH, page 437**
>
> Explain that because English is not a language with a formal and informal form of *you*, there are other ways to express formality. Direct questions are an example of this. They can sound abrupt to native speakers; noun clauses and additional words are more polite. On the board, write: *Where's the restroom?* Ask students how to make this more polite. Write possibilities on the board, e.g., *Excuse me/I'm sorry, would you mind telling me where the bathroom is?* Show that more words = more polite.

Chart 16.4, page 437　　　　　　　　　5 min.

- **Note:** Students often try to add *that* to a noun clause with *if/whether* because that may be correct in their native language. Explain that this is not possible in English. On the board, write: *I wonder whether that we will have a quiz today.* Ask students to correct the sentence. Note that *that* should be eliminated. For higher-level students, explain the difference in meaning between *if/whether* and *that*, e.g., *We didn't know that you would be here. We didn't know if you would be here.* In sentence 1, this was a surprise. In sentence 2, it was a possibility, but we weren't sure of the outcome.

- **Note:** *Whether* is often considered to be more formal than *if*. *Whether* is used more often in academic writing and newspapers.

6 page 438　　　　　　　　　　　　　　5 min.

1. period	4. period
2. question mark	5. question mark
3. period	6. question mark

7 page 438　　　　　　　　　　　　　　10 min.

A 1. Diego speaks Japanese?

2. I turned the TV off.

3. Alex is on vacation.

4. Joanne was at the lecture.

5. the bus goes to the park.

6. the concert is tonight?

7. Shari left.

8. they are happy.

B *Answers will vary.*

- **Expansion Tip:** Have students repeat the statements in exercise **7** to a partner, and then continue the conversation with an additional sentence, using their own imagination. Model an example. A: *Do you know whether or not Diego speaks Japanese?* B: *I think he does because he lived in Japan for ten years.*

PRACTICE

8 page 439　　　　　　　　　　　　　　5 min.

- **Tip:** Have students look at the photo and read the caption. Ask students what they know about Mumbai. Explain that Bollywood is the Indian equivalent of Hollywood. More people view Bollywood movies than Hollywood movies, and many of these are filmed in Film City, outside of Mumbai. If possible, show the class a short clip of a Bollywood movie or images of Mumbai to create interest.

1. where the Gateway of India is

2. if/whether there is time

3. if/whether it is a long way

4. how we can get

5. if/whether we will be able to see

6. which street goes

7. where Crawford Market is

8. if/whether we need

9 LISTEN & WRITE, page 440   20 min.

A 1. a   2. b

B *Answers will vary.*

- **Tip:** Students may be wary of guessing answers before they hear the information. Explain that there are often times when it is necessary to guess information. Explain that they will listen for the correct answers in exercise **D**, but first they should compare their answers for exercise **C** in pairs.

C *Answers will vary.*

D 1. a   3. b   5. a
   2. a   4. b   6. b

10 WRITE & SPEAK, page 441   15 min.

A 1. where the zoo is?

2. how I can get to the theater?

3. if there is a good bookstore near here?

4. when the bus to the castle leaves?

5. what time the stores close?

6. whether the museum is open today?

B *Answers will vary. Sample answers:*

1. The zoo is just outside of Castletown on Highway 15.

2. The Main Street Theater is on the corner of Main St. and 7th Ave.

3. Yes, the Old Towne Bookstore is on the corner of Main Street and 4th Ave.

4. The bus leaves every hour, starting at 10 a.m.

5. The bookstore closes at 8 p.m.

6. Yes, it's Tuesday, so the museum is open until 6 p.m.

11 APPLY, page 441   15 min.

Answers will vary.

- **Expansion Tip:** Have students ask and answer questions about additional places that aren't on the map such as Italian restaurants or movie theaters. Have students add this new information to their maps.

- **Alternative Apply:** Have students work in pairs to create a conversation between a new student and an experienced student at their school. First, have them write a list of possible questions (e.g., *Do you know whether Ms. Brown gives a lot of homework or not?*). Then have them write a conversation with at least four noun clauses. Have students act out their conversation for the class.

Student Learning Outcomes	• **Read** a blog about space exploration. • **Complete** conversations using reported speech. • **Find** and **edit** errors in an article about the first Hispanic American woman in space. • **Rewrite** a conversation about spiders in space using reported speech. • **Listen** to two students discussing a project. • **Write** and **punctuate** sentences with quoted speech. • **Interview** a classmate about their opinions on space exploration.
Lesson Vocabulary	(n.) achievement (ph.v.) deal with (adj.) leading (adv.) nowadays (n.) step (n.) astronaut (n.) gravity (n.) moment (n.) species (n.) survival

EXPLORE

1 READ, page 442   5 min.

• Ask students to look at the photos and read the title, the captions, and the quote by Carl Sagan. Ask, *Who was Valentina Tereshkova? Do you agree with Carl Sagan? Why, or why not?* Have students read the blog and decide whether they agree with the writer of the blog.

Be the Expert

• In 1961, Russian Yuri Gagarin was the first human in outer space. In 1969, American Neil Armstrong was the first person to walk on the moon, followed by American Buzz Aldrin.

• Carl Sagan was a professor of Astronomy and Space Sciences. He was also a consultant for NASA (National Air and Space Association).

• Some engineers predict that as soon as a planet similar to Earth is discovered in another solar system, the public will be ready to allocate more money for space exploration.

• Today, private companies are investing in space exploration. Planetary Resources, with Google founders as investors, plans to send robots to mine platinum on asteroids. Elon Musk has founded a company called SpaceX, with a goal to land astronauts on Mars and create a permanent human colony there.

2 CHECK, page 443   5 min.

1. T   2. F   3. T   4. T   5. F

• **Tip:** Ask higher-level students to correct the false sentences.

3 DISCOVER, page 443   10 min.

A 1. My grandmother told me that it was an incredible moment.

2. . . . Neil Armstrong said, "That's one small step for a man, one giant leap for mankind."

3. . . . , scientists tell us that we have learned a lot from space travel.

4. Some people even say the survival of humankind may depend on space exploration.

5. Carl Sagan said, "We have a basic responsibility to our species to venture to other worlds."

B 1. 2, 4   2. 1, 3, 5

• **Tip:** Ask students to look at the examples in exercise **A** and notice what other differences there are between the exact words and the noun clauses (e.g., *quotation marks, commas, the word* that).

LEARN

Chart 16.5, page 444   5 min.

• **Note:** In spoken English, speakers usually use reported speech (see chart 16.6). However, if a speaker wishes to say exactly what someone else has said, he/she may say, *The president of the company said, quote, no one will be fired, endquote/unquote.* Saying *quote* and *endquote/unquote* show that this is quoted speech.

• **Note:** Quoted speech is mainly used in writing, and students should be aware of the importance of using a quote rather than repeating the same words without giving credit to the original speaker. This may be a time for a discussion on plagiarism.

4 page 444   5 min.

1. b   3. b   5. a
2. a   4. b   6. b

5 page 445   10 min.

A 1. Julie said, "I'd love to be an astronaut."

   2. "Why is that?" Hector asked.

   3. Julie said, "I want to see the Earth from space."

   4. Hector said, "Yes, that must be an amazing sight."

   5. "Are you worried about the dangers?" Ratna asked.

   6. "It's worth the risk," Julie said.

   7. Ratna said, "I don't like the idea of spacewalks."

   8. "I think they sound amazing," said Hector.

B 1. "I'd love to be an astronaut," Julie said.

   2. Hector asked, "Why is that?"

   3. "I want to see the Earth from space," Julie said.

   4. "Yes, that must be an amazing sight," Hector said.

   5. Ratna asked, "Are you worried about the dangers?"

   6. Julie said, "It's worth the risk."

   7. "I don't like the idea of spacewalks," Ratna said.

   8. Hector said, "I think they sound amazing."

- **Expansion Tip:** Have students work in pairs to write three questions about space and astronauts (e.g., *What qualities do you think you need to be a successful astronaut?*). Have students ask a new partner their questions, and write exactly what they say using quoted speech. Then have them show their sentences to a partner to see if they wrote down and punctuated the comments correctly. Have volunteers write some of the sentences on the board.

Chart 16.6, page 446   5 min.

- **Note:** Many languages do not follow the same tense shift patterns. To remind students to change the verb tense, make a gesture to mean *shift to the past*, such as waving a hand behind your shoulder. Use this gesture if students forget to change the tense.

- **Note 2:** There are times when it is possible to keep the same tense. For example: (1) general fact: *He said that the Earth revolves around the sun*, (2) when one person reports something that was just said: *I asked if you want milk in your tea*, or (3) when the speaker wants to emphasize that a situation is still true: *He told me he loves you!* Explain to students that although there are exceptions, it is generally a good idea to shift tenses when using reported speech.

6 page 446   10 min.

   1. he was coming

   2. if the assignment was due on Friday

   3. there was going to be a storm

   4. he was doing

   5. she was too busy

   6. he had too much work

   7. she wasn't enjoying the movie

   8. he didn't think so

- **Tip:** Ask students to work in groups of three, and assign numbers 1–3 to each person. Have person student 1 whisper a statement to person student 2. Have student 2 whisper the same comment to student 3, using reported speech in the present. Then have student 3 repeat this aloud, to see if this matches what student 1 said. Switch roles and repeat the activity until everyone has had at least two turns.

> **REAL ENGLISH, page 447**
>
> Explain that there are times when the tense does not need to shift. One of these times is when someone reports what has just been said.

7 SPEAK, page 447   5 min.
Answers will vary.

Chart 16.7, page 447   5 min.

- **Notes 1 & 2:** Students often have difficulty remembering whether *said* or *told* takes an object because the two verbs have very similar meanings. One way to help student remember this is with a mnemonic: *Say is solo, but tell needs two people.* Write the following examples on the board: *I said goodbye. I told him goodbye.*

- **Note 3:** Explain that it is possible to have *answer* + object or *answer* + noun clause but not both in one sentence (e.g., *I answered my teacher.* Or, *I answered that it was cold outside.* Not, *I answered my teacher that it was cold outside.*). Explain that *replied* cannot take an object (e.g., *I replied that it was cold outside.* Not, *I replied my teacher.*).

8 page 447   5 min.

1. asked/asked me   5. told me/said

2. replied   6. asked

3. told me   7. answered

4. said   8. asked him

9 page 448   10 min.

1. Will asked Mei what she was watching.

2. Mei said (that) it was a video from the space station.

3. Will asked who was talking.

4. Mei said (that) the mission commander was giving a report.

5. Will asked why the woman's hair was like that.

6. Mei said (that) it was because of zero gravity.

PRACTICE

10 page 449   10 min.

A 1. , "What are you watching?"

2. "It's a video about insects in space,"

3. , "Are you serious?"

4. , "Yes, astronauts sometimes take spiders and ants into space."

5. "Oh, why do they do that?"

6. , "They study their movements and feeding habits."

B 1. what she was watching.

2. it was a video about insects in space.

3. if she was serious.

4. astronauts sometimes took spiders and ants into space.

5. why they did that.

6. they studied their movements and feeding habits.

> **REAL ENGLISH, page 449**
>
> Ask students to work in pairs and discuss what they like to watch on TV. They should continue the conversation for one minute. Then have each student write their own sentences about the conversation using at least three different reporting verbs.

11 SPEAK, page 450   5 min.
Answers will vary.

12 EDIT, page 451   15 min.

For this assignment, I watched an interview with Ellen Ochoa, who became the first Hispanic American woman in space in 1991. She went on to make several more flights and has spent over 950 hours in space.

When the interviewer asked her what ~~was~~ NASA training **was** like, Ochoa replied that everything was harder in training than in space. Next, the interviewer asked Ochoa how ~~did it feel~~ **it felt** to float in zero gravity. She replied that it was fun to be weightless. She ~~told~~ **told the interviewer/said** there was really nothing to compare it to on Earth. She said the closest activity was probably swimming. Ochoa ~~said her~~ **told her/said** that astronauts had to prepare for all sorts of problems and accidents. The interviewer then asked the former astronaut ~~did she miss~~ **if/whether she missed** her family when she was in space. Ochoa said it ~~is~~ **was** difficult. She ~~said~~ **told** the interviewer she used e-mail to communicate with her husband when she was in space.

13 LISTEN, page 451   15 min.

A 1. asked   5. why it

2. was reading   6. replied

3. asked if   7. if

4. said that   8. answered

B 1. , "How is your research going?"

2. , "Great. I'm reading about the Voyager 1 space probe."

3. "Is it a useful article for the assignment?"

4. , "Yes, the mission is at a very exciting stage."

5. , "What's happening?"

6. "The probe is no longer in the solar system,"

7. "Does that mean a man-made object is flying around the galaxy?"

8. , "Yes. It's the first time in history."

14 APPLY, page 452   20 min.
Answers will vary.

- **Tip:** Have students reread the blog on page 442. If possible, have students prepare their answers at home before discussing them with a partner.

- **Alternative Apply:** Have students work in groups of three and prepare a list of 3–5 interview questions to ask prospective astronauts. Each member of the group should have a copy of the questions. Then have students role-play interviews with other classmates. Explain that they should use their imagination. Have students take notes and then return to their original group to discuss the interviews using reported speech. Have the groups decide who they will send to space. If time permits, have each group announce who they will send and why they chose them.

1 page 453   10 min.

1. when/whether   6. said
2. that   7. if/how
3. the city."   8. whether
4. I'm not sure   9. that
5. I believe/I believe that 10. asked/asked them

2 LISTEN & WRITE, page 453   15 min.

A 1. a   3. b   5. a   7. a
    2. a   4. b   6. b   8. a

B *Answers will vary.*

C *Answers will vary.*

3 EDIT, page 455   10 min.

Often we ask ourselves why we are ~~we~~
here. This semester, I have learned a lot about
this question. After learning about fossils from
different parts of the world, I am convinced that
humans began a great journey out of eastern
Africa around 60,000 years ago. Evidence shows
that early humans explored all areas of the globe.
How did they survive? Scientists say ~~us~~ that these
early humans discovered plants and animals to
eat and found ways to stay warm. But, they are not
certain how ~~did they move~~ they moved across
wide oceans and over rough terrain. I'm sure
many didn't survive.

The question is why they did it~~?~~. I believe
the reason is that humans have an innate desire
to explore, learn, and take risks. The author T.S.
Eliot said, "~~only~~ Only those who will risk going
too far can possibly find how far one can go." This
suggests that being an explorer and taking risks
helps us to survive and succeed. We should all ask
ourselves, "What ~~I am~~ am I doing to improve life
for the people who will live after me?"

4 WRITE & SPEAK, page 455   15 min.
Answers will vary.

• **Expansion Tip:** Have students write a report
of the interview. This should be one to two
paragraphs, and should include at least four
instances of reporting verbs and reported speech.
If possible, students should try to have one
example of quoted speech as well. Allow students
time to complete this in class or assign it for
homework. Then have students peer-edit and
compare their reports.

Connect the Grammar to Writing

1 READ & NOTICE THE GRAMMAR, page 456   20 min.

A *Answers will vary.*

- **Tip:** If students have a difficult time thinking of one thing that they learned, make this question more general, by asking, *What do you think people can learn by going to new places?*

B *Answers may vary. Sample answers:*

1. I also learned that we had a lot of work to do./I wanted to believe that I could be that strong.

2. I was surprised that many of them could still laugh./I was amazed that complete neighborhoods were flattened.

3. My friend Bo asked me if I wanted to take a trip to Illinois./He said that some volunteers at the university were going to help people affected by a terrible tornado.

4. One man said, "My family is safe; nothing else really matters."/An older woman said, "Life is too short to be sad for too long. We will rebuild and make new memories."

C

Where did she go?	to Illinois, to a town hit by a horrible tornado
What did she do?	cleared broken furniture, bricks, papers, and pieces of cars and household appliances; moved branches and fallen trees; talked with people whose homes were gone
What did she learn?	She learned that some things are more important than others.
Quotes	"My family is safe; nothing else really matters." "Life is too short to be sad for too long. We will rebuild and make new memories."

- **Expansion Tip:** Ask students if they would like to go on a trip like the one in the reading. Why, or why not? Explain that many U.S. colleges arrange service learning trips (trips that incorporate volunteer work with learning opportunities). Have students discuss whether this is an important aspect of a student's education.

2 BEFORE YOU WRITE, page 457   15 min.
Answers will vary.

- **Expansion Tip:** If time allows, have students interview someone who went on a similar trip and include a quote from this interview.

3 WRITE, page 457   20 min.

WRITING FOCUS, page 457

Have students choose two quotes that are meaningful to them and help them *connect* with a topic. These can be from the textbook, quotes they have found on their own, or quotes they found through an online search of *quotes for English learners*. Have them share their quotes in groups of 3–4 and explain why the quotes have meaning for them.

- **Alternative Writing:** Have students research a famous explorer online and create and deliver a 1–2 minute presentation on the explorer's life. The presentation should include at least one example of quoted speech and two examples of reported speech. Have the other students take notes, and then work in groups of 3–4 to write one sentence for each presentation, using reported speech. Have volunteers share their sentences with the class. Then have the groups discuss which adventure they would most like to have been a part of and why.

- **Alternative Writing:** Have students review the textbook and choose one article that they wish to research in more detail. Have them research and prepare a 1–2 minute presentation. Follow the same steps as in the first alternative writing assignment above.

UNIT 1

LESSON 1

1 READ, page 4   CD1–Track 2

9, page 9   CD1–Track 3

Valerie: Tell me, Kofí . . . How do people usually celebrate birthdays in Ghana?

Kofi: Well, I am Asante, and the Asante people don't celebrate our birthdays on the date we were born. Instead, we celebrate on the *day of the week* we were born. It is a special day, called *krada*. For example, I was born on a Friday, so I always wait until the first Friday after my birthday to celebrate.

Valerie: Oh, that's interesting. When does *krada* start?

Kofi: For the Asante, a new day never begins at midnight. The day always starts at sunrise.

Valerie: What do you usually do to celebrate *krada*?

Kofi: Well, for children, parents often prepare a special breakfast for *krada*. They usually make a dish called *oto* from sweet potatoes and eggs. They always fry the *oto* in palm oil. Later in the day, the child has a party. At the party, children usually eat meat with rice and a sweet dish called *kelewele*.

13B and 13C, page 11   CD1–Track 4

Sally: On today's show, we're talking to Professor Kent Northam about rites of passage. Professor, remind us exactly what a rite of passage is.

Professor: Well, Sally, a rite of passage is a ceremony that marks a change in a person's life. Many rites of passage celebrate the change from child to adult.

Sally: OK, so do you have some examples for our listeners?

Professor: Yes, I do. Now, this first one happens on Pentecost Island in the Pacific. A tribe there builds a tall tower. To prove their bravery, young boys climb to the top and tie themselves to the tower with strong vines. They cut these vines from trees and use them like ropes. Then, the boys jump off the tower head first! The idea is that their heads just touch the ground, so it's important that the vine is the right length, of course.

Sally: Oh, but that's frightening! Do the boys ever get killed?

Professor: Well, that's the surprising thing—people rarely get killed, although they do sometimes get hurt. The men in the tribe dig the ground below the tower to make it soft.

Sally: That's amazing! So, this rite of passage sounds a lot like bungee jumping . . .

Professor: Well, yes, I guess there is a strong similarity.

LESSON 2

1 READ, page 12   CD1–Track 5

11, page 18   CD1–Track 6

Conversation 1

Midori: Hi Sally, how are you doing?

Sally: I'm OK, you?

Midori: Great. You know, I usually hate big crowds, and I think people are too noisy in big groups. Well, guess what? Right now I'm in New York at the Thanksgiving Day parade!

Sally: You are? I don't believe it!

Midori: Yes, I am! And I am having a wonderful time!

Conversation 2

Angela: Mmm . . . this soup tastes delicious! Do you want some?

Kara: No, thanks.

Angela: Are you sure? It's really good.

Kara: No, thanks. I don't feel well, and I don't want you to get sick.

Conversation 3

Mike: Hi, Kemal. Are you OK? You don't look very happy. What's the matter?

Kemal: Oh, I . . .

Andy: Hey, Mike, do you have a minute? I need to ask you something.

Mike: Sorry, but Kemal and I are talking right now. Can I call you later?

REVIEW THE GRAMMAR

3, page 21   CD1–Track 7

Professor: . . . Now, let's look at the next slide, and you will see what I am talking about. Yes, there we are. Now, look at the young man in this photo. He's standing in tomatoes almost up to his waist. And do you see what's happening . . . ?

Student 1: Someone's throwing more tomatoes at him!

Professor: Yes, Kim, that's right. And he's smiling about it.

Student 1: Are you sure? I don't think he's smiling.

Professor: Hmm. . . well, I guess you're right. But do you think he is complaining?

Student 1: No, he's not trying to get away. He's just waiting for the tomatoes to hit him.

Professor: Yes, that's right. He's having a good time.

Student 2: So, you're telling us that people actually do this for fun? They get covered in tomatoes! What's the point of that?

Professor: You know, Philip, that's a very good question. We live with so many laws and rules. . . . Sometimes, people like to feel that there are no rules. Many ancient celebrations include a time like this. For a few hours or a couple of days, no one needs to obey the usual rules. I mean, you can't just go to Buñol and start throwing tomatoes in January, right?

UNIT 2

LESSON 1

1 READ, page 26   CD1—Track 8

9A, 9B and 9D, page 31   CD1—Track 9

Derek: So Andrew, how long did it take to make your last nature film?

Andrew: Well, Derek, we spent all last winter in Antarctica. Then, the editing and production took several more months.

Derek: That's a long time to be in the cold. Why did you choose Antarctica?

Andrew: I wanted to tell the life story of the emperor penguin. I remember when I was a child, I thought penguins were just funny birds at the zoo. The truth is they are very tough, and they survive the coldest winter on earth.

Derek: Really? So, what did you see?

Andrew: Well, we arrived just in time to film a wonderful sight. We filmed huge numbers of emperor penguins as they climbed onto the ice and began a fifty-mile walk away from the sea.

Derek: Fifty miles? Why did they walk so far?

Andrew: They were trying to find the perfect place to lay their eggs and raise their chicks. When they found a good place, the female penguins each laid one egg and then left! The male penguins stayed behind with the eggs. The males kept the eggs safe through the terrible winter. The temperature fell to minus 40 degrees Fahrenheit, and there were very strong winds. Anyway, we got some great shots of the male penguins. . . . They survived the extreme cold by crowding together. They kept moving so that each penguin was able to spend time in the middle of the group. That's how they survived. And during all this, the male penguins didn't have anything to eat!

Derek: Really? Wow. When did the females return?

Andrew: They came back in the spring. Then, the sea ice began to melt, and the penguins were in the best possible place to teach the new chicks to swim.

LESSON 2

1 READ, page 33   CD1—Track 10

LESSON 3

1 READ, page 39   CD1—Track 11

9A and 9B, pages 44–45   CD1—Track 12

Diane: What are you reading?

Julie: It's a biography of Ernest Shackleton.

Diane: Who's he?

Julie: Shackleton? He was an explorer. In 1914, Shackleton sailed to Antarctica with a crew of 27 men. His goal was to reach the South Pole. Their ship, the *Endurance*, was approaching Antarctica in January, 1915, when it became locked in the ice . . .

Diane: Locked in the ice?

Julie: Yeah. When the ocean water froze, ice surrounded the ship.

Diane: Wow. That's terrible.

Julie: I know. . . . Anyway, when the disaster happened, Shackleton became determined to get all his men home safely.

Diane: So, what did he do?

Julie: Well, Shackleton and his men stayed on the *Endurance* at first, and then they made a camp on the ice. . . They waited for nine months but the ice didn't release the ship.

Diane: That's awful. Didn't they have a radio or something?

Julie: No, they didn't . . . No one in the world knew where they were. Then one day, while some of the men were arranging supplies on the ice, the ship began to break up. When the *Endurance* started to sink, Shackleton decided to take his men across the ice on foot. They took small lifeboats with them. He and his men camped on the ice during their five-month journey . . .

Diane: So, then what happened?

Julie: Well, at that point, Shackleton decided to risk an 800-mile trip in one of the lifeboats. While Shackleton and five of his men were trying to reach the island of South Georgia to find help, the others spent several more months at the camp on the ice.

Diane: So did he go back and rescue them?

Julie: Yeah, he did. Shackleton went back for his men in a small ship. Every single one of his 27 men survived. It's amazing, isn't it?

Diane: Yeah, it is. It's incredible!

Julie: I know. And when Shackleton and his men arrived in Chile, they received a hero's welcome.

LESSON 4

The Iceman

Back in 1991, hikers in the mountains near the border of Austria and Italy discovered the body of a man in the ice. Scientists soon learned that the body was over 5000 years old. They called the man the "Iceman."

Scientists used to think that the Iceman died from the cold. Five thousand years ago, people of central Europe used to hunt wild animals for food. They would go up into the mountains in all kinds of weather, and sometimes they wouldn't come back. Then, in 2001, scientists found part of an arrow in the Iceman's body. Somebody killed the Iceman, and we will probably never know why.

After more recent tests, scientists now think the Iceman was not just a hunter. They think he probably had a higher position in society, and didn't spend a lot of time in the mountains. Before the most recent tests, scientists believed that people in the Iceman's community didn't grow crops. However, they found small pieces of stone in the Iceman's stomach. This suggests that the Iceman's people used stones to grind flour for some kind of bread.

Even though the Iceman died over 5000 years ago, we know a lot about his life thanks to scientific research.

REVIEW THE GRAMMAR

While Eric Nerhus was diving in Australia, a shark attacked him. He survived because the shark bit his belt.

Ben Nyaumbe was working on a farm in Kenya when a python attacked him. He survived because he bit the python's tail.

While Kootoo Shaw was sleeping in his tent in Canada, a polar bear attacked him. He survived because a hunter shot the polar bear.

An alligator attacked James Morrow when he was swimming in Florida. He survived because his facemask protected him.

UNIT 3

LESSON 1

LESSON 2

Sarah: Welcome to *Healthline*. Tonight we take another look at healthy eating and what a human body needs to look and feel good. With us in the studio is Dr. Chris Keating. His new book *Vegetables and You* goes on sale . . . um . . . this week, Dr. Keating?

Dr. Keating: Yes, that's right, Sarah. Thanks so much, it's great to be here.

Sarah: So, Dr. Keating, let's get straight to it. What vegetables are really good for our bodies?

Dr. Keating: Well, Sarah, I've brought along a few of my favorites, and the first one I'm going to talk about is squash. Now this is an excellent source of vitamin A. Vitamin A is important for our eyes.

Sarah: So, it helps you see better?

Dr. Keating: Yes, it does. And it's also good for your skin.

Sarah: Hmmm. Good to know . . . Now, I see some green vegetables there. I have to say, I don't like those very much.

Dr. Keating: Well, you need to change your mind, Sarah. Lettuce, cabbage, and other leafy green vegetables are probably the best source of nutrition there is.

Sarah: Really?

Dr. Keating: Yes, really . . . They contain a lot of vitamin K. Vitamin K helps cuts heal quickly and also makes your bones stronger.

Sarah: OK, now my parents used to give me a lot of oranges to eat . . . So, what can you tell us about oranges?

Dr. Keating: Well, Sarah, your parents did the right thing. Oranges are a great source of energy and they are full of vitamin C.

Sarah: Which is good for . . . ?

Dr. Keating: Well, it's important for general health, and it helps build strong muscles, so it's great for athletes.

Sarah: So, that's Dr. Chris Keating, everyone, with some helpful advice on healthy eating. We'll be back with Dr. Keating right after these commercials . . .

LESSON 3

Carlos: Hey, Julie. Hi, Ken.

Julie and Ken: Hi, Carlos.

Julie: Carlos, you look great! Have you been working out?

Ken: Let me guess, you are trying another fashionable diet!

Carlos: Ha! Yes, in fact, I am! I really like it. Do you know about CrossFit? It's an exercise program that has a different workout posted online every day. People at my gym follow the Paleo diet, so I'm trying it out.

Ken: Oh, yeah. I just saw something about it on TV. You don't eat *any* grains or sugar, right?

Carlos: Yes, that's right. I don't eat any added sugar or other sweetener, like honey or syrup, either. I do eat some fruit, though.

Julie: *Paleo*, so you eat like a caveman, then?

Carlos: Yep, that's about right. Fruits, vegetables, and meat, a lot of meat! The Paleo diet is very different from vegetarian or vegan diets, for sure.

Julie: Uh oh. It might be difficult for us to find a restaurant, then. I'm still a vegetarian, and I only eat a little seafood, but no other meat.

Ken: I thought you were a vegan, Julie?

Julie: I was for a few months, but I stopped. I had to avoid all meat, dairy, and any product made using animals—including shoes and clothing. It was too difficult for me.

Ken: No cheese or milk? That *is* tough.

Carlos: Wait, Ken. You eat cheese and milk? I didn't think you ate much dairy. Aren't you on a low-fat diet?

Ken: Yes, but I eat low-fat cheese and other dairy. I eat lean meat, too, but not a lot.

Julie: Carlos, do you eat dairy on the Paleo diet?

Carlos: A little, but not a lot. Some people don't eat any. There is some debate about it. I love cheese, though!

Ken: Full fat does taste better, but my doctor said low-fat foods were good for my heart and weight. I never seem to lose weight, though.

Julie: Neither do I. Some people say that avoiding sugar is more important than avoiding fat, but that would be really hard for me!

Ken: Me, too! There are some tasty low-fat sweets. . .

Carlos: Well, often those *low-fat* products, such as yogurt and cookies, have a lot of added sugar. Grains also become sugar in your body, so eating a lot of bread, rice, or other grains is not good for you. You will never lose weight. Try the Paleo diet! You'll lose weight in one week!

Ken: Really? I can have a steak and lose weight?

Carlos: Absolutely!

Julie: Don't get me started about animal conditions and all the problems with meat. It's awful.

Carlos: I know. You're right. I always try to eat organic meat and produce from good farms.

Ken: That can be so expensive!

Carlos: True, it costs a lot of money to eat well. But I figure it *is* for my health.

REVIEW THE GRAMMAR

5A, page 83   CD1–Track 23

Speaker 1: I'm a good swimmer, and I do a lot of running to keep fit. Then a few months ago, a friend of mine did a triathlon, which is a race with swimming, running, and cycling, and it sounded like a lot of fun . . . So anyway, I borrowed his bike this week and went for a ride, and you know what? I am having the best time! I can't wait to enter my first race!

CD1–Track 24

Speaker 2: Well, I'm on the basketball team this semester, but I'm not sure if I want to keep playing or not. I mean, I like basketball, but I have practice every day, and I want more time to do other activities, too. I enjoy tennis, and I love sailing . . . I go whenever I get the chance, which isn't very often these days. Then, there's swimming and volleyball . . . There just isn't time for everything! Also, my basketball coach says I need to run more to keep fit, but I hate running, so I don't do a lot of it. I like being on a team with other people and the games are always fun . . . I'm not really sure what to do.

CD1–Track 25

Speaker 3: I don't like to play team sports very much. Winning and losing become the most important things, and for me, well, I just like to relax and keep fit, so I love yoga. I exercise at home mostly, but I take a class once a week and that's a lot of fun. It's great to hear other people's ideas and advice about keeping fit. I learn something new every time I go.

CD1–Track 26

Speaker 4: The thing about skiing is you need to pay attention, all the time. I mean . . . one mistake and you can end up in the hospital, so you really have to think about what you are doing. Also, sometimes the weather is not so good, or there's a lot of ice on the mountain—or a lot of other skiers! All of these things can be very dangerous, so you really need to be careful. Some of my friends do cycling, running, and other sports, but skiing is the sport for me . . . there's no question!

CD1–Track 27

Speaker 5: I play football at college. I just love it—it's such an exciting game, and I enjoy the physical side of it, too. We're lucky because we have an excellent coach. Actually, he's my roommate's father, so I get to hear a lot of interesting and helpful information about the games. He knows a lot. Sometimes I ask him for advice. He used to play football, too. Anyway, football is great. It's my favorite sport. The only problem is that I get hurt almost every week. I hurt my arm one week, then I hurt my knee . . . , and last year I actually broke my ankle. It still hurts sometimes.

UNIT 4

LESSON 1

1 READ, page 88 CD1–Track 28

12A, page 94 CD1–Track 29

A couple years ago, my wife Eva and I went on a cruise with our good friends, Lara and Aaron. What a nightmare! The Mediterranean was beautiful, and we saw many amazing things, but we had a bit of bad luck.

First, I forgot to bring my medicine for seasickness. I was OK in the beginning, but as soon as we left Gibraltar, I felt terrible. I didn't leave our room the whole time. Everyone else enjoyed themselves. They met people from different countries, and saw lots of beautiful scenery. Luckily, when we got to the island of Ibiza, Eva bought me some medicine and soon I felt better.

The next day, on the island of Ibiza, Eva and I spent our day on a seabird watching tour. Lara and Aaron relaxed on a beautiful white sandy beach. Lara likes collecting seashells, and while she was digging in the sand for one, she cut herself on a piece of broken glass. Luckily, the lifeguard had a bandage. It wasn't easy for her to swim after that, but at least she was OK.

Then, when we were heading for Sardinia, an island that belongs to Italy, there was a storm. The ship was a bit rocky. As we were arriving to the port, Eva lost her balance and fell down. She hurt her shoulder badly. Right when we arrived to Sardinia, we went to a hospital. Luckily, Eva was OK and able to continue the trip, but I felt sorry for her. It's no fun to travel with an injury.

Finally, when we were near Malta, a small island country south of Italy, we were very excited to see dolphins jumping not too far from the ship. Aaron was taking some great video with his phone when one dolphin jumped closer than expected! He was so surprised that he dropped his phone . . . right into the Mediterranean!

Well, we have laughed a lot about the trip since then, so I guess it wasn't a complete disaster!

12B, page 95 CD1–Track 30

A couple years ago, my wife Eva and I went on a cruise with our good friends, Lara and Aaron. What a nightmare! The Mediterranean was beautiful, and we saw many amazing things, but we had a bit of bad luck.

First, I forgot to bring my medicine for seasickness. I was OK in the beginning, but as soon as we left Gibraltar, I felt terrible. I didn't leave our room the whole time. Everyone else enjoyed themselves. They met people from different countries, and saw lots of beautiful scenery. Luckily, when we got to the island of Ibiza, Eva bought me some medicine and soon I felt better.

The next day, on the island of Ibiza, Eva and I spent our day on a seabird watching tour. Lara and Aaron relaxed on a beautiful white sandy beach. Lara likes collecting seashells, and while she was digging in the sand for one, she cut herself on a piece of broken glass. Luckily, the lifeguard had a bandage. It wasn't easy for her to swim after that, but at least she was OK.

Then, when we were heading for Sardinia, an island that belongs to Italy, there was a storm. The ship was a bit rocky. As we were arriving to the port, Eva lost her balance and fell down. She hurt her shoulder badly. Right when we arrived to Sardinia, we went to a hospital. Luckily, Eva was OK and able to continue the trip, but I felt sorry for her. It's no fun to travel with an injury.

Finally, when we were near Malta, a small island country south of Italy, we were very excited to see dolphins jumping not too far from the ship. Aaron was taking some great video with his phone when one dolphin jumped closer than expected! He was so surprised that he dropped his phone . . . right into the Mediterranean!

Well, we have laughed a lot about the trip since then, so I guess it wasn't a complete disaster!

LESSON 2

1 READ, page 96 CD1–Track 34

11, page 102 CD1–Track 35

Professor: Hello, everyone. This week, we're going to start the lesson with a talk by Melanie Hopkins. Now, Melanie, you took a special vacation in the summer. You went on a writing course in Europe. I'm sure we'd all like to hear what it was like.

Melanie: Yes, thank you Professor Jameson, and good evening everyone. So, this was such a good vacation, I almost don't know where to begin. The course I attended was terrific, and the teachers really helped me with my writing style and my creative process. The course took place in Paris for a month from July 6th to August 6th. It was a great opportunity to concentrate on my writing.

We stayed in the Latin Quarter. There has been a writer's community there for hundreds of years, and the atmosphere was very exciting.

We had formal classes of course, just like here, but in Paris we would also get together—the students I mean—at about eight o'clock and sit outside a bookstore or beside the river and just share our thoughts about the day's work and life in general. There were students from all over the world, so there were a lot of different ideas in those discussions, as you can imagine. The professors encouraged us to spend time in a café observing life and watching the world go by.

The whole experience changed my life. Before the trip, I just felt like a student, like someone learning to write. Now, I feel connected to something bigger than myself. I feel I have something important to say. That probably sounds a bit strange, but I have much more confidence in my writing now . . .

LESSON 3

1 READ, page 103 CD1–Track 36

9C, page 109 CD1–Track 37

Radio Field Report 1

This is Alex Harley, speaking to you live on July 14th from the town of Bend, Oregon, where local gas station owner Kent Couch and his Iraqi co-pilot, Fareed Lafta, took off at 10:20 this morning in a two-seater lawn chair—yes, you heard right—a *lawn chair* attached to 150 giant party balloons filled with helium gas. The two men are planning a 508-mile flight from Oregon to Montana, and they expect to travel at a height of between 15,000 and 18,000 feet. To control their height, they are carrying three large containers of soft drinks. They will empty these out a little at a time if they get too low. When they want to land, they will shoot some balloons. This will make them start to come down. Each of the men has a small gun for this purpose. They are also carrying sleeping bags—it gets pretty cold at 15,000 feet—parachutes, and an emergency flare, in case they need to attract attention, and other emergency equipment. Listen for reports later in the day as we bring you all the details of this fantastic journey . . .

Radio Field Report 2 CD1–Track 38

Welcome back to Bend, Oregon. Once again this is Alex Harley, reporting on the amazing flight of Kent Couch and Fareed Lafta in their lawn-chair balloon. The good news is that the early part of the flight is going very well. After take-off, the two men climbed rapidly over a coffee stand, a light post, and a two-story hotel and started safely on their journey. However, we are beginning to get some reports of bad weather coming in just north of here, and that's right where the two adventurers are at the moment! There's talk of electrical storms later, and of course, that is very bad news. Check back with us later for more developments.

Radio Field Report 3 CD1–Track 39

This is Alex Harley in Bend, Oregon. Well folks, it's now a little after 7 p.m. local time and sadly Kent Couch's amazing balloon flight ended a short time ago. He and his co-pilot flew for around seven hours, but the wind kept changing direction, so they didn't cover a lot of distance. They landed around 40 miles away near the small town of Post, Oregon. It may be a disappointing end to the flight, but the end doesn't take anything away from today's story of courage and adventure. We already hear that Kent and Fareed are planning a flight in Iraq in the fall . . .

LESSON 4

1 READ, page 110 CD1–Track 40

REVIEW THE GRAMMAR

3A and 3B, page 117 CD1–Track 41

I live in Boston. I used to live in Chicago, but about three years ago, I got a new job at a company in Boston, so I moved. Boston's a wonderful city—I love it. It took some time to find an apartment, but finally I found one on Beacon Hill. It's small, but that's OK, I mean, I live by myself, so I don't need a lot of space or anything, and it's in a great location—right near Boston Common and the Public Garden. The Public Garden is beautiful, especially in the spring and summer with all of the flowers. It's a nice place to go for a walk or just sit on a park bench and read and relax. . . or even have a picnic. It's very peaceful. And in the winter, there's ice skating. That's a lot of fun even though I'm not very good at it!

Boston's a small city—a lot smaller than Chicago, but there's lots to do here . . . and the public transportation is good, so it's easy to get around. You really don't need a car. There are a lot of great museums, like the Museum of Fine Arts—that's a fantastic museum. I go there every couple of months or so, and then there's the Museum of Science. I went there for the first time last month and really enjoyed it. And I love Newbury Street and that whole area . . . Newbury Street's a beautiful street and a popular shopping area, but some of the shops are *very* expensive. Even so, it's a nice place to meet friends and at least *window* shop . . . There are a lot of good restaurants in the area, too. In the summer, some of the restaurants have tables outside. I like to go there on Friday nights after work. I also like go to the Prudential Center—it's a nice place . . . the shopping and restaurants are good there, too.

There are so many great places in Boston, but I think my favorite is Faneuil Hall Marketplace. It's near the waterfront and easy to get to by public transportation, so it's a good place to meet up with friends. I often go there on weekends to shop, walk around, or have dinner with friends. There's one restaurant I go to all the time—the seafood there is fantastic! Anyway, Faneuil Hall is a popular tourist spot and an important part of the city's history, it's a good place to take visitors from out of town. When my parents visit, I always take them there. My mom loves the shopping, and my dad's very interested in the history.

UNIT 5

LESSON 1

1 READ, page 122 CD2–Track 2

12, page 129 CD2–Track 3

1. He's just found a new apartment.
2. I've just changed jobs.
3. We've eaten at that restaurant a few times.
4. Where have you been all week?
5. Who's finished the assignment?
6. Has she ever been to Alaska?
7. I've never flown in a helicopter.
8. Have they sold their house yet?

LESSON 2

1 READ, page 130 CD2–Track 4

7A, page 134 CD2–Track 5

Conversation 1

Agent: Hello, this is Brianna. How may I help you today?

Caller: Oh, yes, hello . . . Um . . . I'm having problems with my new MP3 player.

Agent: I'm sorry to hear that. How long have you had it?

Caller: Well, let's see . . . I bought it in January, so I've only had it for about two months.

Agent: OK, so two months. And what's the problem?

Caller: Well, for the last week or two, the sound has been terrible—really unclear, and sometimes it stops in the middle of a song.

Agent: Hmmm. Did it fall, or did you drop it or anything like that?

Caller: No, but I used it once in the rain, and it hasn't been the same since.

Agent: OK . . . let me take down your information.

Conversation 2

Agent: Good morning. My name's Tyler. How may I help you?

Caller: Hello. I hope you can help me. I've had some problems with my phone recently.

Agent: I do apologize, and I'll certainly try to help you. What's the problem, sir?

Caller: Well, I dropped it a couple of days ago. I was running to catch the train, well, anyway . . . ever since I dropped it, the screen's been really unclear.

Agent: OK. How old is your phone?

Caller: Let's see. . . . I bought it about two years ago.

Agent: OK . . . and have you ever had this problem before?

Caller: No, this is the first time it's happened.

Conversation 3

Agent: Good afternoon. This is Denise.

Caller: Finally! I've been on hold for twenty minutes.

Agent: I'm sorry, sir. Thank you for your patience. We've had a lot of calls today. How can I help you?

Caller: It's my computer . . . My Internet connection hasn't worked since we lost power yesterday.

Agent: Was that because of the storm?

Caller: Yes.

Agent: I see. And how long have you had your computer, sir.

Caller: Oh, I guess I've had it for about six months.

Agent: Well it's possible the storm caused the damage . . .

7B, pages 134–135 CD2–Track 6

Conversation 1

Agent: Hello, this is Brianna. How may I help you today?

Caller: Oh, yes, hello . . . Um . . . I'm having problems with my new MP3 player.

Agent: I'm sorry to hear that. How long have you had it?

Caller: Well, let's see . . . I bought it in January, so I've only had it for about two months.

Agent: OK, so two months. And what's the problem?

Caller: Well, for the last week or two, the sound has been terrible—really unclear, and sometimes it stops in the middle of a song.

Agent: Hmmm. Did it fall, or did you drop it or anything like that?

Caller: No, but I used it once in the rain, and it hasn't been the same since.

Agent: OK . . . let me take down your information.

Conversation 2 CD2–Track 7

Agent: Good morning. My name's Tyler. How may I help you?

Caller: Hello. I hope you can help me. I've had some problems with my phone recently.

Agent: I do apologize, and I'll certainly try to help you. What's the problem, sir?

Caller: Well, I dropped it a couple of days ago. I was running to catch the train, well, anyway . . . ever since I dropped it, the screen's been really unclear.

Agent: OK. How old is your phone?

Caller: Let's see . . . I bought it about two years ago.

Agent: OK . . . and have you ever had this problem before?

Caller: No, this is the first time it's happened. . .

Conversation 3 CD2–Track 8

Agent: Good afternoon. This is Denise.

Caller: Finally! I've been on hold for twenty minutes.

Agent: I'm sorry, sir. Thank you for your patience. We've had a lot of calls today. How can I help you?

Caller: It's my computer. . . My Internet connection hasn't worked since we lost power yesterday.

Agent: Was that because of the storm?

Caller: Yes.

Agent: I see. And how long have you had your computer, sir.

Caller: Oh, I guess I've had it for about six months.

Agent: Well it's possible the storm caused the damage . . .

LESSON 3

1 READ, page 136 CD2–Track 9

LESSON 4

1 READ, page 144 CD2–Track 10

10A and 10C, pages 149–150 CD2–Track 11

Marina: . . . and it really is a great place to live . . . OK, so now that I've told you everything about my hometown, Lars, tell me something about yours.

Lars: All right, well, I come from a small city called Kiruna in Sweden. It's the northern most city in the country, about 90 miles above the Arctic Circle.

Marina: Wow! It sounds cold! Have you lived there your entire life?

Lars: Yes, I've lived there—in the same house—all my life, but my family won't be there for much longer.

Marina: So, you're moving?

Lars: Not just us . . . the whole center of town needs to move.

Marina: What? I don't understand . . .

Lars: Well, it's because of the mine there. There is a big iron mine near the town. Recently, because of the mine, the ground under the city has been cracking.

Marina: Really? That's terrible! Has anything happened so far because of this?

Lars: The railroad, roads, and electricity lines have already started to move. They are going to take some of the old buildings apart and rebuild them in the new location.

Marina: Does everyone agree with the idea?

Lars: Well, a lot of people in the town are sad about it. My grandmother has been there for 70 years. She doesn't want to leave, of course, but she has seen the cracks in the ground and she knows she can't stay. And there are also the people who already live in the area the town is moving to, and they're against the idea.

Marina: Who are they?

Lars: Many of them are Sami. The Sami people have been taking care of their reindeer in the Arctic for hundreds of years. They were living in the area long before the mine came. The new railroad cuts across the land the Sami use for their animals.

Marina: Hmmm. That sounds like a problem.

Lars: Yes, their lives have already changed in many ways. For example, the Sami have been using modern vehicles to help move their reindeer for a long time now.

REVIEW THE GRAMMAR

4B and 4C, page 153 CD2–Track 12

Greg: So, today's show is about the use of technology at work. So, let's get right to it. Caller number 1, what do you have to say to our listeners?

Caller 1: Yes, hello Greg. Um, well, the way we work has changed a lot in recent years, but young people like me often feel that it hasn't changed enough.

Greg: Oh, yes? Why is that?

Caller 1: Well, for example, we've been using social media since it first appeared. My friends and I all have the most up-to-date phones and other technology. But I work for a company that still uses old computer software to run its business. Some of their programs came on the market before I was born! I mean, the e-mail system is so old. I can't believe people still use stuff like that.

Greg: And how do you feel about that?

Caller 1: I just think it's crazy. When I leave my home in the morning and go to the office, I feel like I am going back in history!

Greg: OK, thank you, Caller number 1, that's a great start to the discussion. Let's see if Caller number 2 agrees.

Caller 2: Uh, no, I really don't. Um, I think it's fine that some businesses haven't started using all the latest software yet. I mean, it's important for them to think about effects of technology on real human communication. I feel like that's disappearing. People hardly talk to each other anymore. They do everything with their phones! I mean, take last week for example, I received six e-mails in one hour from the same coworker.

Greg: Did they waste your time?

Caller 2: No, they were all important, that wasn't the problem. The strange thing was that this person was sitting in the cubicle next to mine, and she didn't say one word to me the whole time!

Greg: You're kidding!

Caller 2: Not at all. My company has noticed this sort of behavior. Our company president has been conducting an experiment recently. For one day each week, she has been shutting down the company's e-mail system. People have been having real conversations again, even if it's only on the phone. I've been getting up from my desk a few times each morning and going to other offices. It's nice to talk to people face-to-face like we used to. Since the experiment, the change in the office has been amazing. I think everybody is enjoying their work a little more.

Greg: Well, that sounds great, but I expect you are losing business, right? . . .

UNIT 6

LESSON 1

1 READ, page 158   CD2–Track 13

9, page 163   CD2–Track 14

Petra: What are you watching?

Alex: It's a documentary about birds. Look, this part is about peacocks.

Petra: Oh, good—peacocks are my favorite kind of bird.

Alex: Really?

Petra: Yes. I love their feathers. The colors are amazing!

Alex: Well, yes, the males are very colorful, but the females aren't. Their feathers aren't green. They're brown.

Petra: I know, but that's the way it is with most birds: the male has beautiful feathers, so he is attractive to females.

Alex: I guess so. Well, they certainly are interesting, beautiful birds, but they make a terrible noise.

Petra: Yes, that's true. When a male calls out to the female birds, he doesn't make a very nice sound.

LESSON 2

1 READ, page 165   CD2–Track 15

10B, page 171   CD2–Track 16

Jessica: OK, welcome back to *Helping Hand*, everybody. I'm Jessica Lane, and today we're talking about interview techniques and how to get that job you want so much. We have Mark Squire with us, he's an expert on this important topic and you can be sure he'll have the answers to your questions. Right, Mark?

Mark: I'll do my best, Jessica.

Jessica: Great, now the next e-mail comes from Kevin in Ohio, and his first interview didn't go so well. Let me read you what he says . . .

Hi Jessica and Mark,

I need some advice. I had an interview for a job as a DJ at my local radio station, but I was unsuccessful. I've had a lot of experience as a DJ, and I work very hard. I wore a nice new suit to the interview, and I felt pretty confident when I left my house.

Before the interview, I read some interview tips and techniques online. For example, one said, "Copy the interviewer's movements closely." Well, I tried that technique, but the interviewers didn't seem to like it very much. Anyway, I didn't get the job. Now I'm really confused. I know I made a few mistakes in the interview, but nothing really bad. At first, I was nervous, but that was because I arrived late. When the interview started, I spoke loudly, smiled frequently, and talked a lot—well, until they asked me to stop. Also, I didn't ask any questions, but in general, I thought it went well. Where did I go wrong?

Thanks,

Kevin in Ohio

10D, page 171   CD2–Track 17

Jessica: OK, well, I hope you're listening, Kevin, because I'm pretty sure Mark has some good advice for you. Mark?

Mark: Yes, well, first of all, Kevin . . . you *cannot* be late for an interview! For any type of job, anywhere, anytime . . . get there *early*, my friend!

Jessica: Um, I suppose some people just want to be right on time, you know, so they aren't sitting around in the waiting area for a long time. That makes some people nervous . . .

Mark: Hmm, yeah, but then there is traffic to think about and finding the *place* . . . and of course *parking*. . .

Jessica: That's true. OK, so what's next?

Mark: Uh . . . clothes. So, you wore a nice, fancy new suit, Kevin? . . . It was a pop *radio* station, not a *bank*, OK?

Jessica: Right, but most people advise you to dress well for an interview . . .

Mark: Yeah, but in this case, dressing well means dressing *appropriately*, you know, wearing the *right* thing for the job and the company. Take my advice Kevin, if you want to be a pop DJ, save the suit for your sister's wedding.

Jessica: All right, now. . . about copying the interviewers' movements—what are your thoughts and advice about that?

Mark: Well, it's about body language, you know . . . the signals we send without speaking . . . how we sit, how we stand, how we move . . . There's an idea that when you behave the same way as the person you're speaking with, they relax more and even like you more, but if it doesn't happen naturally, just copying someone can be *extremely* dangerous! That person might think you are making *fun* of them!

Jessica: Hmm, OK Kevin, I think we're beginning to understand why you didn't get this job. Any other advice, Mark?

Mark: Sure. Smiling is very good, but talking loudly or very fast is generally a bad thing in an interview. It's also important to ask questions. It's shows you're interested. This is very basic. Everyone knows this. Next time try to think of a few good questions and write them down—and bring them with you. Maybe spend more time on questions and less time picking out a new suit, OK? And back to the issue of talking in an interview. You need to know when to stop yourself, not wait until someone asks you to. Speak clearly and say what you want to say. Answer the question and make it good, then stop. And make it clear that you're finished. Don't just go silent in the middle of a sentence . . .

Jessica: Uh, Mark? . . .

Mark: There, you see? That was an example of what not to do. You'll never get a job behaving like that. You have to know when to stop talking in an interview—or in any situation, really.

Jessica: OK, well, that's all good advice for you, Kevin, and good advice for all of our other listeners, too. We're going to take another short commercial break. Don't go away!

REVIEW THE GRAMMAR

3A, page 173   CD2–Track 18

Marion: Did you record that show you wanted to watch—the one about bowerbirds?

Ken: Yes, I did. In fact, I've already watched it. It was really interesting.

Marion: Oh, that's too bad! I wanted to watch it with you.

Ken: I know. I'm sorry, but I'd like to see it again, anyway. I just put it on to check the recording, but the photography was wonderful! I watched the whole thing straight through. Some of the bowers the birds build are amazing.

Marion: What is a *bower* anyway?

Ken: It's something that the birds build out of sticks.

Marion: Like a nest?

Ken: Well, no. Not exactly. The male birds build them to attract females. Some species of bowerbird build tall, round bowers with roofs. . . . Others build two walls with a path between them. Scientists call the path an *avenue*. . . . Some birds even paint the sticks in their bowers with a plant mixture.

Marion: They *paint*?

Ken: Yeah, and if the female likes the taste of it, she'll stay longer. Anyway, the bower is where the female goes to watch the show.

Marion: The *show*? What show?

Ken: Oh, the males dance and sing for the females. But first, they fly off and collect materials to make a sort of stage in front of the bower.

Marion: So do the different species make different types of bowers or something?

Ken: Well, that's the surprising thing! The stage depends on the bird itself, not the species. The documentary showed three bowers, all from the same species. One had a stage made of leaves, and another was made of nuts. The third bird had collected old drink cans and other shiny pieces of garbage.

Marion: Ew! That sounds terrible!

Ken: Well, the females clearly didn't agree with you. That bower bird was the most successful one!

UNIT 7

LESSON 1

1 READ, page 178   CD2–Track 19

5, pages 182–183   CD2–Track 20

Carl: I'm so glad it's Friday. Are you going to do anything special this weekend, Valerie?

Valerie: Yes, I'm going to go to the opening of the new Space Museum. I'm sure it'll be crowded, but I really want to see it.

Carl: What are you going to see there?

Valerie: Well, Phil and I are going to take the children on some of the rides. There's one called "A Trip to the Moon."

Carl: That sounds fun.

Valerie: Yeah, they're going to love it.

Carl: What are you and Phil going to do?

Valerie: Oh, an astronaut is giving a lecture in the afternoon. We're going to attend that. How about you? Are you going to the game on Saturday?

Carl: No, I'm not, unfortunately. I have to study.

Valerie: That's too bad. Are you going to study all weekend?

Carl: No, on Sunday, I'm not going to do any work. I'm going to sleep late and just relax.

Valerie: Oh, good. Well, have a great time.

7, page 183   CD2–Track 21

1. This book about the planets looks great. I'm going to buy it.
2. My brother enjoyed the astronaut's lecture. He's going to go to another one next month.
3. Governments aren't going to spend much money on space research in the near future.
4. The astronauts will be on the space station until the end of the month.
5. A: Don't wait for me. I'm going to be here for a long time.

    B: I'm not in a hurry. I'll wait for you.
6. The museum gift shop will open at 10:00 a.m.
7. There won't be any lectures next week.
8. Sarah won't like that movie. She doesn't like science fiction.

9A, page 184   CD2–Track 22

Glenn: Hi, my name's Glenn Lopez, and I want to be an astronaut. I'm taking flying lessons now, and in two years I'll be a pilot. Then, I'll need to get some more flying experience. My plan is to start astronaut training in five years. The basic training takes two years, and then there is a lot more to learn before you can go on an actual mission. Ten years from now I'll be in space!

Sylvia: I'm Sylvia Moretti, and I'm a medical student. I think medical research in space will help people here on Earth and that's why I want to become an astronaut. I'm going to finish medical school in two years. In five years, I'll be a doctor. Then, I'll start thinking about astronaut training. If everything goes according to plan, I'll be ready to go on my first space mission in about ten years.

Mark: My name is Mark Johnson, and I'm still in college. I'm going to join the Air Force in two years, after I graduate. That'll be a good place to develop my skills, and five years from now, I'll be an experienced flight engineer. I've always wanted to go into space. Everyone knows it's very tough to become an astronaut, but I'm going to work hard. Then, in ten years, I'm going to work for NASA as an engineer.

LESSON 2

1 READ, page 186   CD2–Track 23

8, page 190   CD2–Track 24

1. I'm giving a presentation about our new product tomorrow.
2. The boss isn't flying to Europe next Thursday.
3. Trisha starts work at 8:30 every morning.
4. I'm waiting for a call from David right now.
5. Do we have a meeting this afternoon?
6. Are they arriving on Friday?
7. Martin prepares the sales figures every week.
8. Are you busy right now?

LESSON 3

1 READ, page 192   CD2–Track 25

REVIEW THE GRAMMAR

3A and 3B, page 201   CD2–Track 26

Matt: I love to learn new things. I always have . . . A few months ago, I took a Thai cooking class, and now I'm trying to learn Russian online. But the one thing I've always really wanted to do is learn to play the guitar, so I'm going to do it. . . . So, anyway, I'm going to take a class at a music store downtown. It meets once a week on Tuesday nights. The music store is close to my office, so it's perfect. I've never been much of a musician—I learned *that* in high school when I took violin lessons—I was terrible, so I know it's not going to be easy for me! Anyway, I really want to learn, so I'm going practice every day. I've heard that it's really important to practice every day—even for a short time—so, I'm going to do that. I'm also going to listen to music a lot. I mean, more than I *already* do. There are some great bands in this area. Anyway, that's my plan—I won't become famous, so don't wait around for my first album to come out or anything— in fact, I probably won't be very good at all, but I think I'll enjoy it, and like I said, it's something I've always wanted to do, so, hey, why not?

CD2–Track 27

Tammy: Every year I set a goal for myself . . . and *this* year, I've decided to run a marathon. That's right, 26.2 miles! Well, I guess I've got some work to do. I started running about two years ago. I run a few times a week, but only short distances—you know, two maybe three miles at a time, so I need to start running longer distances. The first thing I'm going to do is buy a new pair of running shoes. Mine are really old. That'll be the easy part! Then, I'm going to join a running club. There's one in my neighborhood that meets every Saturday morning at nine o'clock. I think running with other people will be helpful, and I'll meet new people. And I'm sure I'll get some helpful tips from the other members of the group. Then, when I feel ready, I'm going to enter some short races. I've read that this is a good way to practice and build up to your goal. Anyway, I know it's going to be really hard. But one thing's for sure, I'll get in great shape. Well, I don't have any hopes of winning a medal or anything. I just want to finish, even if I come in last.

UNIT 8

LESSON 1

1 READ, page 206   CD2–Track 28

11, page 212   CD2–Track 29

Speaker 1: I like both of these coats very much. The blue one is a little cheaper, and the collar is prettier. The green one is a little longer. But it's also a little tighter, and the green one is more comfortable. So, I think the green one is the one I'm going to buy.

Speaker 2: I'm going to get a family car. A sports car is faster and more fun to drive, but a family car has more room and is more comfortable. The main reason for my choice, though, is that the family car is cheaper to run.

Speaker 3: It's my mom's birthday, and she loves red roses. But she likes yellow roses too, and these yellow roses are much fresher than the red roses. I'll take a dozen yellow roses, please.

Speaker 4: Wow! This apartment is huge! It's further from my office, but it's much bigger than the downtown apartment I looked at last week. It's quieter out here in the suburbs, too. But I think I'm still going to go with the downtown apartment. It's just so much more convenient for work.

Speaker 5: I love walking boots! They're so much more comfortable than the shoes I wear to work. But I can't make up my mind between these brown boots and the black ones I tried on before. The brown ones are better looking and they're a little cheaper, but I think the black ones will last longer. That's really more important to me, so I'll get the black ones.

Speaker 6: This TV is really big, but the picture isn't very clear. The picture on this smaller TV is much clearer. I don't really need a big TV anyway, so I'm going to buy the smaller TV.

LESSON 2

1 READ, page 213   CD2–Track 30

LESSON 3

1 READ, page 220   CD2–Track 31

5A, page 223   CD2–Track 32

1. At what time of day do you work most efficiently?

2. Who is the most beautiful person in the world?

3. What is the worst movie you've ever seen?

4. What kind of book do you read most frequently?

5. What is the most important thing to do in a storm?

6. What is the most interesting sport to watch?

7. What is the closest place to have lunch in this area?

8. Who is the smartest person in your family?

REVIEW THE GRAMMAR

3A and 3B, page 229   CD2–Track 33

Professor: Now you've all had time to read some of the other information from the Greendex Survey. Martin, did you find anything interesting?

Martin: Um, yes. Most people think that their country is greener than the results show. Also, many people think they buy goods more carefully than they really do. I guess we like to think we're trying as hard as we can to be green... You know, we like to think that all the problems with the environment are someone else's fault.

Professor: OK... that's an interesting idea. Karin, did anything surprise you about the survey?

Karin: Well, I wasn't surprised that the United States got low scores for most of the categories. I don't think most people here are very careful about the goods they buy.

Professor: OK. Any other thoughts?

Karin: Yeah, also, life in the United States is much more difficult without a car. I mean people travel long distances to go to work, shop, visit friends and family, so people really *need* cars.

Professor: True, but maybe more Americans could drive smaller cars.

Karin: Yes, and cars that use less gas *are* becoming more popular in the U.S. But there's a new Greendex Survey every year, and the results show that attitudes aren't changing as quickly as people think. I mean, people don't really want to change the way they do things.

Professor: Good point. Thank you, Karin. Andrew, what do you think about the survey as a whole?

Andrew: Well, to be honest, I'm not sure what to think. Most people want to make life more comfortable for themselves and their families if they can... I mean, everyone wants an easier life. So, it doesn't surprise me that many countries get low scores on surveys like these.

UNIT 9

LESSON 1

1 READ, page 234   CD3–Track 2

12A, page 241   CD3–Track 3

California is home to several types of redwood trees, but the most famous is the Sequoia, or giant redwood. This huge tree only grows in a narrow area along the coast. Most of the world's giant redwoods are in California, but you can also find these trees in Oregon.

Redwoods can grow to a height of 379 feet. Their circumference, or the distance around the outside of the tree trunk, can be up to 26 feet. They have long, flat leaves, and they have surprisingly shallow roots for such big trees. But of course, these roots are extremely strong.

The tallest and oldest trees grow in deep valleys where the conditions are perfect for them, and some of the biggest trees have even become tourist attractions. People love to take pictures of themselves standing in front of one of these giants of nature.

LESSON 2

1 READ, page 242   CD3–Track 4

11A, page 249   CD3–Track 5

Professor: OK, so today we're going to talk about the connection between two of the biggest geological features on Earth: the Sahara Desert and the Amazon rainforest. Now, you probably think there is no connection because the two places are so far apart. However, although the Sahara is thousands of miles from the Amazon, there is an important relationship between them. Now, who can tell me what a desert is made of? Come on, it's not a trick question...

Student 1: Um... sand?

Professor: Yes! Sand! Thank you, Alan. And what *is* sand? Where does it come from?

Student 2: From rocks. Over millions of years, rocks break down and become sand.

Professor: Right, and when scientists study sand, what do they find?

Student 1: Um, minerals . . . metals and salts and stuff like that. . . Everything that was in the rocks.

Professor: Right. Good. Now, plants need minerals to grow, right? And the Amazon rainforest has 2.7 million square miles of hungry plants, so you can imagine that those plants need a lot of minerals to survive!

Student 2: OK, but I still don't understand the connection between the Amazon rainforest and the Sahara. I mean, no one *takes* the sand to the Amazon, right?

Professor: Well, that's the thing, Carmen. No one *needs* to take sand from the Sahara to the Amazon because it gets there by itself.

Student 2: It does? How?

Professor: Well, one thing everyone knows about deserts is that there are a lot of sandstorms there. During a sandstorm, the wind picks the sand up and moves it at high speeds. And although most of the sand comes back to Earth, large amounts are carried high into the sky every day. The normal direction of the winds carries the sand from Africa to South America.

Student 2: So, you're saying that the wind blows the sand all the way to the Amazon?

Professor: That's right.

Student 1: How much sand? Is it a lot?

Professor: Yes. Scientists believe it's around forty to fifty million tons of sand a year.

Student 1: Wow.

Student 2: That's amazing.

Professor: Then the sand, with all its minerals, falls over the Amazon in the rain. . . So, even though the Sahara is a place where not many plants grow, the minerals in its sand are helping create new life on the other side of the Atlantic.

LESSON 3

1 READ, page 250 CD3–Track 6

8, page 254 CD3–Track 7

Ivan: If I don't work late tomorrow night, my wife and I are going to go see a movie. What are you doing this weekend?

Meg: My sister Carla is coming for a visit. If the weather is good, we're going to go hiking. If it's not, we'll go shopping downtown.

Ivan: The weather report said it's going to be sunny all weekend.

Meg: Great! We'll go hiking, then!

Ivan: When you get out in the woods, you'll see a lot of wildlife, I'm sure. I always see interesting wildlife when I go hiking around here.

Meg: I know. I saw a lot of deer when I was hiking last weekend. I really hope we see some deer this weekend. Carla will be so excited if we do. She loves deer.

Ivan: Really? Does she like bears, too? I hear there are a lot of bears around this year!

Meg: Bears? That sounds dangerous.

Ivan: Don't worry. If you see a bear, it probably won't come near you. In fact, if you make a lot of noise, it will probably run away.

Meg: Well, if we go hiking, we'll try to make a lot of noise, then!

REVIEW THE GRAMMAR

1, page 258 CD3–Track 8

Andy: Do you want to take the afternoon off and go to the beach? It's a beautiful day, and the beach is never crowded on Tuesdays.

Kerim: I'd like to come with you, but I don't know if I can. I need to finish my science assignment. What time are you going?

Andy: It takes an hour to get there, so I'm going to leave here at about one o'clock.

Kerim: OK. If I work for a few hours now, I think I'll be able to finish it by then.

Andy: OK, great. I'll make some sandwiches for us. Do you want cheese or turkey?

Kerim: Cheese, please! I'll call you when I'm ready.

Andy: Take your time. We'll leave when you finish.

4A, page 259 CD3–Track 9

Shawna: So, our task is to make a list of the similarities and differences between gorillas and chimpanzees. I'll take notes.

Mark: OK. Let's start with the similarities between them. Gorillas live in Africa, and so do chimpanzees.

Shawna: Right.

Mark: Also, chimpanzees don't have tails, and neither do gorillas.

Shawna: OK, got it . . .

Mark: And I know that both animals have large brains, so they are quite intelligent.

Shawna: That's true . . . although chimps are actually more intelligent than gorillas, since a chimp's brain is bigger in comparison with its body size.

Mark: OK . . . that's one difference between them, then. Let's talk about the other differences.

Shawna: Hmmm. OK. Their diets are different, too. Chimps eat meat, but gorillas don't.

Mark: Yes. Also, gorillas are bigger and heavier, and they have bigger muscles in their arms, chest, and legs than chimps do.

Shawna: That's true. Gorillas are stronger than chimps. But both animals are very strong, . . . and both chimps and gorillas can be violent and aggressive.

Mark: Well, even though both animals can be aggressive, people are usually less afraid of chimps. Chimps' behavior is often funny to humans, so many people think they're cute.

Shawna: That's true.

UNIT 10

LESSON 1

1 READ, page 264 — CD3–Track 10

8, page 268 — CD3–Track 11

Gail's Story

Well, I had a choice between taking a job at a bank in my hometown or becoming a ski instructor. It was a very easy decision! I love skiing, so doing it as a job was a dream come true for me. I enjoy being outdoors and helping people. I'm good at teaching, too! I certainly don't miss sitting in front of a computer all day. I feel really lucky. I've found the perfect job!

Nick's Story — CD3–Track 12

Finding a job isn't easy these days, but I finally found one. I work for a sports website. I got the job posting photos on the website. I'm really good at taking action photos, and they needed a photographer. When they saw my photos, they offered me the job immediately. I was very excited about working as a sports photographer, so of course I said yes. It's a fun job. I really enjoy getting up and going to work every day.

Miyoko's Story — CD3–Track 13

I'm really interested in seeing the world, so leaving my teaching job to become a tour guide was a good choice for me. Traveling is stressful sometimes, so I make sure everything goes smoothly for my clients. It's such a great job. I don't think I'll ever consider going back to teaching again!

10A and 10B, page 270 — CD3–Track 14

1. On weekends, I go for a hike with my husband. It's the highlight of my week. I feel so alive when I'm outside.

2. No, I don't think so, thanks. It's nice of you to ask, but I don't think I'll ever watch another action movie. They're all so similar, and most of the time I don't find them exciting at all.

3. Yes, I've been all over the museum—it has some really great collections! I wouldn't visit it again just for myself, but you really should see it while you're here, so I'll be very happy to come with you.

4. Look, Pete, I'm sorry, I really am. There was this big business meeting the same weekend. My company chose me to give the opening talk, so I had to be there! You know I didn't want to miss your birthday party, right? But I really had no choice.

5. Wow! There are so many attractions in this town—we'll never get around to them all in one day!! There's the castle, the zoo, and I'd like to find that bookstore I told you about. I know we were going to take a boat trip up the river, but it takes such a long time. You know, it really doesn't matter to me if we do that or not.

6. Oh, it was great, thanks. I mean, you don't often have much time to yourself on business trips . . . but this time I was able to get to the beach for a couple of hours, so that was a nice break from the serious stuff.

7. So, ladies and gentlemen, those are some of the things you can do on this wonderful ship. While you are traveling with us, please feel free to contact me at any time. Remember, my name is Cindy, and I am here to help passengers throughout the trip. It's my job to deal with any problems you may have. Just call 379 from the phone in your cabin.

8. You know what? I have no idea why we're still here. I mean, Harry's obviously not going to come now—he's already half an hour late . . . and we're going to miss the start of the show if we don't leave now. I'm not going to wait any longer. Are you coming or not?

LESSON 2

1 READ, page 271 — CD3–Track 15

9 PRONUNCIATION, page 277 — CD3–Track 16

9A, page 277 — CD3–Track 17

10, page 277 — CD3–Track 18

Jenna: So, I was visiting my brother in Australia and he said, "Do you want to climb down a slot canyon with me?"

Trish: A slot canyon?

Jenna: Yeah, I know. To be honest, I didn't know what they were either. Slot canyons are very narrow passages where a river cuts into high land. Some of them go down hundreds of feet. They're a bit like caves but they're open to the sky.

Trish: That sounds like hard work . . .

Jenna: Oh, trust me, it was! I nearly said no because I didn't have the right clothes, but John's wife lent me some of her equipment.

Trish: You still didn't have to go . . .

Jenna: No, but I really enjoy climbing at home in Colorado. And the thing is—it was a wonderful chance for me to spend some time with John. So I said, "Yes, I would like to make the trip."

Trish: Where did you go?

Jenna: To the Blue Mountains. They're a few hours' drive outside Sydney where John lives.

Trish: And did you have any problems?

Jenna: John's wife told me to be careful because the rocks in the canyon are always wet. You know me—I usually hate getting wet, but the canyon was such a beautiful place. I really didn't mind!

Trish: So you enjoyed yourself?

Jenna: Oh yes, it was a great experience . . . but I still like climbing mountains better.

LESSON 3

1 READ, page 279 CD3–Track 19

11A, page 285 CD3–Track 20

1. Our company doesn't have enough money to buy the equipment.
2. The police arrived too late to catch the criminal.
3. The article was too long for me to complete in an hour.
4. The text on this screen is too small for me to read.
5. The TV show was on too late for the children to watch.
6. The patient wasn't well enough to have visitors.
7. Paul isn't strong enough to run a marathon.
8. The video game was too difficult for my little brother to play.

REVIEW THE GRAMMAR

1, page 287 CD3–Track 21

Milan: Sorry I've been too busy to get together recently.

Amy: Yeah, you need to take more breaks!

Milan: I know. So, how is your hockey going?

Amy: Well, I'm getting better at defending the puck, but I still don't skate very fast. The coach has advised me to do more training.

Milan: So, are you going to agree to do that?

Amy: Well, I don't mind working hard, but I want to avoid getting injured. I don't want to hurt my knee again. It's still not strong enough for me to play at full speed.

Milan: Well, listen . . . I'm going to the park to get some exercise tomorrow morning. Why don't you come along?

UNIT 11

LESSON 1

1 READ, page 294 CD3–Track 22

8 PRONUNCIATION, page 298 CD3–Track 23

8A, pages 298–299 CD3–Track 24

1. I like visiting places that are warm, sunny, and relaxing.
2. I have friends that don't like to fly.
3. I don't like guides that talk all the time.
4. My friend likes trips that allow plenty of time to shop.
5. I don't buy souvenirs that break easily.
6. My classmate likes places that aren't very crowded.
7. I like to stay in hotels that have exercise rooms.
8. My mother likes to eat in restaurants that have fixed menus.

9, page 299 CD3–Track 25

Neville: I've been reading an article about the World Cup that took place in South Africa in 2010. We watched some of it on TV. Do you remember?

Cindy: Oh, yes. Almost everyone who watched the games had one of those awful musical instruments that made a terrible noise.

Neville: Well, I suppose the people who were using them had a good time. Anyway, this article is all about things that have happened since the competition.

Cindy: And what does the writer say?

Neville: She says it was an event which brought the South African people together. The people who thought it would be a big waste of money were completely wrong. Researchers interviewed people during and after the competition. Tourists who came to South Africa for the World Cup were very impressed, and most South Africans that spoke to the researchers were very proud of the way their country organized the Cup.

LESSON 2

1 READ, page 301 CD3–Track 26

8A and 8C, pages 305–306 CD3–Track 27

Photo 1

Student 1: I think this is a beautiful photo of a fisherman on Inle Lake, Myanmar. The photo that this photographer took looks almost like a ballet, doesn't it? But the technique this fisherman is using looks very difficult. The boats the fishermen on Inle Lake use are so long and narrow. I understand why they stand up to row. Tall plants cover parts of Inle Lake, and the fishermen have to stand to see where they are going.

Photo 2   CD3–Track 28

Student 2: Most of the people who live around Inle Lake are called Intha, but there are other ethnic groups, too. They build simple houses of wood and bamboo. They run their own farms and produce enough food to live on. They catch fish called Inle carp from the lake, and they grow vegetables and fruit in floating gardens like the one in this picture. It takes a lot of hard work to create these gardens on the surface of the lake.

LESSON 3

1 READ, page 308   CD3–Track 29

REVIEW THE GRAMMAR

3A, page 315   CD3–Track 30

Brian: Good evening, everyone. Brian Evans here with another vacation report. This week, I'm in Cappadocia, Turkey, talking with some brave tourists about balloon rides. So, let's say hi to Scott from Toronto and Julie from Boston. Julie, tell us about your experience. How was the balloon ride you just took?

Julie: Oh it was incredible, Brian! The balloon was huge and so colorful. The other people who went with me were really friendly and were from all over the world. It was an experience that I'll never forget! The views were amazing!

Brian: Well, that's one satisfied customer! Now, Scott, what did you think about the company that you chose to go with?

Scott: Well, the pilot who flew our balloon was excellent, and we had a guide whose mother was from New Zealand, so his English was great.

Brian: Great! Any final words?

Julie: Yes! If you're a person who loves travel and photography, you'll love Cappadocia! I hope the photos I took are half as beautiful as the real thing.

Brian: OK, there we have it. Thanks and enjoy the rest of your vacation.

UNIT 12

LESSON 1

1 READ, page 320   CD3–Track 31

5 PRONUNCIATION, page 323   CD3–Track 32

5A, page 323   CD3–Track 33
1. My teacher can draw very well.
2. I can't understand modern art.
3. My friends and I can't get together often.

4. I can speak more than one foreign language.
5. In my opinion, art can change how people think.

9B, page 327   CD3–Track 34

Director: Hi, Clare. I just got a call from Nomi, and she isn't able to help us set up the art exhibit today. She's not feeling well. Are you able to come and help us?

Assistant: Sure, but I won't be able to get there until around two o'clock this afternoon. Is that OK?

Director: Two is fine. We were able to do a lot of work last night.

Assistant: Great. I'll see you then. By the way, who is the artist?

Director: His name is Yong Ho Ji.

Assistant: Oh, yes, I know his work. He's able to create such amazing sculptures with those old car tires. I really look forward to seeing his work. I wasn't able to see his last exhibit because I was out of town. By the way, will I be able to meet him? I'd love to ask him about his work.

Director: Sure. Once we set everything up, you will be able to relax and enjoy the reception. I'll introduce you then.

11, page 329   CD3–Track 35
1.

Woman: Oh, I really hated that movie.

Man: Why was that, Jane?

Woman: It was so loud! And the actors all spoke so fast, I couldn't understand half of what they were saying.
2.

Woman: Hello?

Man: Hello! Alice?

Woman: Oh, hi Marc. How are you?

Man: I'm fine, thanks. Listen, I have two free passes to the new exhibit at the art museum. Do you want to go with me on Saturday?

Woman: Oh, I'd love to, but I can't go on Saturday. I can go on Friday night, though. Is that good for you?
3.

Woman: Do you like this painting?

Man: I can't decide. It's very dark, but I like the subject.
4.

Man: This is hopeless! Just look at my drawing!

Woman: Take it easy! Faces are difficult.

Man: I was able to draw better than this when I was a child! I don't know why it's so hard.
5.

Man: Did you like the ballet, Jean?

Woman: Well the performance was excellent . . .

Man: But . . .

Woman: Well, I didn't feel very well, so I couldn't really enjoy myself.

6.

Man: Thank you Luz for helping me get my photos off my phone and onto my computer. I couldn't figure it out.

Woman: Oh, that's OK. It was fun to see those pictures of your trip.

7.

Man: I've really been looking forward to this concert.

Woman: Me, too. I saw this singer last year and she was fabulous.

Man: Can you see all right? There are some tall people in front of you.

Woman: Uh, well, not really.

Man: You can have my seat.

Woman: Thanks!

8.

Woman: Hi, Richard. How did your art exam go?

Man: I'm not sure. I finished everything before the time was up, at least.

LESSON 2

1 READ, page 330   CD3–Track 36

10A, page 335   CD3–Track 37

LESSON 3

1 READ, page 336   CD3–Track 38

7 PRONUNCIATION, page 340   CD3–Track 39

7A, page 340   CD3–Track 40

1. Could you tell me your full name?
2. Would you lend me five dollars?
3. Could you repeat the last question?
4. Would you speak more slowly?
5. Could you tell me the time?
6. Would you raise your hands in the air?

REVIEW THE GRAMMAR

2, page 344   CD3–Track 41

1. Oh, yes, the concert was great, thanks. She is a fabulous singer, but unfortunately I was in the back, so I couldn't see very well from my seat.

2. Look at Steve! He's falling asleep in his chair. He must not like the movie.

3. The train journey takes about four hours, so I'll need something to do. I might buy a novel to read.

4. My brother gave me this guitar years ago, but I still don't know how to play. Would you teach me?

5. My daughter started ballet classes a few weeks ago. The teacher says she moves very naturally and may become a really good dancer.

6. My father retired several months ago. He wanted a new hobby, so he decided to take an art class. He loves painting. He'll be able to paint realistic faces pretty soon.

7. The club next to my apartment is really loud. I could hear the music from the band last night perfectly.

8. Can I use your computer? I want to e-mail this invitation to the art gallery opening to Jill and Tim.

UNIT 13

LESSON 1

1 READ, page 350   CD4–Track 2

8 PRONUNCIATION, page 355   CD4–Track 3

8A, page 355   CD4–Track 4

1. You have to practice a lot to become good at any sport.
2. My friend has got to stop watching football! It takes up all his time.
3. I've got to get new running shoes. Mine have a hole in them.
4. Students don't have to know all the answers.
5. A student has to be responsible.
6. Did you have to study a lot last weekend?

9B, page 355   CD4–Track 5

Sunil: Hi, Jay. It's Sunil. I can't find my schedule. When do we have to be at the ice rink for tomorrow's game?

Jay: Hi, Sunil. Um, 3:15 or 3:30, I think. I'll have to check. It's right here on my phone. Hold on . . . Uh, no, I was wrong—we don't have to be there until 4 p.m.

Sunil: Thanks. I've got to remember these things! Are you feeling confident?

Jay: To be honest, I'm nervous. We were terrible last week.

Sunil: Yeah, you're right . . . but we had to compete without our best player.

Jay: Well, Kurt is still sick, and a sick player can't play. The coach says we can't stay on the team if we do badly again tomorrow.

Sunil: Why does he have to say things like that?

Jay: I guess it's his job! Look, I've got to go—I have a ton of homework to do.

12A, page 357 CD4–Track 6

Folk Racing

Susie: This week on *Sports for All*, we're going to take a look at a special type of car racing from Finland. Our reporter Johnny Evans has just come back from Finland. Now, Johnny, young children usually can't compete in a race themselves. But, as you're going to tell us, things are a bit different in Finland . . .

Johnny: That's right, Susie. In Finland, racers don't have to be adults. Finland is the home of Folk Racing—a sport in which people of all ages can compete against each other. They drive old cars that are no longer used on public roads. In some races, the only people who can't compete are children under the age of five.

Susie: So they can compete at the age of five? Wow! That's young! And are there a lot of these races?

Johnny: Yes, definitely. Events take place most weekends all over Finland. And you don't have to be a great driver to try Folk Racing. You don't even have to have a normal driving license! The only things you must have are a special license and, of course, a car.

Susie: Do you have to have a special car for Folk Racing?

Johnny: No, but there are some important rules. For example, people must not spend a lot of money on their car. The competition must be between the *drivers*, not between the cars. In 2013, drivers could only spend 1400 euros.

Susie: OK, thanks, Johnny. Johnny will be back later to tell us about other unusual sports . . .

LESSON 2

1 READ, page 359 CD4–Track 7

REVIEW THE GRAMMAR

2, page 366 CD4–Track 8

1. I am supposed to play softball tomorrow.
2. I must speak to the coach immediately.
3. We have to buy three tickets for the game.
4. I ought to ski more often.
5. I was supposed to go swimming yesterday.
6. The referee's got to write a report after the game.
7. The players should receive free tickets for their families.
8. We didn't have to train hard for the race.
9. In tennis, players must not touch the net.
10. Players must not speak while the coach is talking.

UNIT 14

LESSON 1

1 READ, page 372 CD4–Track 9

12A and 12B, page 380 CD4–Track 10

Student 1: George Stephenson was a nineteenth-century British engineer whose ideas changed the way we travel. He is known as "The Father of the Railways" because he built a steam engine, the *Locomotion*, for use on railroads. Other engines already carried goods, but in 1825, Stephenson operated the first train for human passengers.

CD4–Track 11

Student 2: Josephine Cochran made the first successful automatic dishwasher in 1886. Cochran was a rich woman. She had servants who washed her dishes for her, but she wanted a machine that worked more quickly and did not break any dishes. Cochran's dishwasher was a great success. She made dishwashers for friends, and soon restaurants and hotels wanted her machines. She soon started her own business. Her company became part of a larger business that still produces dishwashers today.

CD4–Track 12

Student 3: Tabitha Babbit was an American woman who lived in the early nineteenth century. In 1813, she invented a large circular saw for use in sawmills—the place where wood is cut for use by house builders or furniture makers. At the time, men used large straight saws to cut wood. She noticed that the men worked very hard, but they didn't produce enough wood. She wanted to solve the problem for the workers and the saw mills. Her new saw was able to cut without stop and could cut more wood in less time.

CD4–Track 13

Student 4: Of course, Johannes Gutenberg did not invent books. Books were around for hundreds of years before his time, but when Gutenberg invented his printing press in 1450, it changed the world. His machine made inexpensive books for everyone, and it allowed ideas and knowledge to reach a lot more people.

LESSON 2

1 READ, page 382 CD4–Track 14

10A, page 388 CD4–Track 15

People like to believe that inventors are brilliant people who dream up new ideas on their own. In movies about innovation, an inventor often wakes up with the perfect solution to a problem. At times these inventors run into problems, but they never give up. They keep on trying to make our lives better, and eventually they succeed.

In fact, these popular ideas about inventors are far from the truth. In reality, most inventions come from a community of people who are all trying to figure out the answer to a problem.

For example, people often bring up the name of Thomas Edison when talking about innovation. Many people believe that Edison came up with the light bulb without any help. However, Edison's light bulb was not completely new. He was just the first one to produce something that people could buy and use.

REVIEW THE GRAMMAR

3A, page 391   CD4–Track 16

Hello! Today I'm going to talk about my invention, a computer disk notebook. I made the notebook with those small square plastic disks for old computers. Remember those disks? Anyway, I came up with the idea because I was helping my uncle set up a new computer, and I came across some old disks that didn't work with his new computer. I was going to throw them away, but then I decided to make something with the disks that my uncle could use. So, I cut some paper to the same size as the disks, put the paper on top of one disk, and then put another disk on top of the paper. At first I couldn't figure out how to keep the disks and the paper together, but then my uncle used a tool to make two holes through the disks and the paper. Finally, I put a piece of plastic through each hole to keep the disks and the paper together. My uncle loves his computer disk notebook! I made some other ones for friends and family members, but so far the invention hasn't taken off.

UNIT 15

LESSON 1

1 READ, page 396   CD4–Track 17

LESSON 2

1 READ, page 404   CD4–Track 18

9B, page 411   CD4–Track 19

Juan: Hi, Val. I'm going to choose Pompeii for my project. I went there last year while I was on vacation in Italy. Would you like to work together on it? That way we can share the research.

Val: Yes, that's a great idea, Juan. I've always wanted to find out more about the real Pompeii. You can't always believe the stories in books and films.

Juan: I took some pretty good photos. Look at these. We should include some of them in the project.

Val: Yes, I suppose we should show some of the bodies. I feel strange looking at them, to be honest. I think we should respect the people who died even though it was a long time ago.

Juan: Well, don't forget, you're not looking at their real bodies. These are plaster casts made from the ash that covered the bodies.

Val: Yes, I know, but I still find them disturbing. I remember seeing a cast of a dog in a magazine once. Did you take a picture of that?

Juan: Um, no, but the official website might show it.

Val: Oh, that's true. I'm sure we can find a lot of good information on that site.

Juan: OK, so we seem to have some good ideas. The only problem is that a lot of students might choose Pompeii—it's a popular topic.

Val: So, let's go find Professor Lopez right now. If we don't hurry, he may not approve our project.

LESSON 3

1 READ, page 413   CD4–Track 20

7A, 7B and 7D, page 418   CD4–Track 21

Conversation 1

Jessie: Ew . . . Hey Tom, what's that smell? It's awful!

Tom: I think it's old milk and produce. It looks like these people threw away a lot of food. What a waste! That drives me crazy!

Conversation 2

Sue: I'm so glad I joined this project. I'm really learning a lot.

Dave: Sue! Tell me you're not serious! We just stare at garbage for hours and hours. I've had enough for today. I want to do something fun!

Conversation 3

Rick: OK, we've finished looking through this pile. Let's start on that one over there. I don't think we have enough information yet.

Angela: Good idea! This is going so well! I think we might be able to make some important conclusions by the end of the day.

Rick: I agree. In fact, I wasn't expecting the type of information we've collected already.

REVIEW THE GRAMMAR

3B, page 421　　　　　　　　　CD4–Track 22

Presenter: Welcome to this week's *History Quiz,* the show that finds out how much *you* know about the past! On tonight's show we have Cindy from San Diego . . . Hi, Cindy!

Cindy: Hi, Bill!

Presenter: . . . and Alan from Chicago . . . Hello, Alan.

Alan: It's great to be here, Bill.

Presenter: So, welcome to you both and let's start the first round of questions. OK, Cindy, let's start with. Your first question is: Where were the first public baths built?

Cindy: Hmm, um, I believe that was in ancient Rome, Bill. The Romans used public baths as social centers.

Presenter: That's the correct answer! Cindy, you have your first ten points, and here's your next question: When was the first moon landing completed?

Cindy: Um, I believe it was 1969?

Presenter: And you have another ten points! Now, this next one is a bit more difficult: Where were scissors invented?

Cindy: Scissors? Um, I'll have to take a guess . . . Let's see. How about Japan?

Presenter: No, I'm sorry, that's the wrong answer. Scissors were invented in ancient Egypt. So, it's over to you, Alan. Here's your first question: When was the first airplane flown—1898, 1903, or 1907?

Alan: Uh, I know it was flown by the Wright brothers . . . I'm not too sure, Bill . . . I'll go for 1903.

Presenter: And you score ten points, so it's Cindy twenty points, Alan ten points. Alan, here's your next question, and it's a tough one: Who was popcorn invented by?

Alan: Actually, Bill, I know this one. I'm a big fan of popcorn. It was invented by Native Americans.

Presenter: Correct answer! Now you both have twenty points. If you get this next question right, Alan, you'll move into the lead . . .! Here we go: When were the first CDs sold?

Alan: Uh, I'm going to say . . . nineteen seventy . . . uh, nine!

Presenter: No, Alan, I'm sorry. It was 1982. So at the end of the first round, Alan and Cindy are tied at 20 points each. We'll be right back with round two, when . . .

UNIT 16

LESSON 1

1 READ, page 426　　　　　　　　CD4–Track 23

10A, page 432　　　　　　　　　CD4–Track 24

If you want to explore a lost city, Machu Picchu in Peru is a popular choice. It is often called the "lost city of the Incas" after the American Indian people who built it. I went there last year, and I'm sure every visitor to the site comes away with very special memories.

It's true that the city first attracted archaeologists over a hundred years ago, but after traveling so far, you can almost believe you have found it for the first time. Of course, if you want to feel like a real explorer, you have to ignore all the other visitors to the ruins. Try early morning or late afternoon, when it's quieter. You should avoid the middle of the day if you can—the place is very busy then. I've heard that Sunday is usually the day with the fewest visitors. I don't think Machu Picchu is as crowded as it used to be, though. I know the government has now limited the number of people who can visit each day, so you should buy your ticket as early as you can.

Remember that Machu Picchu is very far away. The only road to the city is from the small town of Aguas Calientes. I know that some people walk to Machu Picchu along the Inca Trail, but you really have to be fit to do that. I believe it takes most people two to four days to walk. Some people say the Inca Trail is more exciting than Machu Picchu itself. Personally, I have to say I was very glad there was a bus! I enjoyed my visit to Machu Picchu very much. I hope to go again one day.

10B, page 433　　　　　　　　　CD4–Track 25

1. Of course, if you want to feel like a real explorer, you have to ignore all the other visitors to the ruins. Try early morning or late afternoon when it's quieter. You should avoid the middle of the day if you can—the place is very busy then.

2. I've heard that Sunday is usually the day with the fewest visitors.

3. I don't think Machu Picchu is as crowded as it used to be, though. I know the government has now limited the number of people who can visit each day, so you should buy your ticket as early as you can.

4. Remember that Machu Picchu is very far away. The only road to the city is from the small town of Aguas Calientes. I know that some people walk to Machu Picchu along the Inca Trail, but you really have to be fit to do that. I believe it takes most people two to four days to walk.

5. I believe it takes most people two to four days to walk. Some people say the Inca Trail is more exciting than Machu Picchu itself. Personally, I have to say I was very glad there was a bus! I enjoyed my visit to Machu Picchu very much. I hope to go again one day.

LESSON 2

1 READ, page 434 CD4–Track 26

9A, page 440 CD4–Track 27

Vasco da Gama was a Portuguese explorer in the fifteenth to sixteenth centuries. In 1497, da Gama made a sea voyage. He was sent by the king of Portugal. Because of political changes in the fifteenth century, it became impossible for Portugal and other European countries to trade with India via land.

9D, page 440 CD4–Track 28

Vasco da Gama was a Portuguese explorer in the fifteenth to sixteenth centuries. In 1497, da Gama made a sea voyage. He was sent by the king of Portugal. Because of political changes in the fifteenth century, it became impossible for Portugal and other European countries to trade with India via land.

The King wanted da Gama to find a sea route to India. The explorer sailed south from Lisbon and around Africa. The voyage to India and back was long and difficult. Two of da Gama's four ships were lost along the way and over 100 people died. However, da Gama was successful. He reached the Indian port of Calicut, not far from modern Mumbai. Calicut was an important city in the spice trade.

The new trade route discovered by da Gama brought wealth to his country over many years. Unfortunately, da Gama is not only remembered for his discoveries. He is also remembered for his great cruelty to people in order to protect the spices for his country.

LESSON 3

1 READ, page 442 CD4–Track 29

13A and 13C, pages 451–452 CD4–Track 30

Maria: Hey, Phil. How is your research going?

Phil: Great. I'm reading about the Voyager 1 space probe.

Maria: That's a very old mission . . . Is it a useful article for the assignment?

Phil: Yes, the mission is at a very exciting stage.

Maria: Oh, what's happening?

Phil: Apparently, the probe is no longer in our solar system.

Maria: Really? Does that mean a man-made object is flying around the galaxy?

Phil: Yes! It's the first time in history.

REVIEW THE GRAMMAR

2A, pages 453–454 CD4–Track 31

Brad: These caves in Vietnam look amazing. They've just been explored for the first time. The pictures are fantastic.

Sylvie: What's so special about them? There are caves all over the world.

Brad: Yes, but Hang Son Doong is different. The caves form the largest cave system anywhere.

Sylvie: Oh really? Can I see the photos? Wow, you're right! They really are amazing!

Brad: I don't like going in caves. The guys who took these photos must be brave.

Sylvie: Why do you dislike caves?

Brad: Going into a cave is a big risk. It's easy to have an accident.

Sylvie: I guess so, but you could have an accident crossing the street. The risk doesn't worry me. I love exploring new places!